SEPT 2021

CONTEMPORARY WOMEN STAGE DIRECTORS

Darling May,

Of course I had to write in this
one too... 😊 🙂

I hope you enjoy these and they
give you some inspiration for
the amazing director — or anything
else you choose to be — that you
can become with all your
talent and visual fantastic-ness
and general brilliance. Plus the
rare and awesome way you talk,
relate and communicate your
ideas and thoughts to everyone
is soooo great, you'll be wonderful (as you are)
Love you, Dad ♡ xx ✡ ♡♡

CONTEMPORARY WOMEN STAGE DIRECTORS

Conversations on Craft

Paulette Marty

methuen | drama

LONDON • NEW YORK • OXFORD • NEW DELHI • SYDNEY

METHUEN DRAMA
Bloomsbury Publishing Plc
50 Bedford Square, London, WC1B 3DP, UK
1385 Broadway, New York, NY 10018, USA

BLOOMSBURY, METHUEN DRAMA and the Methuen Drama logo are trademarks of
Bloomsbury Publishing Plc

First published in Great Britain 2019

Cover design: Eleanor Rose
Cover image © Johan Persson / ARENAPAL

A catalogue record for this book is available from the British Library.

Library of Congress Cataloging-in-Publication Data
Names: Marty, Paulette, author.
Title: Contemporary women stage directors : conversations on
craft / Paulette Marty.
Description: London ; New York, NY : Metheun Drama, 2019. |
Includes bibliographical references and index.
Identifiers: LCCN 2018038775 | ISBN 9781474268578 (hb) |
ISBN 9781474268530 (pb)
Subjects: LCSH: Theater–Production and direction–Great Britain. |
Theater–Production and direction–United States. |
Women theatrical producers and directors–Great Britain–Interviews. |
Women theatrical producers and directors–United States–Interviews.
Classification: LCC PN2053 .M3725 2019 | DDC 792.02/33082–dc23
LC record available at https://lccn.loc.gov/2018038775

ISBN: HB: 978-1-4742-6857-8
PB: 978-1-4742-6853-0
ePDF: 978-1-4742-6854-7
eBook: 978-1-4742-6855-4

Series: Theatre Makers

Typeset by Newgen KnowledgeWorks Pvt. Ltd., Chennai, India
Printed and bound in Great Britain

To find out more about our authors and books visit www.bloomsbury.com
and sign up for our newsletters.

This book is dedicated to all women directors—past, present, and future. Thank you for catalyzing collaboration, envisioning new worlds, and telling the stories that need to be told.

CONTENTS

ACKNOWLEDGMENTS

First, my profound thanks to the directors. In spite of their busy schedules, they were generous with their time, patient with follow-up questions and administrivia, and unfailingly gracious. It was a privilege to collaborate with them on this project.

Thanks also to Anna Brewer, Lucy Brown, Camilla Erskine, and the rest of the editorial team at Methuen Drama (including the anonymous reviewers). Their advice and guidance were invaluable in shaping the form and content of this book. It is a far better volume than it would have been without the influence of their wisdom.

I could not have completed (or even begun) this project without funding from the College of Fine and Applied Arts, the University Research Council, and the Department of Theatre and Dance at Appalachian State University. I am grateful to my colleagues for this financial support, as well as for granting me leave in the fall of 2014 to launch my research.

Thanks also to the many colleagues, friends, and family who listened to me effuse and fret, gave me feedback on pieces of the draft, and supported me in so many other ways. Particular thanks to Kym Bartlett Schmauss and Brad Schmauss for graciously hosting me on multiple trips to London, and to my mother, Norma Wojtalewicz, for never wavering in her belief that I'm capable to doing anything I set my mind to (even when my own belief falters).

Finally, all my love to my husband, John, and two daughters, Fiona and Zea. They are my motivators, sounding boards, and best friends. I am deeply thankful that I have them beside me in this glorious journey through life.

INTRODUCTION

This book captures the wisdom and vision of mid-career female directors and artistic directors. These women have all reached or are approaching the apex of their careers; thus, they have both extensive knowledge from years of experience in the profession and the curiosity and creative restlessness of artists who anticipate years of work ahead. This combination of expertise and forward momentum makes them fascinating, inspiring people who have much to teach us about today's theater.

These directors are making some of the most exciting work in English-language theater today and running some of the most influential organizations in the field; yet if you look at the books profiling directors that have been published over the past two decades, you will find few mentions of these women. Such books overwhelmingly favor male directors, and the female directors they include tend to be drawn from the same small group of women, most of whom are at a later stage of their careers. Even Anne Fliotsos and Wendy Vierow's excellent volumes *American Women Stage Directors of the Twentieth Century* (University of Illinois 2008) and *International Women Stage Directors* (University of Illinois 2013) feature only a few mid-career British and American women. In short, a scan of the existing books available on today's shelves gives the impression that there are few influential mid-career female directors in the field, which is simply untrue. This book begins to fill this omission in the literature and gives readers a chance to hear these directors' insights in their own words.

Interviewees

The directors featured in this book have a wide variety of perspectives and experiences. They come from different ethnic and racial backgrounds. Some were born in other countries before emigrating to the UK or the United States. Many are based in London or New York, others work primarily in regional theater centers. Some almost exclusively direct new plays, others focus more on classics. Most work freelance, others run theaters, and some teach as well as direct. With their varied backgrounds, these directors have a breadth as well as a depth of knowledge to share. They are current and future leaders in the field and their aesthetics and diverse perspectives will continue to shape the future of live theater in the decades to come.

Maria Aberg started her career as a literary associate at Royal Court Theatre in London. She has since directed new plays at many major London theaters, including the National, Royal Court, and Kiln Theatre (formerly Tricycle). A native of Sweden, she also directs regularly in northern Europe. In recent years, she has become known for her innovative, feminist productions of Shakespeare and other classics at the Royal Shakespeare Company and various other theaters in the UK.

May Adrales has worked in New York and at many regional theaters developing new works with playwrights like Katori Hall and Thomas Bradshaw, as well as directing established plays. She has received numerous directing fellowships from national organizations, including Theatre Communications Group and the Stage Directors and Choreographers Foundation, and has taught at NYU, Julliard, Yale School of Drama, American Conservatory Theatre, and American Repertory Theatre, among other institutions.

Sarah Benson is a British-born director who became Artistic Director of New York's Soho Rep at age twenty-seven and led the company through its transition from Off-Off Broadway to Off-Broadway status. She has shaped Soho Rep into an important center for the development of new artists with programs such as the Writer/Director Lab. Benson has also helped disseminate diverse writing by producing new writers, alerting other producing organizations to new plays, and editing Methuen Drama's *Contemporary American Theatre* anthology.

Karin Coonrod is a professor at Yale University School of Drama and has directed extensively in both the United States and Italy for such theaters as the American Repertory Theatre, the New York Shakespeare Festival/Public Theater, New York University, and New York Theatre Workshop, among others. She is known for her imaginative stagings of Shakespeare and dramatic adaptations of literary works. She is also founder of the international company Compagnia de' Colombari, which is jointly based in New York and Orvieto, Italy.

Rachel Chavkin and her New York-based company The TEAM have devised numerous productions, several of which have been featured at international festivals. She has also directed new plays by various playwrights, including Dave Malloy's acclaimed immersive work *Natasha, Pierre, and the Great Comet of 1812*, for which she was nominated for a Tony Award in 2017.

Lear deBessonet is the founding director of the Public Theatre's Public Works project, which brings together hundreds of New York City community members and a small core of professional actors to create professional-quality musical versions of classics in the Delacorte Theater in Central Park. Artistic Director Oskar Eustis invited deBessonet to create this innovative community-based program after seeing her other community-based projects at cities across the US.

Nadia Fall began working as an assistant at the National Theatre early in her career and, though she has worked at numerous theaters across the UK, she still considers the National her "home." She is currently an associate director for the theater and has directed in all of the building's spaces, most recently in the Lyttleton and Olivier. Among her productions for the National was Alan Bennet's *Hymn*, which transferred to the West End in 2012.

Vicky Featherstone is currently Artistic Director of the Royal Court Theatre in London. Formerly Artistic Director of Paines Plough Theatre Company and founding Artistic Director of the National

Theatre of Scotland, Featherstone has been a national leader in new play development for nearly two decades. She has received many awards and honors for her directing and artistic leadership and her insights and opinions on the arts are regularly featured in national and international media.

Polly Findlay has directed a wide variety of classics and modern plays at venues across the UK. She has become a regular at the National Theatre in recent years and has also directed multiple times at the Royal Shakespeare Company. Aside from her work on plays, Findlay directed the solo magic show *Derren Brown: Svengali* on the West End, which won the 2012 Olivier for Best Entertainment.

Leah Gardiner has directed the US premieres of plays by prominent British playwrights debbie tucker green and Roy Williams, as well as other world and regional premieres throughout the United States. In 2015, she directed the premiere of Anna Deavere Smith's new solo work, *Notes from the Field: Doing Time in Education, The California Chapter*, at Berkeley Repertory Theatre.

Anne Kauffman won a 2015 Obie Award for Sustained Excellence in Directing, as well as a 2007 Obie for her direction of Adam Bock's *The Thugs*. She has been directing new plays Off-Broadway and in regional theaters for years and is widely regarded as one of the finest new play directors in the country. She has worked repeatedly with several prominent playwrights, such as Lisa D'Amour and Jenny Schwartz.

Lucy Kerbel founded Tonic Theatre in 2011 with a mission "to support the theater industry to achieve greater gender equality in its workforces and repertoires." Through Tonic, Kerbel has partnered with theater companies throughout the UK on a variety of projects that promote gender equity in the industry. In two of the most visible of these projects, she collaborated with the National Theatre to write and publish the book *100 Great Plays for Women* and collaborated with the Royal Shakespeare Company and ten other theaters on the Advance Project, in which they gathered data about gender in their organizations and developed action plans for increasing equity.

Young Jean Lee's self-named Young Jean Lee's Theater Company is based in Brooklyn, but has performed at festivals and venues across Europe and the United States. Lee writes and directs the company's work, which varies in form, style, and theme. For example, *We're Gonna Die* is a monologue/rock show about mortality, *Songs of the Dragons Flying to Heaven* is a scathingly hilarious parody of Asian racial stereotypes, and *Straight White Men* is a relatively conventional play about a father and sons grappling with their identity politics. Lee has received numerous awards and accolades for her plays and, in 2018, became the first Asian-American female playwright to have a play produced on Broadway.

Patricia McGregor completed her MFA in Directing at Yale School of Drama and then worked as a stage manager for Deborah Warner before launching her directing career at the encouragement of playwright August Wilson. She gained Off-Broadway acclaim in 2012 for her world premiere production of Katori Hall's *Hurt Village*. In addition to new plays, McGregor has directed revivals of plays, musicals, and classics, as well as collaboratively developed unconventional pieces such as *Burnt Sugar Freaks the JB Songbook, an Opera in Progress*, a re-orchestration of the music of James Brown performed by the band Burnt Sugar and select actor/musicians.

Blanche McIntyre is known in the British theater community for her directorial precision and clarity. She gained widespread recognition when she won the 2011 Critics' Circle Most Promising Newcomer Award for *Foxfinder* and *Accolade* at the Finborough Theatre, and the 2013 TMA UK Theatre Award for Best Director for *The Seagull* with Headlong Theatre. She continues to direct at theaters across the UK, including Shakespeare's Globe, English Touring Theatre, Nuffield Theatre, and others.

Paulette Randall became the first black woman to direct in the West End with her 2013 production of August Wilson's *Fences*. She has also had an active career in television as a producer, director, and writer. In 2012, she combined her knowledge of televised and live production to serve as the Associate Director of the London Olympics Opening Ceremony. In 2015, Randall was awarded an MBE for services to drama.

Diane Rodriguez is a national leader in American nonprofit theater. She has served as Chair of the Board of Directors for Theatre

Communications Group since 2013 and, in 2016, was appointed to the National Council on the Arts by President Obama and the US Congress. Rodriguez has worked at Center Theatre Group in Los Angeles for over two decades, first as Associate Producer/Director of New Play Production, then as Co-director of the Latino Theatre Initiative, and now as Associate Artistic Director. In addition to being a director, Rodriguez is also a published playwright and Obie-winning actor.

Indhu Rubasingham spent nearly two decades working as a freelance director in many prominent UK theaters, including the National, Royal Court, Young Vic, Almeida, Birmingham Rep, Chichester Festival, Gate, Hampstead, and Kiln Theatre (formerly Tricycle), where she came to specialize in directing plays by international writers from diverse backgrounds. In 2012, Rubasingham took over as Artistic Director of the Kiln Theatre (then Tricycle Theatre) in Kilburn, one of the most racially and ethnically diverse neighborhoods in London. At Tricycle/Kiln, she has made a commitment to helping the unheard voice become part of the mainstream and refocused the theater's mission and programming away from the overtly political toward plays that offer different lenses on the world.

KJ Sanchez is currently the Head of the MFA Directing program at the University of Texas, Austin. She has directed Off-Broadway and at numerous regional theaters and is director, coauthor, and producer of *ReEntry*, a documentary theater piece about Marines returning from deployment that has toured to over fifty military bases and hospitals in the United States and abroad. She is also a stage and television actor and a playwright whose work has been performed at regional theaters across the United States and internationally.

Tina Satter is founder and Artistic Director of Half Straddle, an experimental theater company in Downtown New York City. Satter writes and directs Half Straddle's productions. She was named a "2011 Off-Off Broadway Innovator to Watch" by Time Out New York, received a 2014 Doris Duke Impact Award and, in 2013, Half Straddle won the Obie Award for best emerging theater company. Satter has also taught as a guest artist at several universities and conservatories.

Kimberly Senior is most widely known for directing the premiere and Broadway productions of Ayad Akhtar's Pulitzer-prize winner *Disgraced*. She also directed the first two productions of Akhtar's *The Who and the What* at La Jolla Playhouse and Lincoln Center Theater 3. Senior has directed dozens of new plays and revivals in Chicago area theaters like the Goodman and Steppenwolf, as well as at other regional theaters across the United States.

Roxana Silbert has served as Associate Director at Royal Court Theatre, Literary Director of the Traverse Theatre, Artistic Director of Paines Plough Theatre Company, and Associate Director of the Royal Shakespeare Company. She is presently Artistic Director of Birmingham Rep. In these leadership roles, Silbert has employed and mentored many women directors, as well as directed more plays by female playwrights over the past decade than any other director in Britain.

Leigh Silverman specializes in new play directing. She was nominated for a Tony Award for Best Direction of a Musical for *Violet* on Broadway in 2014 and also directed the Tony-nominated Broadway production of Lisa Kron's *Well* in 2006. She has won several awards for her Off-Broadway work and has directed numerous world premieres of plays by such prominent playwrights as Neil Labute and David Henry Hwang.

Caroline Steinbeis started her career by winning the prestigious JMK Award, which funded her critically acclaimed 2009 production of Caryl Churchill's *Mad Forest*. Her work has been selected for the Radikal Jung Festival in Munich and she has won a Manchester Theatre Award. From 2011 to 2013, she served as International Associate for the Royal Court Theatre. Over the past several years, she has directed numerous productions in the UK and Europe.

Liesl Tommy began directing while pursuing her MFA in Acting from Brown University/Trinity Repertory Company. She has directed at venues across the United States, from Broadway to Disneyland. Her resume includes everything from large-scale commercial musicals to world premieres of intimate dramas. She has won numerous awards and in 2016 became the first woman of color to receive a Tony nomination for Best Direction of a Play for Danai Gurira's *Eclipsed*.

Lyndsey Turner gained international renown for her 2015 production of *Hamlet* at the Barbican featuring Benedict Cumberbatch in the title role. She received an Olivier Award in 2014 for the premiere production of Lucy Kirkwood's *Chimerica* with Headlong Theatre. Formerly an associate director at Royal Court (where she directed Laura Wade's *Posh*, resulting in a West End transfer), Turner is now an Associate at the National Theatre.

Erica Whyman was Artistic Director of two London theaters—Southwark Playhouse and The Gate—and Chief Executive of Northern Stage in Newcastle-upon-Tyne prior to assuming her current position as Deputy Artistic Director of one of the UK's largest theaters, Royal Shakespeare Company. In 2012, Whyman won the TMA Award for Theatre Manager of the Year and was awarded an OBE for services to theater in the UK.

Research Process

This book is the result of a research project I began in 2014. I had been visiting the UK and seeing theater productions fairly regularly since the mid-1990s. Over time, I began to notice that an increasing percentage of the most captivating productions I saw were directed by women. I wanted to find out more about these female directors; unfortunately, as I described above, I discovered that there was little to no literature on them except profiles and reviews by journalistic media. While these pieces were often informative, they did not satisfy my thirst for detailed knowledge about these women's work, ideas, priorities, and careers. I decided to go to the source and interview several of them myself.

Initially, I thought I might use the interviews to write a journal article about gender in the directing profession, but as I talked to more directors, I began to reconsider the scope of my research project. These women offered such insight into the process and profession of directing that I felt strongly their underrepresented voices should be heard. I determined that a book would be the best format for amplifying those voices within and beyond the theater industry. Serendipitously, I learned that Methuen was launching a new series called Theatre Makers and that they wanted to include a book about British and American women directors; to that end, I conducted interviews with twenty-seven directors between June 2014 and June 2017—some in person, others via Skype, and a few over the phone.

Our conversations ranged over a wide variety of topics, shaped by the particular things that intrigued me about each individual director's work and by what each director felt most passionate about discussing at that moment. The topics we covered fell into four general areas: artistic process; artistic priorities; career; and the impact of gender, race, ethnicity, and identity on their work. Eventually, I used subdivisions of these four broad areas to create the organizational framework for this book.

Organization of the Book

Most interview-based books about theater artists are structured in a question-and-answer format with one chapter dedicated to each interviewee. I have opted instead to take a thematic approach. Each chapter has a main topic and is divided into subtopic sections, and each of those subtopic sections contains quotes from multiple directors (framed by contextual information from me in italics). This thematic organization allows the reader to see several directors' insights into a subject in one place. I hope that as you read, you feel like you are sitting with these women, hearing each of them share their thoughts on various topics of interest.

One drawback of a thematic rather than question-and-answer organization is that usually it makes it difficult for readers to get a clear picture of one individual interviewee's ideas and personality because her quotes are buried in text throughout the book. To alleviate this problem, I've included the director's name in bold above each quote and created an Index of Director Names at the end of the book. If you want to learn about one specific director, use the index to find the relevant pages and that director's name should leap out at you from the page.

Each chapter has a distinct topic, but their contents overlap. Because directing is by nature an integrative task, the various facets of it do not pull apart neatly into discrete categories. For example, I initially planned to include a chapter about "audience" but quickly realized that the subject was inextricable from the other chapter topics because, ultimately, every aspect of the directing process is focused on shaping an audience experience; therefore, I opted to include the directors' ideas and insights about audiences in the other chapters rather than attempting to pull them out of context. As you read, you will find that such disparate-seeming topics as "visual storytelling," "work–life balance," and "empowering actors" might all overlap and inform one another.

The deep integration of topics in this book mirrors the directing process itself. A director's job is to integrate many diverse pieces into a coherent whole. To do so, she must utilize a wide array of skills and knowledge, partially developed in the classroom and rehearsal hall, but also developed through the other activities of life: observing human behavior, reading about ideas, listening to and viewing many types of media, and simply noticing the shape of people's stories. Arguably, every aspect of a director's life is training for her craft. To better understand that craft, let us turn to these directors as they describe their myriad experiences as theater artists, industry professionals, and inquisitive, fascinating people.

1
CHOOSING PROJECTS

Many factors influence a director's choice of projects. For most, the ideal is to produce a script you love, for an audience receptive to the work, in a venue suited to the piece, with collaborators you connect with and resources sufficient to realize your collective vision (all while getting paid enough to make a living); however, individual directors' preferences and priorities for the details of this ideal vary widely. Some directors will only direct plays they feel deeply connected to, while others are willing to be quite flexible about the play as long as they can produce it in a particular venue or for a particular audience. Some directors focus almost exclusively on new work, others prefer classics, and most direct some of each. Some work repeatedly with the same collaborators (especially designers) because they value the synergy they've established with those artists, while others value the fresh perspective of new collaborators on most every project.

Directors also have to consider broader implications when deliberating whether to sign onto a project. Individuals build a body of work that influences how they are perceived in the industry and, consequently, what projects they are offered. One of the quandaries young directors often face is whether to specialize in a particular style of theater or type of story. Carving out a niche for oneself can be a quicker path to visibility in the field, but it can also lead to pigeonholing and a limited toolbox of skills. Those in leadership positions at theaters have to consider an astounding number of factors when choosing plays for their seasons. No single production exists in a vacuum, so directors must think about the long game whenever they choose projects. In this chapter, the directors describe the myriad factors they consider when making choices about what and where to direct.

What Draws You to a Piece?

Maria Aberg

I need to find myself in it

I've got to feel like I've got a strong connection to the piece—a need to do it. I need to be able to find myself in it somehow. Not a representation of myself, but some aspect of something I struggle with or feel strongly about.

I think exploring our own vulnerabilities in front of an audience is the biggest risk we as theater makers can take. And I also believe it's the most precious thing we can offer an audience. Creating an arena where it's okay to expose and explore vulnerability is probably the most valuable thing I can imagine doing.

One vulnerable area that Aberg has explored in her work is the effect of sexism on women's lives and identities. She has a keen awareness of how women and their bodies are depicted and perceived in contemporary culture and has used cross-gender casting and pop culture images to expose sexist assumptions and misogynistic behaviours in plays such as Shakespeare's King John[1] *and Webster's* The White Devil *and* The Duchess of Malfi.[2]

Roxana Silbert

The play has got to speak to you at an emotional level

The play has got to speak to you at an emotional level. I directed *Khandan* at Birmingham Rep, and I am not Punjabi like the characters, but I am an immigrant.[3] I came to this country from Argentina when I was seven years old, my parents were not from this country, and I understand the immigrant experience. I understand what it means to come from one culture and to try and find an identity that belongs in this

---

[1]Royal Shakespeare Company, 2012.
[2]Royal Shakespeare Company, 2014 and 2018 (respectively).
[3]Birmingham Repertory Company, 2014.

culture without losing where you come from. That play is about people from a different culture than me, but a lot of the themes and ideas in it were things that I had struggled with and I was very interested in. So, at the heart of it, there's got to be an emotional attachment.

At first blush, choosing only pieces one is emotionally attached to may seem somewhat limiting; but Silbert, who has been directing professionally for over two decades, observes that "what speaks to you on an emotional level changes all the time."

I remember one of the first main stage shows I was offered was at Bolton Octagon and I was given a choice between *The Price* by Arthur Miller or *Woman in Mind* by Alan Ayckbourn.[4] I was thirty years old and the one that I emotionally responded to was Arthur Miller, because my father, as an immigrant, was trying to make his mark and better his family, so I understood the experience. Interestingly, we programmed *Woman in Mind* last year at Birmingham Rep and I had a very different response to that play as a middle-aged woman.[5] I realize now that that's a play about how the choices you've made have led you down a certain road, yet there's a whole other life that you could have had if you'd made a slightly different choice. I see that play from a completely different perspective now. It's an ever-changing thing.

Anne Kauffman

My work is the way I process the world

As you get older, time becomes a precious thing. A play is a six-month commitment, normally. You're thinking about it, casting it, designing it, and then you have go into the actual rehearsal and preview process, which, in and of itself, is at least two months. It's a commitment. So I lead with the question, "Do I resonate with the play?" I've turned down a lot of stuff that I think is very good, but I just don't resonate with it and decide I don't want to give my time to it. I've also become rather selfish in that my work is the way I process the world. So, if the play

---

[4]Bolton Octagon, 2001.
[5]Birmingham Repertory Company, 2014.

isn't resonating in terms of a path I'm interested in exploring, chances are I won't take it on.

KJ Sanchez

Complicated and ambivalent feelings

I only choose work that I have complicated and ambivalent feelings about. For example, I've been offered some commissions to do work on Mexican immigration, but I didn't accept because I knew exactly what I felt about it. It would just become propaganda. I am now writing and directing a piece on refugees for the Guthrie, but my way in to it is to pay attention to not only the people who are for refugee immigration and the people who are experiencing it, but also to the people who are against it and why. Another example was *Jane Eyre*, because I loved the script, but it also made me furious at points.[6] I had conflicting feelings about what [playwright] Polly Teale was saying about who Jane was and how a woman is required to move in the world. I didn't have easy answers, so I really wanted to get in and wrestle around with how she was telling the story. If I can read a play and go, "Boom, I know exactly how I feel about this issue, or I know exactly how this story should be told," then I pass. I want to get my hands dirty in rehearsal and be changed by the work. I want a good puzzle, otherwise I'm not interested. I'm a terrible director if I'm too comfortable. I love living on that edge of "this could be great or it could all fall apart." That's the place that makes me the happiest.

Leigh Silverman

The next good idea

The thing that drives me is the next good idea. I am always looking for scripts where the writer is transforming their style, exploring new themes, or pushing themselves into new territory. For example, David Henry Hwang's *Kung Fu*[7] is a play that acted like a musical and Jeanine Tesori and Brian Crawley's *Violet*[8] is a musical that acted like a play. To

---

[6]Cincinnati Playhouse in the Park, 2017.
[7]Signature Theatre, 2014.
[8]Roundabout Theatre, 2013, and American Airlines Theatre, 2014.

be able to work on plays that are stylistically that adventurous? It's the greatest.

Silverman almost exclusively directs new work. On the rare occasions when she does direct revivals—as in the case of Violet—*she prefers to work with the authors to reinvent the piece. She is fundamentally interested in collaborating with writers to explore themes, styles, and ideas.*

Some directors consider themselves auteurs. I really respect that vision, but it's not mine. That's not how I see myself. The next good idea is not my thing, not your thing, but the thing we can get to together.

Patricia McGregor

You can feel the physical and emotional pulse

What excites me most are pieces where you can feel the physical and emotional pulse right in front of you.

Whatever genre or style of play McGregor directs, her productions are distinguished by animated physical energy and rhythmic movement. From the abstract, simulated violence of Spunk[9] *to the jookin' in* Hurt Village,[10] *McGregor's productions make a play's physical and emotional pulse very visible onstage. She traces the roots of her aesthetic back to childhood.*

The first big performances I saw were street performances that involved a lot of dance and movement. Then, in middle school, I was drawn to Shakespeare because there was something about his linguistic athleticism that I was really interested in. Shakespeare's language is muscular in your mouth and in its rhythms and that felt very active to me. So while I'm sure there's going to be a time where I decide I really want to do a Pinter piece and figure out what's bubbling underneath all of that, I am most drawn to physically engaged, muscular pieces.

---

[9]California Shakespeare Theater, 2012.
[10]Signature Theatre, 2012.

Blanche McIntyre

Human behavior explored theatrically

There are two things I go for when choosing plays to direct. One is how well the writer observes human behavior, which is not necessarily the way that people think behavior works. Sometimes you get a script that seems strange in its depiction of how people operate, but actually, it has observed something with delicacy and accuracy. The other thing is a script that knows theater is a presented medium and is excited by the theatricality of that. I am a total sucker for a script that manages to combine these things.

In 2013, McIntyre directed a critically acclaimed production of Chekhov's The Seagull,[11] *which she cites as an example of a script that combines theatricality with accurate observation of human behavior.*

The thing that seemed strange about *The Seagull* was that the play broke all the traditional rules. The characters were unclear or inarticulate, sometimes they talked to the audience, sometimes they shared an in-joke between themselves without letting the audience in on it; the scenes started and stopped in places that seemed to be arbitrary, and the play seemed to record chaotic, rather than understandable, behavior. When I talked with my designer, we realized that the characters were putting narratives on the events unfolding around them, and it seemed to us that one of the play's concerns is how people take the chaos that they experience and make order from it, inventing characterizations and narratives that often aren't there—the handles that one uses as a human in society to make sense of one's experience.

So the strangeness of the action and construction, and the irrationality of the characters were pointing us to look at a fundamental part of human experience. It was a way of using the tools of theater to do something unusual and interesting, as opposed to turn a trite moral about how if you run away with the wrong guy you'll likely be ruined (as

---

[11]Headlong, 2013.

a lesser piece of theater would have done). So the play is not "theatrical" as we traditionally understand it, but it's very theatrical in the sense that it pushes the boundaries of what theater can achieve in order to explore subject matter or a theme or characters that are not necessarily what traditional theater expects.

Paulette Randall

The characters are honest

I know I want to direct a play when I start reading it and suddenly realize that an hour or two has gone by and I didn't know—when something interrupts me and I realize I've been in that world (and I probably should have been doing something else). I'm seeing images and hearing sounds and imagining the way the characters move. Then all that has to happen is that the play doesn't disappoint in the end and I'll be sold. It's the worst when they disappoint in the end. I've had easier breakups!

Randall has directed most of the ten plays in August Wilson's acclaimed Pittsburgh Cycle, *including a production of* Fences *that transferred to the West End.*[12]

I'm especially drawn to plays where the characters are honest. It's where the truth is told (and it's not always pleasant). So, for example, in *Fences*, you have this extraordinary central character, Troy, who is quite aggressive and a womanizer and all of that. And that's true. But he's more than that. Because he's such a broken character who didn't have the best of beginnings and has had to struggle incredibly hard, you go, "It's not that simple, is it?" You can't just dismiss him as somebody who's a womanizer and can't commit, who does all of these bad things. He's someone who's broken and actually needs to be fixed in some way. So how do you allow that character to come alive and be shared and be given the respect that he needs? A lot of the time you see people who are down and out and you don't know what's taken them to that point. Those voices aren't the norm, but I'm far more interested in

---

[12]Duchess Theatre, 2013.

hearing their stories rather than the typical voices you hear onstage. You can have a character that's charming and witty and entertaining with a twinkle in their eye, but that ain't the truth because if you're that way permanently, you're crazy. So, what else is there? I'm always looking for a character that the audience might really meet and my job is to find out how that character got to where he is.

Randall has also directed devised work, which requires a different process than an existing script.

When there's no script to read before you begin, the subject matter is the thing that has to grab you and make you feel passionate. And you've got to make sure that whoever else is involved is as passionate about the initial idea and feels very strongly that you've all got something to say. So, for example, I directed a devised piece called *Urban Afro Saxons* with two writers who'd never worked together before, Kofi Agyemang and Patricia Elcock.[13] Because I had given myself a ridiculously short amount of time, I knew that I needed two writers to share the writing so that we could be rehearsing while something was being written at the same time. They were both very passionate about the subject matter and started sparking ideas off each other. I worked with the actors to improvise the beginning of it so that we could at least all start on the same page, then the two of them wrote, then we would improvise ahead, and then they would come back and rewrite, and so on. It was bonkers, but it worked.

Indhu Rubasingham

The unexpected voice

I'm interested in the unexpected voice or the unexpected story, in writing that shows me something that I haven't seen before. It could be a scene, it could be a speech—it's not necessarily the whole play—just something that makes me look at the world differently or a thought that I haven't heard on stage before or a perspective we don't see or a voice we don't hear. It could also be fascinating characters or fantastic

---

[13]Talawa/Theatre Royal Stratford East, 2003.

dialogue that feels both real and musical. Or a mixture of these things. The other thing that I'm really drawn to is narrative. More than form, I think. I get frustrated with form without substance, and so I want things to be led by the narrative and then let the narrative instruct and influence the form. So, really, I look for a good story that's unusual and told by people you wouldn't expect. For example, I was attracted to *Belong* by Bola Agbaje because it was looking at characters who wanted to emigrate back to Nigeria from the UK, which is unexpected as plays are always about the desire to emigrate to the West.[14]

In 2012, Rubasingham was named Artistic Director of the then Tricycle Theatre (since changed to Kiln Theatre), where she has commissioned and programmed plays on diverse subject matter by a wide range of playwrights.

I directed *Multitudes* by John Hollingworth.[15] It's a play that looks at the various British Muslim identities in the northern English town of Bradford. The playwright is a white man from Bradford and this was his first play, which we had worked on for a number of years. I encouraged him to go into this world (which he knows inside out) as I saw he had a natural empathy and a real ear for these voices. He was naturally reticent because he felt he would be judged and he wanted it to be accurate. For me, it's important to encourage and support writers to write the worlds they want to (as long as they have respect and empathy). If we limit writers to write only from their own background, we limit their imagination and reinforce the ideas that only black playwrights can write black plays and white writers can only write white plays. We ghettoize playwrights out of a sense of political correctness.

One of the Kiln/Tricycle's biggest successes under Rubasingham's tenure has been Red Velvet, a play about nineteenth-century African American actor Ira Aldridge. The play was written by Lolita Chakrabarti, a British playwright and actor of Bengali descent. Rubasingham and Chakrabarti spent years unsuccessfully trying to get British theaters to

---

[14]Royal Court Theatre, 2012.
[15]Kiln Theatre (then Tricycle Theatre), 2015.

produce the play until Rubasingham took over the Kiln (then Tricycle) and programmed the play in her first season.[16] *It was a critical and box office success and transferred to New York in 2014*[17] *and the West End in 2015,*[18] *demonstrating that an unexpected voice can create artistically exciting and financially viable plays.*

Nadia Fall

Recognizable yet original

I feel you have to fall in love with some aspect of the play you're embarking on while remaining mindful not to overfocus on that particular affinity at the cost of other important themes or ideas within the piece. I'm usually interested in plays that excavate human emotions and behavior that feel completely authentic and recognizable yet deliver these in ways that feel completely original. And most of all, I'm drawn to plays that say something relevant about the world we live in and can help us make sense of it.

Tina Satter

Don't keep repeating what's "good"

If we just keep repeating what's "good," we close off growth. "Good" is what we already know. If you push beyond the known good you might fail. That's what's really exciting.

Satter's approach to choosing projects is different from the above directors because she writes and directs her own plays for her New York-based experimental company Half Straddle. In her plays/productions, Satter circumvents and skews typical dramatic forms and conventions to create highly detailed examinations of various types of characters, from high school football players to dance studio owners to Chekhov's landed gentry. Her willingness to "push beyond the known good" and

---

[16]Kiln Theatre (then Tricycle Theatre), 2012.
[17]St. Ann's Warehouse, 2014.
[18]Garrick Theatre, 2015.

*risk critical and artistic failure has freed her to develop creative pieces
that explore new possibilities in form and style.*

New Plays versus Classics

Indhu Rubasingham

New plays: A magnifying glass to society

I'm most interested in new writing because I think it's the cutting edge
of current social issues, a mirror, a magnifying glass to society. It's contemporary social commentary and is relevant and immediate.

*Rubasingham has directed many new plays about contemporary social
issues, from* Clubland[19]*—Roy William's exploration of sexual and racial politics in London—to* Handbagged[20]*—Moira Buffini's shrewdly hilarious study
of the power dynamic between Queen Elizabeth II and Margaret Thatcher.*

If you think about the history of theater, we remember and talk about
the plays that give us the zeitgeist of their time, or examine the issues
of their time, or give an understanding of the world where they were
created. We rarely talk about the productions. We talk about the plays
and the scripts. That's what we study. So when you're directing the first
production of a play, you're implicit in realizing that vision and those
ideas and thoughts because new plays are rarely judged on the script
alone. They're nearly always judged by its first production. So, as a
director, you're part of the process of helping the playwright realize
their vision. If it works well, you're in true collaboration with the playwright, and you're systematically, intrinsically part of the vanguard of
commenting on something about now. Some directors like classics
because you can really put your stamp on it. Often the director is the
focal point of directing a classic—especially if they're trying to do something bold with it—because audiences aren't judging the play, they're
looking at that director's interpretation of that play, or the director is

---

[19]Royal Court Theatre, 2001.
[20]Kiln Theatre (then Tricycle Theatre), 2013, and Vaudeville Theatre, 2014.

asking us to look at the play in a new way. With a new play, it's harder for a director to put a stamp or, more realistically, for the director's work to be seen. However, it's imperative to support and release the writer's vision and, as it's untried as a piece of work, it therefore becomes more risky and more exciting, in my opinion. I mean, I've seen Shakespeare and been greatly moved, but I remember seeing *The Normal Heart* as a teenager and it blowing my mind away because it was something that was speaking to me about now.

Lyndsey Turner

New plays: Not mere journalistic responses to the world

Turner has directed a range of classics, established scripts, and new works. She has a particular interest in collaborating with writers on plays that explore current social and economic issues, such as Laura Wade's Posh[21] *and Lucy Kirkwood's* Chimerica[22] *(for which Turner won an Olivier Award for Best Director).*

Some of the new plays that have been the most exciting and most pertinent to the world we're living in the last few years have been written by women. You've got Lucy Prebble daring to talk about the financial crisis in *Enron* and the big pharmaceuticals in *The Effect*. You've got Laura Wade on the class system, Lucy Kirkwood on the big economic story about China and America, Sam Holcroft who's writing about stem cell research or the horrors of the surveillance state. My generation of female writers have distinguished themselves by their willful assertion of the right to write about anything and everything. And they're putting the leg work in: they're going out to talk to the big pharmaceutical companies, they're reading endless books about how the Chinese economy is structured. All these plays took years to write. There's a kind of diligence in that, but they're not dour blue stockings who happen to be good at research. They're writers of real flair, humanity, and depth: these

---

[21]Royal Court Theatre, 2010, and Duke of York's Theatre, 2012.
[22]Headlong/Almeida Theatre, 2013, and Harold Pinter Theatre, 2013.

are not just well-behaved plays or mere journalistic responses to the world; they are sparkling with metaphor and life. These writers are my major source of inspiration: I want to get better at what I do in order to be up to the task of directing what they're writing.

Rachel Chavkin

New plays: It doesn't quite know what it's trying to be yet

Each new project is a new way of thinking about some aspect of the world. I like being a part of enriching the world's tools in that way. I like saying something that no one's ever said or looking at something from an angle no one ever quite has before.

Many of Chavkin's projects seek new ways of thinking about historical eras, including those she has created with her company The TEAM and those she has collaborated on with playwright Dave Malloy, such as Natasha, Pierre, and the Great Comet of 1812.[23] *Although she is interested in subject matter from the past, she is drawn to innovative forms and staging; thus she works primarily on new plays. She collaborates closely with playwrights to help them find the best narrative structure for expressing their ideas.*

I like figuring out puzzles and working on a new play is a harder puzzle than a classic. Because it's lumpy. It doesn't quite know what it's trying to be yet. There's just something quite thrilling about that.

Lear deBessonet

Classics: No one is the authority

One of the amazing things about classics is that no one is the authority. I learned this from Michelle Hensley, who ran the company Ten Thousand Things in Minneapolis and who has been a very big influence for me. So many contemporary American dramas are set in a

---

[23]Ars Nova, 2012, American Repertory Theater, 2015, and Imperial Theatre, 2016.

particular sociological reality, and whenever you produce them, there are going to be people who know a lot about that particular reality. So if the show is set in a wealthy apartment on the Upper East Side of Manhattan, there are going to be people in your audience that have more and less authentic relationships with that material. With classics, no one is the authority. No one knows what the island is in *The Tempest*. It's a place that we create together. Even *Winter's Tale*, which is set in Sicilia and Bohemia, you could think of them as literal places but you don't have to—I think with all Shakespeare there's the invitation to make it as much a fairy tale world as you want. Classics invite this act of collective imagining in a way that naturalistic plays often don't.

The productions deBessonet has directed for the Public Theatre's Public Works project were all ambitious acts of collective imagining. In collaboration with lyricist/composer Todd Almond, deBessonet has created three musical adaptations of classics—The Tempest,[24] *A Winter's* Tale,[25] *and* The Odyssey.[26] *Each production featured a cast of over 200 New Yorkers, including a small core of professional actors alongside skilled community performers (for example, Caliban's tormentors in* The Tempest *were teen ballet dancers, Penelope's suitors in* The Odyssey *were played by leather-clad bikers, and Big Bird made an appearance in* A Winter's Tale*). To pull these large-scale spectacles together at the open air Delacorte Theater in Central Park, deBessonet drew on the expertise and imagination of diverse musicians, choreographers, dancers, actors, designers and other creative thinkers, giving hundreds of people a degree of authority over each production.*

Roxana Silbert

Classics: You know you have a play that works

Early in her career, Silbert focused on directing new plays and held leadership positions in three theaters focused on new work (Royal

---

[24]Public Theatre, 2013.
[25]Public Theatre, 2014.
[26]Public Theatre, 2015.

Court, Traverse, and Paines Plough). She began directing Shakespeare in 2009 when she joined the Royal Shakespeare Company (RSC) as Associate Director, then four years later moved into her current position as Artistic Director of Birmingham Repertory Company, where she directs a combination of new plays, established scripts, and classics.

When I started at RSC, I found it very, very difficult to go from the world of new plays to the world of Shakespeare. As a director of new work, you're trying to work really closely with the writer to get into their head and then put as close to what you think is in that head onstage in the best way you can. For example, when I went into rehearsals with *Dunsinane* by David Greig, which has now been touring for five years, it was ten pages long.[27] He made that play in the rehearsal room. But when you're directing a classic like Shakespeare, the pressure is "What are *you* going to *do* with it?" When I came to RSC, I didn't bring to the table the knowledge of someone like the current Artistic Director Greg Doran, who is a brilliant Shakespeare scholar and has seen several productions of every Shakespeare play. Before then, I did not go and see many Shakespeare productions. I read the plays and loved them, but I spent most of my theatergoing days at new plays or experimental work. So I didn't go into my RSC Shakespeare productions responding to all the other productions. I'm not a director's director in that sense—there isn't a certain style that I bring to a play. I hoped to achieve a sort of freshness and immediacy in my productions because I was coming to them as if for the first time. I tried to literally just look at the text and tell the story. It was sort of the George Devine approach, which is to direct a new play like a classic and a classic like a new play. And I loved it, because with Shakespeare you know you have a play that works. When you go into rehearsal with a new play, you rarely have a play that works. There's only one new play that I've directed that we didn't radically rewrite through the rehearsal process. So you can't sit safe in the knowledge that a new play works. But you can with Shakespeare.

During my time at RSC, I absolutely fell in love with Shakespeare. He writes about fundamental issues like moral values in an extraordinary way. For example, in *Richard III* (which I directed in 2012), the audience

---

[27]Royal Shakespeare Company, 2010.

love him until he kills the children.[28] Then you feel them withdraw, like there's an unspoken agreement that it's okay for him to kill all these other people, including his wife, but it's not okay to kill two kids. And the audience—five hundred people—have all decided that at the same time.

Blanche McIntyre

Classics: Sometimes I have to try not to be a fan

When I direct established plays, I like to see what other people have done; but no two directors can ever direct alike, and I tend to get ideas from the script and the actors, however famous the play is. That said, there are a handful of productions I've seen—the Donmar *The Real Thing* is one and the Tim Carroll *Twelfth Night* another—that made such an impression on me that I know I should really stay away from the play, because subconsciously I would be trying to recreate it. So sometimes I have to try not to be a fan.

Karin Coonrod

It's always about text in space

Some of Coonrod's best known productions have been of Shakespeare's plays.

With Shakespeare, there's an enormous generosity on the part of the writer. He gives lots of room for the director to write in space (I think the most confident writers are those who let directors write in space!) In my aesthetic, I like to create a strong shape or form for the company and then to explode that form with the humanity of the character as presented by the actor. What's important is to calibrate the humanity of the characters with a large metaphysical frame, all of which go beyond the quotidian, beyond the mere political.

Coonrod's Shakespeare productions typically feature striking stage pictures and soundscapes filled with characters portrayed in rich,

---

[28]Royal Shakespeare Company, 2012.

empathetic detail—from her La MaMa music-theater production of The Tempest[29] *to her minimally staged, lust-filled comic production of* Love's Labour's Lost *at The Public Theatre.*[30]

Shakespeare smells out the dark and light in our nature, the psychic cartography spills far beyond the confines of the civil, and it is our business to penetrate the mystery of what is not seen. That is the Artaudian infection in the theater that, if we think it and know it and mine it, will be felt by an audience. In this way, I believe the ephemeral becomes eternal.

Coonrod has also directed a number of new plays and her own adaptations of literary texts. She explains that her approach is similar for both classics and new work.

There is a great rigor attached to the preparation of classical work in the theater: rhythm, scansion, rhyme, and an understanding of rhetoric and all the tropes of literature come into play. When one turns one's attention to the directing of newly minted plays, the same kind of visceral focus in the preparation of the text brings great aliveness in the hearing of the text. In the end, it is always about the text in space, not talking heads on a screen. And when one treats the language—whether classical or newly minted—with muscularity the piece has more vitality for the audience.

Kimberly Senior

It's a world premiere every night

Senior questions the binary between "classics" and "new work."

We must always be beginning. That's a phrase that I use all the time— when I'm talking to my children, when I'm talking to my actors, and when I'm just speaking in general. I feel like we live in this culture that is constantly about finding the ending. What's the end goal? What's the goal? What's the result? There is a use to that and I'm sure my ambition and

---

[29]La Mama Annex, 2014.
[30]Public Theatre, 2011.

tenacity has been tied into that theory of thinking, but there is also value in looking at things fresh. What if we start at the beginning every time?

My standpoint is that there is no such thing as an old play. That we are always beginning. When I'm directing *Hedda Gabler*,[31] it's a world premiere every night because no one has ever seen that combination of audience members with that performance in live theater. That ephemeral nature is what ties into always beginning.

Polly Findlay

It's an irony

In both the United States and the UK, it is very common for theaters to hire young directors to direct studio productions of new plays; thus, many directors (including a large proportion of those included in this book) cut their professional teeth on new work.

In some ways, of course, it's strange that new directors are so often given new plays. Your responsibility as the director of a new play is generally speaking much greater than your responsibility to a playwright that's already had several versions of their play produced, or who is dead. That's an irony in the way that our system works, that as a young director you're so often handed that responsibility so often at a stage where you don't quite know what you're doing yet.

Influences and Inspirations

Kimberly Senior

Influences and inspirations are ever changing

Directors are constantly influenced by the work of other directors—both their peers and people they've never met.

There's a local director who is on the faculty at DePaul here named Damon Kiely, and he has just been my number one go-to. He and I, we

---

[31]Writers Theatre, 2014.

exchange books constantly. He turned me on to Katie Mitchell's book and then we would talk about it and then we would talk about like, "Did you try that in rehearsal and did that work?" He would shoot me in the head for calling him my mentor. He calls me his guru and I say, "I'm not your guru, I'm your peer." But we have this exchange. Charlie Newell, who is the artistic director at the Court Theatre, is another influence. I was on their education staff fifteen years ago so I know him, but I've never worked there as a director. We don't really have much of an artistic conversation, but I see everything he does. It's been so inspiring to me in the way that he's someone who grabs onto a big idea and does it 200 percent. Sometimes it works and sometimes it doesn't, but that's been really inspiring to me. In moments where I'm feeling not so confident in my idea, I ask, "What would Charlie Newell do in this moment?" I also admire the highly, highly detailed work of Sam Gold. He stands moments to their fullest and shows us the full horizon of what a moment can be. I'm quick, quick, quick, and sometimes I think, "I need to Sam Gold this moment." These are the people in my mind right now, but in a year there will be others. The truth is, influences and inspirations are ever changing.

Liesl Tommy

Taking risks and fighting

I've been influenced by directors like Peter Sellers, Ariane Mnouchkine, Robert Lepage, and Christian Lupa, and what I think I got from them is just always reminding myself to take risks. So even if I'm in an Off-Broadway 200-seat theater, I push the lighting designer, push the set designer, push the sound designer, push myself to make provocative and surprising design choices. Just because we live in a society that doesn't get multimillion-dollar grants for the arts and therefore can't have really expansive, cutting-edge design like our brothers and sisters in Berlin, that doesn't mean that the vision must be small or safe.

I have also been very influenced by growing up during the Apartheid era of South Africa. There's just a part of me that will always be obsessed with issues of freedom, racial equality, civil rights, and how you build or tear down a civil society. Even when I do a thing like *Frozen* at Disneyland, suddenly I'm fighting for civil rights.[32]

---

[32]Disneyland California, 2016.

May Adrales

Discovering Asian American characters

Adrales is Filipina American and grew up in rural Virginia.

I was a Modern Studies and Literature major in college and, in a literature class, I came across David Henry Hwang's *M. Butterfly*. That was so eye-opening because I had not seen or read plays at that point that offered a political perspective from an Asian American point of view. I started reading all of his work and became so enthralled with it that I began to see a different path for myself. I've since worked with Hwang and now consider him a colleague, but I also credit him for the fact that I got involved in theater.

After college, when I moved to New York, one of the first shows I saw was Jessica Hagedorn's play *Dogeaters*. I almost cried upon walking into the theater because I'd never seen so many Asian people together. And I'd certainly never seen anybody that looked like me or my parents on stage before. I imagine that, for most other people, that's what they usually see when they walk into the theater. I realized that I'd been missing that all this time. Even though many family dramas are universal in their theme, there's a difference if you have that cultural familiarity with the characters.

Rachel Chavkin

Suzuki and athleticism

Athleticism is a hallmark of my work. I spent years training with the SITI Company, and Suzuki as a form is entirely based around creating a sense of athleticism in even the simplest of gestures like walking across space. When you slow walk in Suzuki, it strains your sensor core because of all the nuance and internal elements of that physical form. I had an interest in athleticism and people doing the extraordinary onstage before I trained with the SITI Company, but I think they (and Suzuki in particular) helped me articulate what that interest was.

Tina Satter

Take your head out of your own tiny hustle

To be frank, in general I get more inspiration from visual art than I do from seeing theater. And there's also some really good television that has been inspiring me recently. Shows where I felt not just the balm of, "I'll put this on and I'll relax," but, "Oh my God, this is exciting me and making me think with what it's doing artistically."

Satter and her company Half Straddle are a feature of the Downtown New York experimental theater scene.

You need to take your head out of your own tiny hustle and remember there's a larger theater world and you're in it. I see a ton of Downtown stuff because it's my friends' work. Everyone I know is making something/doing something. You need to know what other people are doing.

On Finding Your Niche

Nadia Fall

I don't fit into boxes very well

We live in a world where we expect to identify things very quickly and simply and in a packageable way. We want to know exactly what we're getting so we can take it or leave it. If you're very mixed in your taste or interests, people don't know what box to put you in and might hesitate to use you as a signature artist. I certainly don't fit into boxes very well. I've grown up in the Middle East and Europe. I have very varied taste as a person in everything: in what I eat, in what I wear, what music I listen to, the artists I like to collaborate with, the actors I'm drawn to. So, I continue to make contrasting work, and I wouldn't want it any other way. I love that I could do Shaw's *Doctor's Dilemma*[33] — a play that's all

---

[33]National Theatre, 2012.

about rhetoric and mind-boggling debates—then do *Home*[34]—a verbatim play with a beat boxer. Honestly, if someone said to me, "Nadia, you can only do one or the other," I would feel quite restricted and saddened.

There are colleagues that I admire who have a very strong identity and flavor to their work because of the plays they choose to direct, their process and their aesthetic. Katie Mitchell, for example. When I see that something is directed by her, I feel excited and want to watch it because I know I'm going to get a very particular production: it's going to feel and look like a Katie Mitchell show and ultimately there will be a quality to the work. In Europe, there is this culture of director as auteur which is very much upheld and I think that idea is increasingly becoming part of UK theater, too. The work I make is so eclectic that sometimes I do worry about the notion of carving out a niche to some extent. When you do a wide variety of work, does it denote a lack identity or vision? I don't know. But personally, I am drawn to so many different types of plays and as I study a given text or narrative, it is the material itself that reveals to me the approach it requires. Ultimately, I'm led by and serve the play and every play has different demands.

Fall, who is Muslim, was born in London and split time between there and Kuwait City throughout her childhood.

I used to avoid doing plays about the Asian diaspora or Islam because that was part of my heritage and I thought, "I don't want to be pigeonholed." And also because those stories tend to bring up all kinds of unresolved ideas in my own head. Working on plays like *Dara*[35] and *Disgraced*[36] forced me to confront some difficult questions, and such pieces about your cultural background or plays that bring up subjects which have affected your own life make you expose yourself. They may be the hardest pieces to do, but I'm a great advocate of doing the things that scare you the most.

---

[34]National Theatre, 2013.
[35]National Theatre, 2015.
[36]Bush Theatre, 2013.

May Adrales

I simply work on my own terms

People will label me as an Asian American director. And I used to worry about that moniker, but now I'm tired of defining myself against a primarily white and male mainstream. I simply work on my own terms and choose projects that fit into a politically conscious, spiritually woke artistic point of view.

I always gravitate towards stories that challenge societal norms and political status quo. As a first-generation Filipina American from the rural South, I've always felt like an outsider. So the theater I aim to do works to reframe the largely accepted historical narrative, namely from a female, subjugated, or person-of-color perspective. The plays I do typically diversify and expand cultural representation onstage and often feature strong, wise, badass women at the center.

I find the beautiful within the terrorizing and ugly parts of human nature. Exposing the ugliness of human nature allows us to dissect and understand the roots of violence. I'm not afraid to find the vulnerability within destroyed characters, as in the case of Tommy Smith's *The Wife*[37] and Betty Shamieh's *The Strangest*[38] or A. Rey Pamatmat's *after all the terrible things I do.*[39] But conversely, my work can include an immense amount of joy and hope as in the case of Qui Nguyen's *Vietgone*[40] and Rey's *Edith Can Shoot Things and Hit Them.*[41] In both those plays, people with seemingly unsurmountable odds find family.

Now I feel like people come to me with a lot of different kinds of plays and I enjoy that. I like pulling different parts of my personality. I've done comedies, really dark plays, and musicals. Every play is different to me, it's a new challenge. I'm still finding who I am as an artist and so every play that I do I try to throw myself into and let it change me as I'm changing it.

---

[37]Access Theater, 2010.
[38]Fourth Street Theater, 2017.
[39]Milwaukee Repertory Theater, 2014.
[40]South Coast Repertory, 2015.
[41]Actors Theatre, 2011.

Lear deBessonet

A personal spiritual shift

DeBessonet, who grew up as a fundamentalist Christian, describes how her spiritual journey paralleled and informed her development as an artist.

In my first four years in New York, I made devised pieces. During those years, I was moving through a real spiritual crisis. I was wrestling with fundamentalism, trying to reconcile the love of God that I felt like I had experienced with the things that I was learning were not true. In American fundamentalist Christianity, there's a lot of emphasis on the afterlife and the idea that this world only exists to the extent that it affects things in the next life. As a child, I found the divisions between people to be very sad. I'm from Louisiana, where the racial and class divisions are really obvious, and I thought, "Well, in heaven, all of those people will be dancing together." Then in those first years in New York, I encountered the possibility that I had been misthinking about time and imposing a linear idea of time onto something that maybe isn't linear. Jesus says, "The kingdom of heaven is here." I realized that maybe we should be investing in this world as a place where both heaven and hell are manifest constantly on a daily basis. That was a central turning point for me, a personal spiritual shift. So I took that image of people of different ethnicities and classes holding hands and dancing and said, "Let's make that now. Let's do that here."

DeBessonet has directed many community-based theater projects that bring diverse people together as collaborators. Most notably, in 2013, she became the founding director of the Public Theater's Public Works program, which creates large-scale musical adaptations of classics using a mix of professional actors and performers drawn from community groups throughout New York's five boroughs.

Leah Gardiner

Resisting choosing a niche

I spent time early on choosing projects that would help me better discover myself as a theater director. I did classics. I did Shakespeare.

I did world premieres. I did musicals. I did French Renaissance comedy. My agent said, "You are going to have to choose what kind of theater you want to do." I said, "I don't want to choose. I want to do all kinds of theater." She said, "Well, that's going to take you much longer. The reality is you're a woman, you're of color, and no one is going to call you to do Shakespeare or direct musicals. You should just focus on new plays." I love new plays, but I didn't want to do just that. I don't know, maybe I made a huge error in my choices in terms of building a career and becoming famous, but I was choosing projects that were helping me build as an artist.

Gardiner describes the unique niche she eventually carved out.

Now I tend to do very complicated, sometimes nearly impossible shows. Shows that are dramaturgically very smart. For these kinds of shows, people call me. I'm not afraid of the material. I like the challenge and it has always been exciting for me. And I seem to work well with people others perceive as "difficult." I do very well with celebrities. Before I worked with Anna Deavere Smith on *Notes from the Field: Doing Time*,[42] someone warned me she could be difficult. So I called George Wolfe, who had worked with her before. He said, "Just leave your ego at the door." That was all I needed.

Polly Findlay

Learning by trying out different things

I've been very lucky in being able to try out all kinds of different things. For example, doing Derren Brown's magic show *Svengali* was probably the biggest learning curve for me in terms of pure directing craft.[43] With a magic show, you can't get it wrong. You can't have any ambiguity at all. Every moment has to be completely clear, and the way the audience reacts provides such an obvious litmus test. You can sometimes get away with telling yourself that an audience's silence is a positive thing, a sign of engagement, whereas in a magic show there is no doubt that if they don't audibly react at precisely the right moment, you've failed.

---

[42]Berkeley Rep, 2015.
[43]Shaftesbury Theatre, 2011.

KJ Sanchez

Specialization

Sanchez cautions that there's not a one-size-fits-all answer to the question "Should a director specialize in one type of play?"

Whether you choose to specialize depends on if it serves you and your goals. I think the real key is knowing what interests you. Stating "I want to be *this* kind of director" doesn't make sense to me. Instead, I think you need to say, "These are the stories I want to tell and here's why I want to tell them." What are you passionate about doing? Why are you telling stories? Why are you doing theater? If you don't know, then something is wrong.

Some of my favorite directors are very, very specialized. I'm not, and that's fine too. I like learning systems, so I loved learning how to build and direct a documentary play, but I also love pulling apart plays that are built like brick shithouses, like *Harvey*.[44] Some specialized directors really gave up a lot to be that specialized; but I have to deal with people who only want to see me in one way and are confused when I'm lobbying to do a play that they think is outside my niche, so there are pros and cons to both.

Season Planning

Sarah Benson

What will I invite thousands of people to see?

Benson became artistic director of Soho Rep in New York in 2007.

What will I invite thousands of people to see? What is going to be worthy of their time? We're asking them to turn out of their homes, go away from their families, get a baby sitter . . . it's a commitment. I don't

---

[44]Milwaukee Repertory Theater, 2014.

want to waste their time. I can't tell our audiences that they will love everything we do, but I can tell them we will try to use the forum to its fullest potential and give them a specific theatrical experience. I read a lot of plays that are smart, insightful writing, but could be an amazing TV show or an amazing movie; I don't understand why I would go to the theater to see that.

At Soho Rep, each play is often very different from each other in terms of how it presents. In one season we had: Anne Washburn's *10 out of 12*,[45] which puts the audience in a technical rehearsal at a theater; debbie tucker green's *generations*,[46] where there was dirt all over the floor and a choir of thirteen people for a thirty-minute experience; and *Washeteria*,[47] which was a design-driven project completely instigated by a designer and led by a designer collaborating with other artists (including a large group of second graders). People often ask me, "What's Soho Rep's style?" We don't ever have "a style." I'm adverse to the concept of style. We offer very different theatrical forms from one production to the next.

Vicky Featherstone

Instinct and urgency and risk

As the artistic director of three theaters that specialize in new plays, Featherstone has spent decades deciding which playwrights to culti-vate and which plays to program. Here she discusses her approach to choosing among the many, many new plays that she encounters.

Each theater creates a shared vocabulary among a group of people as a tool that enables us to share an understanding of plays and why we put them on; but actually we choose plays by instinct. And audiences only have instinct as well. You can get a very literate theater audience—like some in London—who have sort of submerged their instinct in the world of knowledge (knowledge of the director and the playwright and

---

[45]Soho Rep, 2015.
[46]Soho Rep, 2014.
[47]Soho Rep, 2015.

the play they saw last week and so on). But really, when I read a play the first time, my response to it is no different than the response of an audience the first time they sit in a space and witness that play. It's instinctual. And your instinct doesn't actually become more refined. It's just that you can trust it more and more.

One of the things I instinctually respond to in a play is a sense of urgency. Urgency can exist in a myriad of ways. So it could feel urgent news-wise, which is the most obvious way. Or it could feel urgent that *this* playwright say *this* thing now because they're saying it in such a way that demands to be heard. And we didn't know that it needed to be said until we read the play. Or it could be that the form is urgent in itself. Urgent doesn't have to be clever or worthy or intellectual. It could be that we really need a brilliant comedy. In 1956, George Devine said that the Royal Court has the responsibility to be alert to a constantly changing set of contexts and truths. That's the cue for finding the urgent: What are the set of contexts and truths that you need to be alert to right now? And they change on a daily basis. So, the work I'm most interested in has some sort of fierceness or risk at its heart. And I don't mean that it is necessarily therefore deeply experimental or avant-garde but that it has to have a sort of transgression, some urgency to exist that will set it apart. When theater just becomes a treadmill, I very quickly find it mediocre and meaningless. So I'm always looking for the surprise or the shift, which is why it's great being here at Royal Court. It'd be really, really hard to have this sensibility and be running a different kind of theater.

As an artistic director, I only feel my organization is progressing when we are taking a journey toward the unknown or into a risk. Otherwise I feel that we're paddling water, which makes me feel uncomfortable and insecure. Some people can handle that uncertainty and risk and some people really can't, but as the leader of an organization, I have to be very confident that that it's alright for everyone to feel uncertain and a little nervous. And I strive to create a climate in the organization where it feels right to exist with those feelings. That was really easy with the National Theatre of Scotland because I was the founding artistic director, so I started from scratch. Every single person there genuinely only felt comfortable when we were saying, "Oh my God, what are we doing? How are we going to do this?" And when you live like that, you mature and gain experience and you bring more and more knowledge to the process of taking risks. The writers I really respect and want to encourage here at Royal Court are the writers who, every single time they write a play, knowledgably go into an unknown. They never tread water.

Indhu Rubasingham
It's about taste, not "quality"

In 2012, Rubasingham became Artistic Director of the Tricycle Theatre in Kilburn (later changed to Kiln Theatre). Kilburn is one of the most racially and ethnically diverse neighborhoods in London. She cautions against using "quality" as a yardstick for measuring the value of new plays.

Who decides what is quality and whose lens are we judging this through? It's really about taste, isn't it? I'm more likely to go for a play that may be rough and not as polished as something by a more experienced playwright but that has an essence or is saying something different or giving a perspective that's different. Our taste is influenced by so many factors, and to ignore this and not understand their influence can make us miss good work and imply superiority of one form over another. Different cultures have different means and methods of making theater and the West's delineation of skills and labor has led to the playwright being separate from the actor and separate from the director. This is not the case in other countries and traditions and, therefore, what quality judgments are we imposing?

In my first season, a fellow artistic director said to me, "Be really bold with your season. Put on what you believe in." So I programmed two new plays—*Paper Dolls*,[48] which had been doing the rounds in America but hadn't had a production, and *Red Velvet*, which had been doing the rounds in England and hadn't had a production.[49] And they were both huge hits. *Paper Dolls*, which is a play with music based on a true story about Filipino drag queens in Israel, ran for eight weeks with no stars, no big name, nothing, and was sold out. *Red Velvet*, which is

---

[48]Kiln Theatre (then Tricycle Theatre), 2013.
[49]Kiln Theatre (then Tricycle Theatre), 2012.

a historical play about the nineteenth-century African American actor Ira Aldridge, won multiple awards and transferred to New York. Then, in my second year, everyone was telling me not to do *Handbagged*[50] because it was going to follow on *The Audience*, another play about the Queen that had just played on the West End starring Helen Mirren. I said, "Look, we're just doing it in Kilburn, it's not going to matter." And then it transferred to the West End. So, I guess what I have learnt is that audiences are interested in good and unusual stories, the unexpected and the less conventional, so I am learning to trust more and more my own taste and knowing that there is an audience out there. Of course, I try to be practical in the programming and not do all new risky world premieres; but actually at times when I've compromised and gone, "Okay, let's try and give the audiences what I think they want," it has never worked as well as I thought. The box office has not done that well when I've played safe.

Roxana Silbert

Giving us a way to think about how we're living

Silbert has been part of the season planning process for five theaters: the Traverse, the Royal Court, Paines Plough, RSC, and Birmingham Rep. Here she talks about her criteria for choosing which plays to program.

In the three organizations that I worked in with new play focus, I was looking for plays that were looking forward in some way. They might be telling a story that was quite well known or dealing in an area of work that had been done before, but they were very experimental formally. Or the form might be quite conventional, but it was the first time that we'd really heard the story. And I was very, very interested in plays by people whose work did not sound like anybody else's. With the writers that I have worked with whom I most admire, like David Greig and Dennis Kelley, I can literally pick up a page from one of their scripts, read it, and know who's written that play. There's something about the quality

---

[50]Kiln Theatre (then Tricycle Theatre), 2013, and Vaudeville Theatre, 2014.

of their line-by-line dialogue that's very attractive (and you cannot teach line-by-line dialogue).

I suppose that I'm also really interested in work that has something to do with the world we're living in. To me, the play's got to be giving us a way to think about how we're living and why we live the way we do. So, when I was Artistic Director at Paines Plough, we wouldn't read any biographical plays because they may be fascinating factually but not interesting dramatically to me. So that's the framework within which I make decisions about what I want to program, but also what I want to direct.

Silbert describes the particular challenges of season planning at a highly specialized theater like the Royal Shakespeare Company.

There are thirty-seven Shakespeare plays and so, if you're at the RSC and mainly what you produce is Shakespeare, how do you decide which plays to do when? Before I arrived, Michael Boyd had done the complete works, which was brilliant, but then after that what do you do? How do you curate those plays? There are lots of different ways of doing it and I think sometimes as programmers we think we're being really, really clever, but audiences don't really notice. They just know that they love that play and they want to come and see it or they don't know that play and they'd like to see it. It's very different from programming a new writing theater where when a brilliant play arrives on your desk, its excellence is the only justification you need to do it. It's also very different from programming at Birmingham Rep where you have the entire global repertoire to choose from.

Erica Whyman

Good, bold decisions

As Deputy Artistic Director of RSC, Whyman is part of the team that plans seasons for one of the largest, most influential theater organizations in the UK. She describes how that visibility affects how she approaches programming.

It is motivating to think that if we make good, bold decisions about programming, particularly decisions we are not expected to make, we can change the perception of the RSC and attract new audiences to our work. And we have special responsibilities to our artists, I think—to make sure Shakespeare and Shakespeare's spirit is alive and inspiring for them, that the next generation want to work with his plays. I feel keenly our responsibility to lead, to ask the big questions, to represent our world on stage, to be ambitiously diverse, to challenge our critics, and widen the horizons of our audiences.

Diane Rodriguez
A parallel universe of art makers

In addition to her job as Associate Artistic Director of Center Theater Group (CTG), Rodriguez serves as Chair of the board of directors for Theatre Communications Group, the national service organization for professional theaters in the United States. In these two capacities, Rodriguez has become familiar with the work of hundreds of theater companies across the country. She identifies two parallel currents running through American theater today and discusses efforts to merge those currents by programming outside companies to perform at a major regional theater.

In the United States, there's an aesthetic and type of art making that runs parallel to what happens in regional, League of Resident Theatres (LORT) theaters. It's found in small companies across the country that are making work together and then either trying to find touring networks or having a space in their own home and getting an audience to come to their space. The Rude Mechs in Austin, Texas, are a classic example. They have been doing work in their space for fifteen to twenty years and in the last five years or so have started to tour nationwide. They're at the forefront because they've been doing it a long time and they're very good, but there are so many other companies across the country that are doing the same thing. I want these artists to have access to a very resourced theater, but because the aesthetics are often very different from what we usually do at regional, LORT theaters like CTG, the two don't necessarily merge. In regional theaters, we are usually about finding plays that are works of literature, and these companies are about creating work that is experiential, or political, or visual theater.

At CTG, I've been trying to bring this parallel universe of art makers into the organization and have had a lot of success. I've tried various ways of getting the work embedded—as part of festivals, as a one-off event for two weeks, or as part of the subscription season. It may not be a very long run and it may not be subscribed, but there is a sense of trying to cross that bridge and see what's on the other side. I think we're very good at that at CTG and other theaters across the country are doing more and more of it too, like La Jolla Playhouse and The Public in New York.

Honestly, the obstacle is money. I look at survey charts of how much money my projects bring in to the organization, versus everyone else's, and it's always on the low end. So you always have to fight to stay relevant and important within the organization with these kinds of shows, because you're challenging the status quo. There are always great reviews and the productions have a big impact on audiences, but the constant question is how can we make them have more impact economically? Because that's how we're going to get more of them in. I want them on the main stage instead of small spaces, partially because it will bring in more money, but really because more people will see it and it will have greater impact.

Nadia Fall

It takes an alchemist

Fall is currently an Associate Director at the National Theatre in London.

I sit in meetings where we're reading plays and vigorously debating which ones to take further. It's incredibly difficult for programmers. You have to give your audience something of what they want and at the same time try to get them to see things they wouldn't necessarily automatically go for. You have to fill big old hungry theater spaces like the Olivier and the Lyttleton. And, as well as choosing plays that will come alive, you have to choose a season that will make the building come alive. It's easy to look at a theater from the outside and go, "Why aren't they doing more of this?" or "Why would they choose that?" But on the inside you see it's a difficult, difficult task. It takes a real alchemist to understand it and the ability to do that alchemy is what makes a brilliant artistic director.

Choosing Collaborators

Liesl Tommy

The vibe

I collaborate with people who I think are not afraid of conceptualizing ideas and of pushing the envelope. I'm interested in a hyperrealism and I like when people go there with me. I try to find out if they'll go there with me by seeing their work but also by just having a conversation with them. I was just hiring a sound designer for a show and I was getting pressure from the theater to hire them quickly. We had had two or three phone calls, but I told the theater we were going to meet in person before I decided. I could sense their frustration, but I was not going to rush the process. I have to spend hours and hours in tech with this person and it has to make sense, so I have to vibe it out. That's a big part of what we do: the vibe. There are a million talented people out there, but are we gonna be able to communicate and is the vibe right?

I have people that I consider my team. We have a good vibe, we have our shortcuts, I challenge them and they challenge me. It's a very satisfying process. Though there are definitely times when I feel like I'm getting too comfortable and need to introduce some new energy into my process just so that I can keep stretching myself.

Lyndsey Turner

Women daring each other

I am increasingly drawn to female collaborators and it's not because they're going to give me an easy ride or a shoulder to cry on. Most of the women I work with know nothing about my personal life: that's not our point of impact on each other. They're all smart as hell and I love the way they think. The way we dignify our gender is to do the best work that we possibly can. And the women I know are daring each other to be braver, more audacious and more ambitious in their response to the work and to the world.

Patricia McGregor

The greatest gift a director can have is a great stage manager

Between earning her BFA in Theater Studies at Southern Methodist and her MFA in Directing at Yale, McGregor worked professionally as a stage manager.

The greatest gift a director can have is a great stage manager who allows them not to have to think with that highly organized side. The director is the one who's creating and spewing energy and investigating and the stage manager is the one who's organizing everything and preparing for the next step of pushing what you're creating forward into performance. I need to work with very, very good stage managers because if I work with a stage manager who is not wearing that hat well, I'll start to slip back in to stage management mind. The stage managers I really love collaborating with really understand the director's vision and use their brand of artistry to translate that to tech and performance.

Leigh Silverman

Managing ego

As a leader, the thing that I care very much about is that it's always about the work. It's never about people's egos and it's never about personality. We're always going to go with what works best, whether it's my idea or your idea. The only times I have trouble (which happens unfortunately more than I like) are when people's egos get in the way: "My part used to be bigger and now it's smaller," or, "I really wanted those costumes to be those colors and now they can't be because the set is that color." Or, with writers, when they see their play a certain way and you get it in front of an audience in 3-D and it's not working, it can be very hard to be honest with yourself about why it is not—for the writer or for me as the director. I want to be honest with the people that I work with and I want them to be honest with me. I think that is where the leadership skill of managing personalities and ego really comes into play.

Leah Gardiner

I tend to be a bully

As a director, you have to have very strong marketing skills with designers, musical directors, and so on. In my case, I tend to be a bully. I'm known for it. I tell people they have to do it and why, then either they jump onboard and commit or they're very honest with me and say, "You know what? You're always too demanding. I can't do it, but so-and-so can." When Sarah Benson called me about directing debbie tucker green's *generations*[51] at Soho Rep, I told her, "I can't sign onto this until I have the right musical director. If I don't have the right musical director, I'm going to have to pass." I contacted a friend of mine who works in the South African community and he said the only person who could do it was Bongi Duma. I contacted Bongi and told him what I was trying to do. Then I basically told him he didn't have a choice, that he was going to have to do this with me, because it was an important piece of theater and a way to showcase black South Africa. Once Bongi signed on, I let Sarah know that I was going to do the show.

Rachel Chavkin

The benefits of a company

After completing undergraduate degrees at New York University's Tisch School of the Arts, Chavkin and several of her fellow NYU alums formed an ensemble company, The TEAM. The TEAM generates and produces

---

[51]Soho Rep, 2014.

work that merges American history with contemporary concerns. They have toured to cities across the world.

I think the greatest experiments in formal inventions have come from companies, because by their very nature they have to constantly do new things or they ossify. The TEAM has made many plays together and we're each other's best friends and family. We know each other so well and have this institutional memory together, so we can remember when we're repeating the same thing we've done before and call each other on it. We have to constantly be pushing into something new.

Where to Work

May Adrales

Urban and regional audiences

New York audiences are very sophisticated and see a lot of theater, so you have a very different kind of relationship with them than when you're going to someplace that doesn't have as much exposure. Regional audiences often have a much fresher perspective, but you also risk losing them sooner if you don't get to the point. I'll never forget I did a reading of Thomas Bradshaw's *Mary* at the Goodman in Chicago and people were so reactionary. After the reading, some stood up exuberant, while others walked out. People either loved or hated it — the exact kind of reaction you want. When we did the same reading at the Public in New York a couple months later, the reaction was very different. People were very analytical and critical about it, but they had seen some of Tom's work before and were able to judge it in a different way. I get that experience a lot when I work regionally. It does feel like people are much more excited by new work.

It can be a particularly satisfying experience when new work connects with a specific regional population.

Qui Nguyen and I worked in conjunction with South Coast Repertory Theatre to create his play *Vietgone* for a Vietnamese Community Center

in Orange County, which has one of the largest Viet communities outside Vietnam.[52] It was an incredible experience to see how the play
ignited a multigenerational audience. Many of that audience had fled
when Saigon fell in 1975; almost all had similar experiences where they
were separated from loved ones. The younger generation knew the
stories but they had not heard them in a style and form that connected
with them. The experience of connecting this community to the South
Coast Repertory community was richly gratifying and rewarding. We
solidified a partnership with the theater through the power of this play.

*Audiences are not the only thing that can vary between locations.
Adrales observes that a change of locale can also shift the working
practices of artists.*

The other good thing about working in the regions with New York actors
is that they don't have all the diversions they have when they're in the
city. In New York, actors are often out to lunch even when they're in
rehearsal; everyone is constantly checking their phones because their
lives don't stop. If you're out of town for a good eight weeks, they're
with you—it's immersive.

Kimberly Senior
Relationship to place versus relationship to content

*One factor that varies from city to city is the audiences' relationship to
theater and theatergoing. Senior is based in Chicago, but works in other
cities as well, including Pittsburgh where she directed Elaine Murphy's
Little Gem at the City Theatre.[53]*

When you're in a major city like Chicago, a theatergoer is someone who
sees a lot of theater. They don't just go to one theater. They're freelance
audience members. A few years ago in Chicago, everyone was producing an Athol Fugard play for some reason. I saw all those plays and

---

[52]South Coast Repertory, 2015.
[53]City Theatre, 2013.

I remember thinking, "I'm subscribing to Athol Fugard plays this year." I would bump into people that I had seen at other theaters because we were all interested in this thing that was happening right then. I think that that happens in a variety of ways, whether it's tracking a playwright or a director. I have people here in Chicago who, bless their hearts, see everything that I do. They don't care what theater it is. That's about seeing Kimberly Senior's work for whatever reason. I think that larger markets have the opportunity to do that.

Then there are smaller markets like Pittsburgh. The theatergoers at City Theatre may see five plays all year and they are the five plays that City Theatre is offering. They're developing this kind of institutional relationship. There it's more about how the plays talk to each other over time or how it reminds them of something they said last season. So their relationship is to a place where I feel like a lot of times in larger cities the relationship is to the content.

I'm in love with Pittsburgh because Pittsburgh loves Pittsburgh. It has this brazen confidence as a city. "We love our sports teams. We love our bridges. We love our rivers. We love our connection to Frank Lloyd Wright. We love our museums. We love our seal. We are so brazenly confident about our city that you can't help but love us too." So I felt my work could be brazen. Confidence attracts confidence, so how does that go into the work? I thought, "This play's in the round and has a bunch of light bulbs hanging from the ceiling and you talk directly to the audience and look them in the eye to form an individual relationship with one audience member—the other audience members will follow along." I feel the audience really responded to that.

Diane Rodriguez

It's the difference between abundance and scarcity

Rodriguez is well attuned to diverse theater audiences. She began her performance career with El Teatro Campesino in San Juan Batista, California, then moved on to perform and direct at various theaters across the country. In the mid-1990s, she joined one of the largest non-profit theater companies in the United States, Center Theatre Group in

Los Angeles. Here she compares the audiences at those two theaters to illustrate how much a director's opportunities and limitations can vary from one audience to another.

El Teatro Campesino is in the small town of San Juan Batista. The theater is in a tomato warehouse; nobody seems to mind. It's general seating; nobody cares, everyone just tries to get there early to get a good seat. The play can be unfinished—what we would consider a workshop production that needs continued work—but if it hooks them, they're standing at the end and crying. It's not that they don't have a critical eye, because they do. The people in San Juan go to these huge shows that they do in the Mission and are always at some event, so they're experienced audience members. It's just that, if they felt something, they're not going to be critical. Their demands of the work are very different than those of an LA regional theater audience.

Audiences at legacy theaters like Center Theatre Group expect work that follows the rules of a well-made play: a narrative they can follow, characters they relate to, a resolution that is cathartic. These days our audiences are less tuned into two-dimensional work that may be political in nature, visual, dance-like, nonlinear. It's not that we haven't tried. We've made a valiant effort to present forwardly aesthetic work, but in the end the audience that we depend on who are our subscribers appreciate mostly that "well-made play." And because they expect to get their money's worth, the experience had better be one they understand or one that makes them feel something.

It's the difference between abundance and scarcity. CTG's audiences have an abundance of choices in Los Angeles. We know that and do everything in our power to keep them by offering them "amazingly produced shows, Broadway offerings, good seats, exciting new plays."

The Teatro's audiences have no other theater choices. They pay less for a theater ticket. And they have few other theater experiences outside of Teatro productions to compare to so they remain loyal because they offer them a rare experience. They entertain them on a Friday night when there is little else to do in town and it is magical.

Erica Whyman

Regional differences in UK audiences

Whyman has been in leadership positions at four theaters that serve very different audiences—Southwark Playhouse in South London, The Gate in Notting Hill, Northern Stage in Newcastle-upon-Tyne, and RSC in Stratford-upon-Avon. She describes the most striking variations and commonalities she has seen in those audiences.

The key difference is how they first hear about or engage with the work and why they choose to come. On the London Fringe, and across London to a degree, audiences are very aware of media coverage, reviews, what's hot. Word of mouth among a culturally knowledgeable audience travels fast and that audience is keen to be stretched and like to feel on the inside track. So you can take artistic risks so long as you have critical approval or can generate some media heat. In Newcastle, as in many cities around the country, the audiences are more concerned with an enjoyable night out, not as confident about taking a bet on something they haven't heard of or don't know how to approach. I found them to be a wonderfully responsive audience—not cynical, not jaded—open to the emotional heart of a play. In the North East, there is also a strong political conscience, which I loved, a desire to see themselves and their points of view represented on stage, but also a real openness to theater makers who choose to bring their work to Newcastle. In Stratford, we have a wonderful mix of audiences—those who come once in a lifetime to visit the birthplace, perhaps traveling a great distance, so expecting the very best performance of Shakespeare, those who are quite local, very loyal, visiting four or five times a year, knowledgeable and confident about the whole repertoire, and then Londoners traveling for a particular opening that has got on their radar, and families coming to the theater for the very first time. We are keen to grow our audience for new work—those people who perhaps don't think Shakespeare is for them but who would really enjoy our more contemporary productions—but we have some very practical challenges around traveling to Stratford and getting home easily and affordably to Birmingham or Coventry. What do they have in common? A tremendous curiosity and openness, so long as you can persuade them to buy a ticket!

Karin Coonrod
Working in Europe and working with students

Coonrod is American and often directs in the United States, but has also worked extensively in mainland Europe.

Typically—for the work I make—it's more favorable to do large productions in Europe than in the United States. I love a large company of diverse actors all in agreement about the making of a theater piece. It makes my heart race. In the United States, there are more financial restraints on this kind of work, so the opportunities are fewer. At the National Hungarian Theater of Cluj in Romania, for example, I had the pleasure of working with a large company of about twenty actors on a translation of Chuck Mee's *A Perfect Wedding*.[54] There the cultural challenges were significant, but the raucousness and irreverence of the humor met with deep understanding. In Orvieto, Italy, I worked with Compagnia de' Colombari on *Laude in Urbis*—the medieval mystery plays for the twenty-first century, which involved more than sixty people (professional American and Italian actors plus some amateurs and a group of children) creating the city as a stage in the piazzas and streets of Orvieto, and thereby launching a new tradition of theater at the time of Corpus Christi.[55] Bringing all this great variety of people together to traverse the city of Orvieto in a marriage of Italian iconography with American rhythm was unspeakably thrilling. It has become much harder to do this kind of work in the United States because of the cost of large casts.

Although most professional theaters in the United States have shrunk their average cast size for financial reasons, most American universities

---

[54]National Hungarian Theater of Cluj, 2011.
[55]Compagnia de' Colombari, 2006.

still welcome large cast productions. Coonrod, a professor at the Yale School of Drama, has directed many student productions at various universities.

One of the delights in working with students is the possibility of involving a large company of actors, thus drawing out the best in the students while also workshopping ideas with their game-ful spirit and energy. Two such occasions come to mind: (1) Lorca's *The House of Bernarda Alba* (a translation I made with Nilo Cruz as a commission from the Public Theater in New York), which I directed with the MFA students at Columbia University and that also traveled to Bologna, Italy, and won a prize;[56] and (2) Euripides' *The Phoenician Women* (my own adaptation), which I directed with the students at American Repertory Theater in Cambridge, Massachusetts, and as part of the ART program and that performed in Moscow for four months.[57]

Leigh Silverman

Broadway

Broadway is the forum that people look to internationally to get ideas about who's doing what kind of work. The more people see you directing (and directing on a high level), the more they believe you can do it and will continue to call you and hire you.

Silverman has directed multiple productions on Broadway and received a 2014 Tony nomination for Best Direction of a Musical (for Violet*).[58] Her first Broadway production was Lisa Kron's semiautobiographical, meta-theatrical play* Well*.[59]*

The thing that's unpredictable about Broadway is that it's the inter-section of art and commerce. Sometimes it lives comfortably and

---

[56]Columbia University, 2004.
[57]Moscow Art Theatre, 2007.
[58]American Airlines Theatre, 2014.
[59]Longacre Theater, 2006.

sometimes it lives uncomfortably. It can be very hard to do a play like *Well* on Broadway. We were one of the best-reviewed shows of that season. One of the most terribly reviewed shows of the season was playing around the corner from us and it was starring a giant movie star. They were grossing two million dollars a week. I would go out of my half-empty theater and see people lining up around the block in front of our theater in hopes that someone would drop dead and they could get their ticket to the other show. That's the thing that is really hard about Broadway—sometimes what's good and what makes money are aligned, but sometimes there's a far distance between the two. The goal of a Broadway show is to do a show that will entice tourists. It needs to have great word of mouth and buzz, not necessarily just from the critics but also in terms of the general population. It has to have such a big appeal. When you're working in institutional, not-for-profit theaters, those concerns are not even part of your discussions as a director. When you do things on Broadway, they're a part of your everyday discussion: the merchandizing, the way the show's going to get advertised, and so on. Your job is just different when you're working inside an institution than when you're working in a commercial Broadway house.

Broadway is not the be-all and end-all. For me, the goal is consistent work that feels varied and challenging and interesting. To go from a two-person, real-time naturalistic play to a nineteen-person dance musical in different very arenas—that's like a dream for me. I feel very lucky that I'm able to traverse a number of different theatrical worlds.

Leah Gardiner

Pressures of commercial theater

Gardiner explains how pressure from producers differs between commercial and non-profit theater.

Working in the commercial arena requires a particular level of respect and understanding for the producers' investment. Not just the financial investment but also the emotional and mental investment. When they decide to pour half a million dollars or more into a project, there's an expectation that they hope for you to meet. Of course they're interested in creating great art, but they're used to money being the driving factor. They will give you notes until you are blue in the face, and sometimes they make perfect sense and sometimes they don't, but you have to make sure that the producers feel like they matter because they have higher stakes than a nonprofit theater on any one production. Nonprofit theaters put together a team they trust and let you go unless something is going very wrong. Nonprofits will have the next season and the next season and the next season, presumably, so out of five shows a season, they can have one that's not as successful. If they have five that are successful, well, fantastic, but if one or two fail, okay, there's next year. When you have an individual or commercial budget, that's it.

Tina Satter

Doors are blown open

Satter describes New York's Downtown theater scene.

When I think of Downtown, I think of stuff coming specifically out of spaces like P.S. 122 or the Incubator or the Kitchen, from playwrights like Mac Wellman and Richard Maxwell and companies like The Wooster Group and Elevator Repair Service; but it isn't just the location that makes it "Downtown." Downtown theater is an ethos, it's an idea, it's a way of working, it's a way people framework what they see. There's a kind of experimentation and working against normative practices in Downtown theaters. You have different expectations of how you're going to work and audiences have different expectations of what they will see, so there's a wider potential for what your work could look and feel like.

People get caught up a lot in where they direct. They want to do Off-Broadway or Broadway, but, compared to Downtown work, those shows are so limited in what they are able to do. Doors are blown open in Downtown theaters and there's a much larger sense of what is possible. For example, Elevator Repair Service's *Gats* was an eight-hour *Great Gatsby* where they literally read every word of the book. No one would ever commission that, but it ran on the West End in London— only possible because it was created here in Downtown. The earliest incarnation of *Natasha, Pierre, and the Great Comet of 1812* was in Downtown. It started with Dave Malloy saying, "What if we make *War and Peace* this weird musical thing?" and Rachel Chavkin casting some amazingly talented cabaret weirdos. In Downtown, incredible directors can do really special stuff. In mainstream theaters, when they are answering to larger sources, they can't quite explode stuff at the core in that same way.

Liesl Tommy

Pushing the envelope at Disney

Tommy directed the live version of Frozen *that opened at Disneyland in 2016.*[60] *She describes the benefits of working at that scale.*

A while back I was saying to a colleague that I couldn't stand the fact that all my work—the hard work I put the actors through, what I put myself through, the political work—is basically for a really homogeneous audience. And a small one at that. I didn't understand what I was doing anymore in theater and I felt like maybe I needed to switch to film and television. Then, six months later, I got this offer to direct *Frozen* for Disneyland. I wasn't really sure I should take it since I wasn't a Disney person, but then they said, "It's a 2,000-seat theater, we're gonna run the show three to five times a day, so at minimum 6,000 people a day will see this show every single day of the year." So I took it and was able to fight for a lot of diversity on the stage, which was new there. I still get Instagram and Facebook messages from strangers with photographs and meaningful, emotional messages about the Asian Anna or the black Elsa or the Filipino King or the Latina Queen. My culture growing up in South Africa wasn't a princess culture, so I didn't quite understand how much that would mean to people, and I am so grateful for the privilege of doing that kind of audience outreach to so many people.

Plus, the budget for the show was tens of millions of dollars. Artistically, I could push myself and my artistry. I was allowed to bring

---

[60]Disneyland California, 2016.

my own team. We used cutting-edge technology that hadn't been used in theater before. The designers were working at maximum capacity. We pushed the envelope on every level and we ended up with a show that is beautiful and I think has a lot of integrity.

Nadia Fall

Having an artistic home

Though I have worked in so many wonderful theaters, the National Theatre in London has been my artistic home for many years. I began as an assistant director there (although I continued to make my own work on the fringe while assisting); eventually I began directing my own work in the building, and more recently, I have been made an associate. Directors are mainly freelance artists, of course, and we cross-fertilize between buildings, but each venue does feel to me like its own family, each with a unique personality and key set of artists. And maybe the notion of an artistic home is a little bit of a comforting tale I tell myself because one can feel so vulnerable as a freelance theater director. I do find a level of stability in being attached to a building. I often joke about the National Theatre being a sort of factory: we workers clock in, eat in the canteen together, and so on. I think that's extremely important to me, the idea that making theater is our work, hard and meaningful work, and that it is an important and joint endeavor. Of course, that's half in my own brain. They could chuck me out on my ear at any time, and not give me another play to direct ever again! But even so, I have really benefited from the invaluable foundation and nurture I was lucky to gain from the former Artistic Director Nick Hytner and the National Theatre. They invested in me as an artist, without which I'm not sure I could have continued.

That said, I do like to work in smaller spaces too. At the National, as soon as they know you can do a big old number in the Olivier or the Lyttleton, they'll be damned to give you show in the Dorfman, which is the smallest space (still it isn't all that small!). Everyone wants to do a show in the Dorfman, so the directors are backed up. In an intimate space, you can make things beautiful and delicate and detailed and forensic, which is my obsession. I directed *Disgraced* at the Bush

Theatre[61] and I'm just about to direct *Hir* by Taylor Mac[62] in their newly refurbished theater, and I have loved working there. The psychological is a lot easier to access up close and it's a skill to keep it on a larger stage.

Polly Findlay

The dynamics of different stages

Findlay gives two very different examples of how a stage's shape affects the dynamic between the play, the actor, and the audience.

The physical dynamic of the Olivier at the National dictates staging in a way that I haven't experienced anywhere else. It's an incredibly wide stage with an even wider house. It's obviously a challenge to play an intimate scene in there; it's also very hard to spring physical surprises or create dynamic entrances because the length of the actor's journey, from where they come on at the side of the stage to the focus point, is just so great.

    Both the Royal Shakespeare Company stages—the Swan and the Royal Shakespeare Theatre—allow you to play with a much greater angularity than a more traditional, end-on space, which is certainly part of the reason that I've enjoyed working there. Engaging with something from a physically different angle to the one you're used to changes the way that you listen to or receive it. For example, you can have actors on the edges of those spaces but still in the room, and I think that people tend to listen in a very different way if an actor is half off the stage.

---

[61]Bush Theatre, 2013.
[62]Bush Theatre, 2017.

2
ENGAGING WITH SCRIPTS AND IDEAS

When Anne Kauffman tells people that she leads an annual directors' retreat, she is dismayed by how many of them—including theater professionals—ask, "What do directors do on a retreat with no actors or writers?" As if directors are simply facilitators with no independent creative role in the production process! Even if their collaborators aren't always aware of it, directors do a great deal of work with the play prior and parallel to rehearsals. They analyze an established script or collaborate with a writer on developing a new play (and sometimes act as both playwright and director), create a guiding vision for the production, engage in extensive research to understand the world they are creating onstage, and develop methods for communicating the play's ideas effectively to that production's particular cast, creative team, and—perhaps most importantly—audience. In this chapter, the directors describe their approaches to each of these crucial, often unseen, tasks.

Analyzing the Play

KJ Sanchez

Finding a concept

You don't have to come up with a brand new concept for every play you do. I just don't buy it. Thankfully, I think we're phasing out of this idea that if I don't put my big, fat stamp on it, if it's not recognized as "a KJ Sanchez production," then I've failed. If you're true to yourself, it's going to be different than other productions. For example, when you see an Anne Kauffman production, you know it's hers—there's a one and only Anne Kauffman—but the production is never self-conscious or self-aggrandizing in any way. I think many of us are kind of bored with the question, "What is my vision for the play?"

By the time you get to opening night, you might have something that looks like a high-concept production even if you actually built that "concept" through the process rather than started with a big vision. That's what happened to me recently with my production of *Jane Eyre*.[1] I simply started with the fact that it was one of my favorite books of all time; it was so important to thirteen-year-old me to find a character in a book that was weird, quirky, not charming, not cute, and despised for it, yet came out okay in the end. I wanted to stay focused on that character and not let her get lost in a scenic shuffle of reading rooms and moors. So the scenic designer Kris Stone and I pursued the bare minimum set we needed to tell the story. And, to keep the focus on the character, we asked, "How can the set be like Jane?" Then with the other designers I asked, "How can the music the actors play be like Jane? How can we have eight actors play sixty characters while making the costumes as essential as possible?" That stripping away, stripping away, stripping away made it seem to audiences like we led with a big concept, but the choices were actually really practical.

Polly Findlay

Finding relevance and an anchor

Findlay describes how she approaches the challenge of making a classic play relevant for a contemporary audience.

Directing a classic text, you are creating a world that exists in the Venn diagram overlap between the time in which the play is being produced and the time in which the play was originally written. The world of *As You Like It* in a production now is clearly not 1599, but it's

---

[1]Cincinnati Playhouse in the Park, 2017.

also clearly not quite the twenty-first century because, for example, the political climate, jokes, and language are completely different. I try to go through the text in a methodical way and ask myself a series of quite strict questions, like "Who is the most powerful person in this world? How is money generated in this world? Who are the people that are inevitably marginalized? What codes are present in the way that people dress?" You answer these questions with the 1599 answers, then try and find the equivalent gesture for the twenty-first century. For example, when I was doing *Antigone* at the National, I ended up feeling that what Sophocles had set out to write was a political thriller.[2] My job was to translate that in such a way that it could be decoded by a contemporary audience. If that means utilizing a different set of trappings than the ones Sophocles would have recognized, then that's a completely legitimate thing to do. Essentially, your job is to create a bespoke world with its own rules and assumptions, vocabulary, and patterns of behavior. And, with a classic text, that world has to somehow occupy a space between the realities of the world in which the play was written and the world in which it's being performed.

For all the plays she directs, whether classics or not, Findlay makes a practice of summarizing the plot to create "a useful anchor."

Right at the beginning of planning a show, I set myself the challenge of trying to summarize the whole plot or drive of the play in a single sentence. For example, *As You Like It* was "a lonely girl obsessed by self-control learns to let go and, in doing so, makes the world a better place" (it's actually the same plot as Disney's *Frozen*, isn't it?).[3] Of course, that in itself is an extremely subjective exercise, but I always find it a useful discipline, a way of articulating what it is about the piece that most grabs my interest. The sentence then informs your edit, or the way that you design the text—it provides a useful anchor, reminding you of the core of the story you're trying to deliver in your particular production.

---

[2]National Theatre, 2012.
[3]National Theatre, 2015.

Liesl Tommy

Finding and landing the metaphor

I'm interested in theater that happens on two levels, the literal and then the metaphorical. I do the unglamorous, literal analysis of the play—just going through beat by beat, figuring out what the beginning, middle, and end is and what the arcs of the characters are, figuring out what the playwright is trying to say. But then I also think about metaphor because that's where imagination and theater magic come in, that's where we start to engage with the play in an exciting way. And that's the director's artistry. Even on a new play, oftentimes I won't tell the writer what I think the metaphor is because, when I have in the past, some just give me this look like, "What?" I don't know that writers always think about metaphor when they're writing. They use different language to get to their depth. But that's the language that I use because "metaphor" is the language of the director.

I did a production of *Appropriate* by Branden Jacobs-Jenkins, and for me the play was a metaphor for the United States of America's very complicated history with its slave past.[4] It's about three siblings who are cleaning out their dead father's house when they discover a photo album of lynched black men. The siblings and in-laws react in archetypal ways to this racist past. For example, there are people in this country who actually feel like we shouldn't even teach about slavery or lynching and we've just got to let it go, like the brother who says, "Throw the album in the garbage. Get rid of it." Then there are people who get absolutely enraged when anybody brings it up and say things like, "Well how can I be held accountable for things I didn't do?" And their rage and frustration at any conversation around race are as palpable as a person of color's rage and frustration when they talk about race. Then you have another group of people who are very confused and have absolutely no idea how to approach it, but want to. You could break down every one of the characters in the play into those subgroups.

That metaphor affected casting, staging, everything. I purposely cast actors who looked alike for the siblings—they were very handsome, tall, slim actors who were kind of Aryan-looking. There was one scene

---

[4]Woolly Mammoth, 2013.

where one of the wives, who is Jewish, was telling this story about how the father said some anti-Semitic things to her. I staged it with the three siblings sitting on the couch with various stages of shock, disbelief, discomfort, and condescension on their faces as she stands separately. It actually ended up being one of the press photos. They all have their heads turned to her, looking at her, and she's just really emotional as she's trying to explain her point of view. That was an example of me playing around with this metaphor in the staging.

There are unquantifiable moments in the theater where the audience feels uncomfortable and don't entirely know why. I'm an avid audience-watcher during previews and, in this particular play, there were moments like this one where people were leaning forward and not breathing. I knew their discomfort wasn't just because the family was fighting; it was because the metaphor was landing.

May Adrales

Excavating the values of this world

I like the metaphor of excavating the play. I grew up in an old mining area and I like the idea of scraping through carefully to find the gem. When you're excavating for gems, you can't do it with a big sledgehammer or a bulldozer. You have to use fine tools. For me, working on a play requires digging deep into it—spending lots of time staring at the pages, scraping away the layers, trying to figure out what it all means. Like excavating gems, it's a long, meticulous process that's not very pretty.

This process is useful for both revivals and new plays. When you're excavating a new play and you find that you've dug yourself into a hole, you can ask the writer, "Where this is leading?" Sometimes they see that they should make a line change or sometimes it reveals something about the play that you didn't understand before. It helps you ask the right questions to the writer.

When I excavate plays, I ask, "Who are the gods in this world? What would hell be like?" In Thomas Bradshaw's *The Bereaved*, maintaining "middle class status" was the god.[5] Every sacrifice and choice was

---

[5]The Wild Project, 2009.

driven by their desire to maintain a middle-class stature. He marries his dead wife's best friend the day after she dies so that there will be money for his kid's private school education and so they can live in a certain house. They start dealing drugs to maintain their middle-class lifestyle. And the characters will die for those values. My job is to identify the values of this world and embolden the actors to make choices within that world.

Lear deBessonet

Excavating the substructure of a piece

When I assisted Bart Sher, he gave me a number of pieces of advice that I think about constantly in my daily work. One of the most influential things was his description of "substructure" as a way of thinking about a piece. He was speaking specifically in terms of its design, but it ends up playing out in all areas. In a director's attempt to reveal a piece—to let the piece be itself and be seen—there is a kind of excavation process where you're trying to understand the deep DNA of the piece in terms of genre. For example, when I was working on Brecht's *Good Person of Szechwan*, I felt like there was a commedia dell'arte influence in the bones of that play.[6] In commedia, both humor and pathos are coming out of poverty. There's this real edge to it, because the situation is dire and the characters feel such urgency (clowns are so transparent in their need) and that drives the humor. After I identified that *Good Person*, in its truest self, has this ancestor in that form, I then wanted the ghost of that to be present in the design. So how we designed the mini-thrust was based on commedia.

Any play you read, you could draw a little diagram of the other things it reminds you of, right? Other plays of course, but you could also extend that into other art forms, as well. You identify all your choices and think, "In its deepest self, this play is trying to be an intimate family drama meets a noir detective story," or whatever. So then you know that the fingerprints of those genres need to be there in all of your choices in some way. It can be in very subtle ways where nobody other than the director and potentially the designers even knows it's there.

6La MaMa/Public Theatre, 2013.

Patricia McGregor

Finding the rhythm of the scene

The text of plays often looks like poetry on the page to me, so when I'm doing text breakdowns, I try to figure out the rhythm of the scene or monologue or whatever. That rhythm can sometimes become almost like music that helps to score the physical life of things on the stage.

Diane Rodriguez

You have to understand the tone

From the very beginning, you have to understand the tone of the play. Then, in auditions, you have to hire actors who are going to be able to manage that tone. Tone is really dependent on the actors. For example, I directed my own play *Living Large—A Tale From Suburblandia* at Teatro Luna in Chicago in 2013.[7] The play starts out as a comedy and then transforms into a serious play that has humor. How can you make that transition without making it jarring to the audience? It purposely starts out as a bright, primary-colored sitcom and then as our main character evolves so does the play. So, tonally you have to begin to layer in the moments of serious transformation amid the comedy. You let a moment breathe when a character is alone and still when lamenting a loss. And then the next moment, she covers up that hurt and puts on her mask as if nothing is wrong and she's managing very well, thank you very much. So, to be able to do that flip, you have to use actors who can transform on a dime in order to maintain the tone of the play that is funny but poignant at the same time.

Young Jean Lee

Finding the right tone is the challenge

Lee is a playwright known for exploring diverse identities through a variety of theatrical styles. She has directed the first production of each of her plays with her troupe, Young Jean Lee's Theater Company.

---

[7]Teatro Luna, 2013.

In every show we do, the tone changes throughout because that's how we create the ride. For *The Shipment*, which was a show about black identity, the first half is structured like a minstrel show, so tone became incredibly crucial because that was the only way to prevent it from becoming an actual minstrel show.[8] There are different sections within it, but the stereotypes section was the most crucial. We created this tone of weird paper doll offness. Everybody moved very stiffly, they spoke very artificially, there was weird lighting. We invented a tone that we had never seen before so that it wouldn't be identifiable.

Even with the one naturalistic play I've done, *Straight White Men*, we messed with the audience with the tone.[9] The first act is very light, very light. The audience is laughing, it's this atmosphere of hilarity and then suddenly one of the characters just breaks down crying in the middle of Christmas dinner. That really brings down the mood. The second act is very, very tense, and then it ends in this explosion of dance. Then the third act starts at this giddy level and ends at this brutally crushing emotional level. It's very up and down and that took us the whole rehearsal process to figure out.

That's the reason why I have to direct the first production of my plays. Finding the right tone is the challenge of the entire rehearsal process. For the play to work, the tone has to be *that* tone. If the stereotype section of *The Shipment* were done with a high comedy tone, it would be horrific. It can't be done that way, so I actually have to write the tone into the script as much as I can and try to make that as readable for future directors as possible. To do that, I have to be there finding the tone during rehearsals.

Kimberly Senior

Inspiration, imitation, integration, and innovation

When she teaches undergraduate students, Senior describes the creative process in four steps, which she labels "The Four I's." Her

---

[8]Young Jean Lee's Theater Company, 2009.
[9]Young Jean Lee's Theater Company, 2014.

description highlights the complex, recursive relationship between analysis, research, and generation of creative work.

As artists, we begin with inspiration. We're inspired by something. We see it, we read it, whatever. It's a sunflower, it's Aristotle's *Poetics*, it's a train going by your window, it's the light of sunset hitting a building, but you're inspired. My sources of inspiration change from day to day—I'm usually quite inspired by fiction and poetry and often bring those resources into the room. I just read Kate Tempest's terrific book of poetry and am currently reading Jonathan Safran Foer's *Here I Am*, and they are bleeding their way into my work. I ship boxes of books from town to town when I travel for work. The inspiration key is knowing it is everywhere.

Next, you attempt to imitate the kernel of your inspiration. How do I capture the bend in the neck of the sunflower? How do I get the feeling of voyeurism of this train going by? Imitation is the work of practice.

The next step is integration. I might attempt to borrow a shape I see in a painting for a staging moment, but it's artificial until I integrate it with intention, with narrative. Integration is taking these moments of inspiration and your own ability to imitate, and—using the collaborative approach of our work—finding something new. Music shows us this with sampling, remixes, and mash-ups. What you create may be reminiscent of your inspiration but is now its own thing. I always take it as a compliment when someone says my work reminds them of something else, intended or not!

Then the holy grail, the bliss of the artist's experience, is the last step, which is innovation. I don't know that I've ever even gotten there. Has anyone?

Working with Playwrights

May Adrales

Build a strong trust

Working on a new play requires a marriage between writer and director. We have to talk about our values and our approach to the work. We need to have a collective understanding of the text and the world we are creating so we have a singular vision for the piece. Like any marriage, you have to talk through the hard stuff—work through disagreements and also love the work at hand. When there are disagreements in casting or design, we just talk through them and arrive at the solution that is best for the production. We have to build a strong trust.

Occasionally, you do have to convince a playwright of something. I worked with Tommy Smith on his show *The Wife*.[10] He envisioned it as just a table and two chairs in a black box, but I wanted to submerge the audience in the quiet drama. I wanted the audience to actually be right next to the action of the play. We got permission to alter the space and, in the design, there were pockets of audience in between these little stage platforms. I was so nervous about showing him that design. I gave him this big philosophical speech about how we ignore tragedy around us. He was dubious, but I just felt so strongly that this was the best thing for the play that he finally said, "Okay, let's see how it works out." Luckily, he liked it in the end.

Sarah Benson

Brutal honesty and trust

Speaking personally, I think the most fulfilling collaborations I've had with playwrights (similarly to designers or actors) have been with those that form organically and that are built on a level of brutal honesty and trust. That is what has enabled me to feel free in the rehearsal room and design process to really ferret out the reason for doing the play and put that on stage. I have to feel like I can put myself on the line. That's when I make the strongest work. If I feel (and this has only happened to me once, but it was awful) that I am trying to create a "good production," then the work by its nature is only competent and it of course fails. In the three-week rehearsal process model, sometimes directors can feel driven to create a "successful" or "good" result quickly and this usually bombs. With a strong collaboration you can create a huge mess at first before honing the production and I find that to be essential. Everyone is

---

[10]Access Theater, 2010.

trying to make something bigger than themselves and that's what ultimately creates a holistic show.

Benson describes the advantages of a strong director/playwright community.

In such a playwright-driven culture (opposed to say the more director-driven model of Europe), sometimes directors feel powerless. I hear this all the time. I remember when I first moved to New York feeling so isolated. I had no idea how other directors made work and I didn't really know playwrights. For me, the Writer/Director Lab at Soho Rep was how I first began to get a sense of community. That and the Prelude Festival which I was lucky enough to curate for two seasons. Those were both huge opportunities for me as I got the chance to participate in a group as a director in the Lab and with Prelude I got to pick up the phone and call a bunch of artists and invite them to be part of something.

Leigh Silverman

Together groping around in the dark

Theater has only ever really made sense to me when I have a writer with me. I'm much more interested in the act of creation with somebody else, someone you have to explain your ideas to, someone you are questioning and that is questioning you. I understand my job completely when a writer is there.

Silverman discovered her passion for new plays while working toward her BFA in Directing at Carnegie Mellon University. She was so drawn to new work that she decided to simultaneously earn an MA in Playwriting in order to better understand the writer's process. She has built her career directing new work by a range of playwrights.

My favorite collaborations are with writers that are rigorous. They challenge me, they inspire me. I got so lucky early on in my career with collaborators that I just loved, including a number of collaborators that I work with still to this day. Tanya Barfield—I just did my fifth play with her; I've known her for seventeen years. Lisa Kron and David Hwang—people that I work with again and again. They're extraordinary, creative artists and I learn about the world from them. Being in the room with them and helping them figure out where they're going and what their next ideas are, giving them a mirror so they can understand the world that they've created, hopefully giving them inspiration—that conversation, that exchange, is the reason why I do it. When I am by myself on a revival and I get to make all the decisions, I bore myself a little bit. I have done it, but it's not really where I live. Where I live is when I have a writer with me and we are together groping around in the dark.

Anne Kauffman

You write the play, I write the production

Kauffman directs new work in New York City and elsewhere. There are several well-known playwrights she has worked with repeatedly, including Lisa D'Amour, Anne Washburn, Jordan Harrison, and Adam Bock.

I often say to playwrights, "You wrote drafts without me standing behind you looking over your shoulder saying, 'Are you really gonna use that word?' So, I need the rehearsal process to scribble and throw things out . . . scribble and throw things out." What gets difficult for some playwrights is that they see the goal of rehearsals as gunning for the result; but the wrong direction, as we all know, often takes us in the right direction. I need the freedom to try things and get it wrong in the rehearsal room.

There's a reason why a playwright asks me and not another director to do a particular play of theirs. Or at least I imagine there is. Them seeing something in my work that they want for their piece and asking me to direct are essentially recognizing me as an artistic partner who will collaborate with them and take what's on the page in directions that reflect who I am as an artist and hopefully end up someplace neither one of us expected. The fact that they choose me as an artist empowers me to say, "I want to give you the best production of your play, but I have to also be an equal partner in this. You write the play, I write the production." There have been productions where I have done exactly what the playwright wants and, ultimately, I don't understand the play. I absolutely do not understand what I'm watching. That's the worst feeling. I know enough now, I *hope*, to avoid having that experience.

My favorite playwrights are those who don't *totally* understand what they've written. A playwright doesn't always understand (and shouldn't) every moment because there's unconsciousness in the act of writing and, therefore, in the play. The director can bring those unconscious elements to the fore. The playwrights who feel comfortable in their not knowing everything are my dream collaborators.

Patricia McGregor

What's in the playwright's head

McGregor earned her MFA in Directing from Yale School of Drama. Here she describes what she learned from the playwriting professors there and how she applies those lessons to her directing process.

I feel happy to have been at school during the bridge time between Richard Nelson and Paula Vogel as heads of the playwriting program. They have very different approaches to working with directors and I use parts of both. From Richard, I got the idea of having the playwright read their play to you. Doing this, I get information about character, rhythm, intensity, and what's really going on in their head. I also ask as many questions as possible, and just try to sponge as much information from them as I can. Also, I try to read as many interviews of them and biographies to really see what it is they're saying and where they're coming from.

So at the beginning of the process I'm asking and investigating and researching how the writer sees the play, but by the end I've gotten more in the driver's seat. One of the things Paula Vogel talks about a lot is the need for the director to decide what *this* production is going to do and say, how *this* production is going to interpret the gift the playwright has given it. For that reason, I think that during table work the playwright's voice should be at the table as much as the director's. And I love actors to do second-week character meetings with the play-wright—one-on-one sessions where they can get their dramaturgical questions answered. Then by the third week of rehearsal, when we're really refining what the production will be before we go into tech, I try to make sure that all actor communication about the play is going through me. I'll still check in with the writer, but I just want to make sure the actors aren't confused and that we have a unified perspective on what's happening for this production. Because the playwright is the parent of the play, but the director is the leader of the production.

Maria Aberg

When the production is allowed to crash into the text

Aberg directs classics and new work in the UK and other central and northern European countries. She describes how, in the UK, the expectations differ for a director working on a new play verses a classic.

There is a bigger sense of responsibility with new work because when I'm working on an interpretation of a classic, I can be quite selfish about which ideas I'd like to communicate to the audience through the prism of the text. With a new play, I'm more focused on finding a creative expression for what the writer wants to communicate rather than on trying to push against the text. Which is perhaps not always a good thing. Sometimes friction between a production and a text can be really exciting, and I think in new writing in the UK we by and large avoid that because the production tends to be much more about enabling the writer's voice. You very rarely have a situation where the production is allowed to crash into the text in an unexpected way. This is much more common in director-led theater cultures where it is more accepted that playwrights and directors have two quite different ways of thinking with equal value and that those different ways of thinking are encouraged to kind of rub up against each other.

Liesl Tommy

The "dramaturgical director"

When you work on a new play in different incarnations at different theaters, you get feedback from a lot of people. Dramaturgs, for example, don't travel with you. They are with their theater. So you have to figure out how to use the awesome feedback you get at one place and then at another, but make sure the playwright isn't applying every single note, or the play could just become a mishmash of different tastes and points of view and agendas. You have to help the playwright trust themselves. People have described me as a "dramaturgical director" because I'm able to hold onto the vision that I have sensed the play-wright is trying to achieve regardless of the point of view of the different theaters and workshops we go to.

Kimberly Senior

Directing multiple productions of the same play

Senior directed the world premiere of Ayad Akhtar's Disgraced[11] *and subsequently has worked with Akhtar on several other productions of the play.*

There was a huge era in this country of world premiere-itis where a lot of foundations got behind new play development but they would only take it as far as the first production of the play. We're never done at that point. I have directed multiple productions of *Disgraced*, and every time Ayad and I have approached it new. We have never been attempting to do the same again. We've held on to certain elements, like an actor has remained, or a designer has remained, but we have, with the text, continued to approach it new. On Broadway, we were changing it up until the play was frozen after twenty-one previews, and now in the latest one (a joint production between the Goodman, Berkeley Rep,

---

[11]American Theater Company, 2012.

and Seattle Rep), we're still changing it. Some of it is that the world has changed around us, that we have grown as artists, and some of it is just the opportunity to get back in there. We keep using the phrase "advancing the thread count." We've created this amazing set of sheets that it is now so much more textured and nuanced and sophisticated because we've had the opportunity to continue to revisit it. Instead of directing to the word, I was able to direct to the sentence or the phrase or occasionally the paragraph. To think in a larger way about the work and its continued life.

Working on multiple productions also gave Ayad and me the opportunities to create a language and a symbiosis that you don't often get with a playwright because normally you're thrown in a room, you have four weeks, and you just have to get the work done. Instead, he and I often had several months in between productions where we could read the same books and go to the movies and listen to music and talk about wine and get to know each other in this way where we developed a language about the work that we were trying to make. It's not rare for us to be in a room with each other where someone's like, "I've never seen two people work together like you do." Because we cut to the chase. He and I will begin on our first day by launching into what makes the work raw for us and try to create an environment in the room where everyone is just ready to give and to start with go. There's not a lot of politeness in that way. There is kindness but not politeness. It's highbrow and it's lowbrow. We can make a dick joke and then two seconds later be talking about Kant. That's the work that Ayad and I are both really excited about. When we found each other we were able to develop that language separate from the plays and then be able to put it back into the plays.

Vicky Featherstone
Enabling playwrights to communicate

Featherstone works with playwrights not only as a director of their work but also as an artistic director who commissions and programs new plays. In this capacity, she frequently meets with playwrights in the early stages of their projects.

Playwrights never talk confidently about their ideas. They just don't. Because they're too internalized. They could be very confident people, but even the most successful writers don't come in here and give me a movie pitch. They come in here and wade around an idea, and it's my job to try and help them find the confidence to be sure about what they're communicating. I feel it's my role to enable that in people.

As the artistic director of three new play theaters, Featherstone has been working with playwrights for decades, so she has extensive experience in enabling writers to find confidence and clarity. While this experience is very valuable to her work, she acknowledges that in one regard it can pose an obstacle.

As you get older, it gets harder to determine if a playwright has an original voice. You've been part of more things, so it's quite hard to see sometimes when things are truly original if they're emulating something that was once original. But individual writers need to go in cycles. So sometimes I have to remind myself that a less mature, emerging writer needs to write that play and have it produced in order to maybe get to another play, even though I've seen another writer write that play before. And that's quite a challenge for me sometimes because I really like the movement of something forward. So even if I'm aware that another writer asked this same question in 1991, I remind myself that everyone has to ask that question, and it's fine because this new writer is asking it in an interesting way. And asking it may lead to another question, then another. As somebody in my position, I can't expect that everyone has the sum of my experience.

Leah Gardiner

Everyone feels heard and seen

Gardiner has worked on numerous new plays. Her advice about working effectively with playwrights demonstrates that the demands of playwright-director interactions are similar to those of other collaborative relationships.

At the end of the day, I think it's really about the delicate balance of recognizing roles and responsibilities in the theater and making certain that everyone feels that (1) they are being heard, (2) they are being seen, and (3) their participation matters.

Playing Multiple Roles

Tina Satter

Directing frees you as a writer

Although I write and direct my shows, it's not devising. I always come in to the first rehearsal with a pretty firm script and then I direct that script. Because I will be the director, I don't have to keep in mind how it will be directed as I write. For example, for *Seagull (Thinking of You)*, I read Chekhov's writing and a lot about him, then wrote a play about those characters using some of his words and some of mine.[12] I would think, "I love this scene in Chekhov and want to imagine what else Masha and Nina might say to each other," then I would write that. I didn't know until we got into the rehearsal room how we would make it come to life. The script I brought into rehearsal was just the language for the most part; all the stage directions in the published script came out once we started rehearsing it. I didn't have to think about staging as I wrote, because I knew that I would know exactly how it should go once I started directing it.

Young Jean Lee

Why play multiple roles?

Lee is a playwright who makes a practice of directing the first production of each of her plays.

---

[12]New Ohio Theater, 2013.

Why not just direct? Why write? I've always found this to be an unsatisfactory answer, but I think that the amount of energy you need to put into a new play (or any play) in order to direct it really well is just so extreme that few people are actually willing to do that work. The really excellent directors are not only gifted, but they also put in way more work and care and thought and time into the direction of a piece than their peers. Excellent directing is a very time-consuming endeavor. I've tried directing other people's work and it was just too hard to give that much of myself to somebody else's words when I am capable of writing. I've actually quit productions before because I just could not commit the same level of care and time and attention to somebody else's play. Directing really is a service role. You're serving the needs of the production. People think of it as you get to be this dictator, a mastermind, boss-in-charge, but it's really not like that. If you're a good director, to some extent, you're in a service position.

Why not just write? Why direct? First, it's hard to find a director who will devote as much time as I would. There are very few of them and they're very booked. They work all the time and they make a lot of sacrifices. Second, when you direct your own work, you have control over every aspect of it. I've more or less self-produced the premieres of almost all of my shows, so I have no idea what it's like to write something and have some aspect of the first production not be under my control. There's something incredibly satisfying about that. If anything doesn't work, you can blame yourself, which is for me a lot easier than having that frustration toward other people. I'm such a perfectionist and my standards are so high, I can't ever really push anybody else to the same level that I would push myself as a writer, director, and producer of my own theater company. I feel nobody will ever care as much as I do. But as I get more interested in filmmaking, and as theater becomes less primary in my life, the idea of letting other people direct my plays is becoming more appealing because, as a filmmaker, I would always want to have time and energy to write and direct my work.

Why film? Being a person who requires a high level of control, it has become increasingly difficult for me to sit there in a theater performance and feel totally helpless to affect whatever is happening on stage while a live performance is happening. I want to be able to capture the performances I want and have them stay that way.

*She discusses the importance of keeping her writer and director hats
distinct during the rehearsal process.*

So much happens simultaneously with the writing and the directing, but
I do feel it's important for me to separate them into two distinct roles
because they are literally separate. If I'm in rehearsal and something
needs to get rewritten, I will leave the rehearsal room and sit outside in
the lobby with my laptop, making the corrections. Then I'll send them to
the stage manager, they'll print them, and we'll do them in the room. That
feels like writing and directing are happening at the same time but actually, I'm going into the lobby. It's actually a separate act. I just don't think
you can sit in a room and write at a computer while people are yelling
stuff at you. I brainstorm with people and take notes while everybody's
throwing out ideas, but that's a very different thing from actually sitting
down and figuring out how to make it work. I just have to do that alone.

Patricia McGregor

Creating pieces that don't start with text

*McGregor has directed a number of pieces that begin with something
other than a dramatic script, such as music or poetry. She describes
the roles she played in two of those processes.*

In my work with poets, musicians, and dancers, they'll come in
with an idea and my job is to make the framework. When Greg Tate
approached me to direct a piece about James Brown that the Apollo
had commissioned from his band Burnt Sugar,[13] I said, "If you're just
looking to do a concert, I probably shouldn't do it because there are a
lot of people who can do lights up, lights down." In this sort of piece, I'm
always interested in finding some kind of narrative strain to give the work
shape while still allowing for what I call "moments of jazz" to happen.
Greg and I spent about a month researching Brown, and one day he
brought me the Christie's catalog for an auction of the James Brown

---

[13]Apollo Theater, 2010.

Collection—everything from love notes to his Kennedy Center award. I became obsessed and said, "If I'm doing this piece, this is what I want to explore—the story of Christie's auctioning off the Godfather of Soul's stuff." So that became the framework for the performance. I brought on the actor Brandon Victor Dixon to play James Brown. Greg probably would have gone with someone in the band to play him, but I thought the show really needed an anchor who could nail both the character and the singing. So with that actor and narrative, we were able to take the audience on a trip with lots of space for abstraction. My job in those collaborations (in addition to lighting and all those things) is to figure out how much form to put on and then where to leave spaces.

I did another piece, called *Holding It Down*, with Vijay Iyer and Mike Ladd.[14] They had interviewed veterans and written songs about them, but the concert event they were working on wasn't telling the story that they wanted to tell about the veterans' return home. When I came in, I wanted to create for the audience the experience of going through a sleepless night as a veteran. What dreams do you encounter? What anxieties do you encounter going from nine at night until nine the next morning? What is that moment where it feels like you can't go on and then daybreak releases you? We added videos of the interviews, first-hand testimonials from performers who were veterans, and a careful build of tension. Vijay is a very famous pianist, and he held back on doing piano solos until near the end. People kept saying, "You should solo more," but I said, "No, I want to build the tension so that when the sunlight has broken and you realize you can make it through the night, you exhale—and that's the moment when the long piano solo comes and all of that tension just releases."

Paulette Randall

Risk in devised pieces

Randall has directed devised work as well as pre-scripted plays. Here she compares the level of risk in the two forms.

---

[14]Harlem Stage Gatehouse, 2012.

I think directing is always a risk. It's a bit like saying, "Here's a recipe for a cake and it's going to be fabulous," but sometimes, for some reason, the cake doesn't rise. You've done all the right things and the thing's as flat as a pancake. That's the same with a play or with devised work. All you're doing is upping the ante a bit if you haven't got a script to begin with.

Sarah Benson

There's a more collaborative model evolving

As Artistic Director of Soho Rep, whose mission is to be "a leading hub for innovative contemporary theater in New York City,"[15] Benson has directed and supported many diverse new plays, including those developed in Soho Rep's annual Writer/Director Lab.

I feel like more and more writers want to make something in a room with a bunch of collaborators rather than sitting at home on a laptop and delivering a draft. Maybe I'm just a blind optimist and this is what I want to think so I'm seeing it everywhere, but I feel like people—writers, directors, actors, designers—want to be making the thing together from the ground up. There is more of a collaborative model evolving. Producing structures are still getting caught on how to support that work—some are doing a great job, but others are flailing around. The progressive theaters are working to find out what artists need and figuring out how to get them in the room with their collaborators.

Rachel Chavkin

Developing a play with an ensemble

In 2004, Chavkin and several other recent NYU graduates formed the theater company known as The TEAM. The ensemble collectively creates work that "crashes characters from American history and mythology into modern stories, drawing unexpected and sometimes

---

[15]*Soho Rep*. http://sohorep.org/about/mission (accessed June 1, 2017).

uncomfortable connections across time to touch the raw nerves of the current moment."[16]

Paulette Douglas, who filmed the documentary *The TEAM Makes a Play*, said, "It's so exciting because obviously playwrights go through the same process as TEAM, but it's all happening inside their head, whereas with you guys it's all externalized in the room because it's a group process." We're all constantly doing different research and bring it into the room. Sometimes that happens in really formal ways, where I'll assign different research projects based on the conversation. Other times people just start reading about something and share it. Then we present what we've found. Some presentations are ten, fifteen minutes when someone doesn't find anything particularly captivating. But other times they're much longer. When we were working on *Anything That Gives Off Light*, I went down this rabbit hole researching the pageant Walter Scott produced for the King in Edinburgh in 1822 and ended up taking an hour and a half of rehearsal time to present the different connections that I made between that pageant and all the different things we were talking about.[17]

After presenting research, we'll go immediately into improvisations — either targeted or very open-ended. Just to see what characters or lines or worlds the research sparks in people's minds. We're immediately trying to figure out how to turn that research into theatrical material.

Preparing for Rehearsal

Diane Rodriguez

We breathe it

We directors surround ourselves with the play. We breathe it over and over—I know I do, I just can't get enough of it. I have to know the play very well, beat by beat. I beat out the play mainly to work with actors,

---

[16]The TEAM. http://theteamplays.org/about/about-the-company/ (accessed July 11, 2017).
[17]Edinburgh International Festival, 2016.

but it also helps me build a story if I understand where each beat begins and ends and how it's going to affect the next thing.

KJ Sanchez

Each production has different needs

Sanchez describes what she looks for and dwells on when analyzing a script.

I think in terms of choreography quite a lot. When I'm reading the script, I daydream about choreographic moments and about the interstitial moments that are not dialogue. What kind of physical life might be happening during all those moments? I make lots of stick figure drawings while I daydream, then eventually I sit with the model and move people around. Even though I don't stick to any of the choreography I design when I actually get into rehearsal, I want to get a sense of flow and understand the *feng shui* of the stage.

While I'm reading the script over and over, I toggle back and forth between thinking choreographically and thinking about the internal design of the character that I can help the actor build based off the character's history. It's rooted in old-fashioned transactional analysis—Where did I come from, what do I need, and how am I getting it?

Research is also an important part of the directors' preparation process, but different shows require different research approaches. Some period productions require more research than others.

I did Kevin Kerr's *Unity (1918)*, which was about the 1918 flu epidemic in a small Canadian town.[18] For that, I just needed to throw myself into as much historical research as possible, because there is so much good, real information in that play. I needed to be as much of an expert as Kevin Kerr was on the time period. In contrast, for

---

[18]Gene Frankel Theater, 2015.

Jane Eyre, I spent more time reading the novel than researching the period.[19] I had such a personal attachment to the character of Jane from the time I read it as a girl; I really wanted to protect that thirteen-year-old girl's connection to the book as much as possible, so I limited my historical research.

Contemporary plays sometimes present unique experiential research opportunities.

For *The Elaborate Entrance of Chad Deity*, I threw myself into research on wrestling culture.[20] And I mean that literally. I joined in on the wrestling training our actors were getting from wrestling great Al Snow—I actually learned to "take a bump!" which is when you learn that very loud, flat-backed fall on the mat. I went to wrestling matches and hung out with wrestlers and learned as much about the culture as I could. When we developed *ReEntry*, I read as many books as possible on training for combat, hung out at conferences where I would meet military leaders, visited Parris Island Recruit Depot, and got a guy who was a former Marine Corp instructor to train us all and put us through a little boot camp.[21] Then for *Noises Off*, I did something that really surprised me, which was to watch the Peter Bogdanovich film version of the play.[22] I think sometimes it's really valid not to see other productions of something you're working on, but sometimes it's really helpful. It was eye-opening to realize that the key to doing that play well is to understand that these actors are really good at what they do. It's just the circumstances have gone wrong. Too often that play is produced in a way that's making fun of the profession of acting, with these actors as bumbling fools from the get-go. But in that film they played it as though these actors were great at their job and it made it so much better, which was so helpful for me to see.

---

[19]Cincinnati Playhouse in the Park, 2017.
[20]Actors Theatre of Louisville, 2012.
[21]American Records/Two River Theater Company, 2009.
[22]Milwaukee Repertory Theater, 2013.

Sarah Benson

Research on and with playwrights

Benson directed the world premiere of Branden Jacobs-Jenkins's An
Octoroon *at Soho Rep in 2014.*[23]

With *An Octoroon*, I read the original melodrama multiple times and
read a lot of criticism of that play. I read a biography of Boucicault, the
Remus stories, *Uncle Tom's Cabin*, and as many slave narratives as
I could. I re-read all of Branden's work (I do the same with all playwrights
I work with because that's very informative). Branden and I took trips to
the museum. I remember us going to see the James Turrell exhibition
at the Guggenheim as we were talking a lot about light and perspective, which of course Turrell's work plays with so incredibly. We were
interested in how to visually undermine what people were looking at.
I think that Act Five of the show, set in the slave cabin, ended up feeling
a bit like some of those Turrell installations. They are far away and float
in space but also feel like you could just reach out and touch them.
When Amber Gray stepped into that scene (the first time there was any
realism in our design), people often gasped because they thought it
was a photograph floating there. The scenic designer, Mimi, Branden,
and I went to a performance art exhibition at NYU's Grey Gallery called
"Radical Presence." I remember that being helpful in a tangential way.
I find in those kinds of settings you start to form a sense of what you
want the design gesture to be by responding to what you are seeing.

May Adrales

Traveling to the play's setting

Oftentimes going to the place where the play is set can give you a
really true perspective. I did *Yellowman* by Dael Orlandersmith, which is
set in South Carolina and New York City.[24] I went to the area of South
Carolina where it takes place, just a little north of Charleston, to get
some dialect samples. It's a very poor, primarily black, area where many

---

[23]Soho Rep, 2014.
[24]Milwaukee Repertory Theater, 2011.

people are of Gullah heritage. I drove by myself and, everywhere I went people stopped and looked at me, this Filipina American. Like stood in the middle of the road to goggle. One man said, "I've seen black people and I've seen white people but I've never seen anyone like you." Another man waved me down (which was initially terrifying), and I asked him about his story and got a voice recording of his dialect. He wanted to keep in touch with me but didn't have access to a computer, and when I gave him my email address, he didn't know what the "@" sign was. He had never seen that before. And he had no understanding of New York City but just thought of it as this violent place. I got all this on tape and brought it to rehearsals and it was great for the actors. His dialect, his perspective, all the pictures I took of the houses and the roads—they really helped the actors understand the world these characters were coming from and how different it was from New York.

I was at a festival in Shanghai while I was preparing to direct David Henry Hwang's *Chinglish*, so I decided, "I'm going to be like the lead character of this play. I'm going to be an American and travel in China."[25] It was probably the dumbest thing I've ever done. I managed to contact one of David's friends who hooked me up with a translator, but she could only be with me half the time. The moment I was by myself I was terrified. No one spoke English. People kept looking at me and talking to me, but I had no idea what they were saying and they couldn't understand me. I felt so stupid. I took a bus by myself, and when I got back to the hotel room I thought, "I can't wait to get out of here." I had the same experience as the lead character in *Chinglish*—a fish completely out of water. But having that deep experience within the spirit of the play did give me a bit more confidence in how to approach it. Sometimes as a director you feel like a little bit of a cultural tourist because you're always doing shows in different worlds, so being able to have real experiences in those worlds can help you find a lens for approaching the work.

Anne Kauffman

Enter the room a little unknowing

I used to plan things out very carefully before I came into rehearsal. But eventually I realized that if you come in and do exactly what you

---

[25]Portland Center Stage, 2014.

planned, you're not actually experiencing what's alive in the room during rehearsal. You're not paying attention to the particular actors that you've cast, the environment that you're in, the incidental action that erupts through mistakes, or how those mistakes and how you choose to respond to them might be the key to what makes the play tick. You're cutting yourself off from what's alive. It took me a long time to realize that but once I did, I started to have a real point of view. When you dictate things according to a plan, you actually rob yourself and the piece you're working on of your personality and your shifting moods. Theater is live; not just live on stage but live in the making. We get something that hardly anyone else gets, certainly not movies and TV. We get time to mess around, we get a process where if on a particular day you feel shitty, you see the work from one perspective, and then your world shifts the next day and you gain another angle which may utterly contradict your initial understanding, but ends up enriching your overall perspective on the piece. That's what makes theater so alive.

Now I actually try to enter the room a little unknowing because if I get too attached to ideas I come up with before rehearsal, I waste a lot of energy disentangling myself if they don't work. I spend time being disappointed rather than being lithe in experimentation. Of course, I have to have *some* ideas and a solid understanding of the play especially after being through the design process, and I have opinions; but if I'm certain that this moment is about *this*, I can only see that idea. If I can detach and notice how things are moving in rehearsal, I can shape them and work on a play live rather than preempting meaning or action.

Communicating with the Audience

Caroline Steinbeis

It's about sharing the joke

The audience are the most vital and the most unpredictable factor in making a piece of work. Process is hugely important, but at the end of the day, the job is to create a dialogue between the play and the people coming to see it. I watch audiences a great deal to learn what people respond to, and the strongest reactions always happen when an audience feels they have been let in on something. So to my mind, the task is to find the key that lets people engage with the work. A lot of the plays I make are concept-led, so a large part of my process is to set up the rules of the game. Once your audience understands your intention, they can switch off their inner critic and go with you. And then you can start breaking the rules together. But there is nothing more frustrating than feeling left on the outside. It's about sharing the joke; it has to be.

Vicky Featherstone

Activating the gap between actor and audience

I'm really interested in the gap between the performance and the audience and the relationship that happens in that gap. Brilliant theater is where that gap is active, not inert. It's where you can feel the intangible dialogue going backwards and forwards in that space. That really excites me.

To create that active gap, a director has to keep an awareness that the piece won't necessarily be architecturally any different as the result of an audience being there, but it will be different tonally. When rehearsing, you need to make sure the performers have confidence in the architecture of the piece so they know that whatever happens, that architecture won't shift. Then you need to create a sort of surface area awareness in the performers so that every part of them is aware of that gap between them and the audience. It's about alertness. It's closely tied to Brecht's idea of *gestus*: the moment of possibility for an audience is the moment after something is presented and they are waiting to see what the response will be. Like if I said, "I love you," the act of saying it is nothing. What's amazing is the moment after I speak—the moment of *gestus*—when the audience becomes the most alert and alive as they anticipate how you will respond and what will change as a result of my having said it. That's where the gap is and that's the most powerful moment you can have in theater. So I really try and make performers aware of that and alert to that.

Featherstone clarifies that, though she references Brecht's techniques, the gap between performer and audience can and should be active in more conventional theater pieces as well.

Sometimes you want to put a very fragile, beautiful piece of art in front of an audience for them to look at in a particular way; but even then you want the audience to have an active relationship with the piece.

Maria Aberg

Porousness

It's crucial to create a space between the production and the text. To make the world of the play or the ideas of the play porous enough for the emotional and intellectual contribution of the audience to penetrate. I think presenting something where the ideas are solid, sealed, and compacted and the statement, mission, and opinions are fully defined is absolutely pointless. I just see no reason to put that in front of a live audience.

Essentially I believe that theater should be a conversation between actors and audience through the play. I think that requires the actors, and the production, to have a certain distance to the material—to have a relationship with it and to let the audience into that. In naturalism, that distance is often missing, and the performance becomes about imitation rather than exploration. And the audience becomes passive. Of course, Shakespeare wasn't particularly interested in the fourth wall, so his plays really invite the actors into a direct relationship with the audience where "imitation of a character" is only one of the ways the actors might communicate with their audience. I also think it's important not to put a finished piece of work in front of an audience—if it is to be really live, it needs to be evolving. That means leaving unanswered questions, not tying up all the loose ends. I don't believe that my job is presenting the answer to a question; I think it is interrogating the question in a complex, surprising, and provocative way.

Young Jean Lee

Provoke a multiplicity of responses

Lee's company (for which she writes and directs) is based in downtown New York City's experimental theater scene, but also tours internationally.

I've always thought of the audience's experience in terms of a roller-coaster ride. I'm very much trying to design a moment-to-moment emotional experience where everybody's going to respond differently to each turn in the ride, but there's definitely going to be some response to each move that gets made. The audience is very much guided through an experience, but from the beginning it's a disorienting one where you're not sure where you are. How each person ends up processing that experience is, to me, the point of the play. I try to provoke a multiplicity of responses by force. To ensure that you're unable to leave with a single interpretation. A bunch of questions get raised, and then there's no satisfying resolve. That's the one thing I've purposely never provided in any of my shows. I want my shows to be an irritant, something that remains with the person and that they have to contend with afterward. This impulse makes my work really difficult for mainstream audiences, because they tend to find that really frustrating. That's why I think I'm part of the experimental theater world because that audience is hungrier for that type of experience.

Lee challenges herself and surprises her audiences by regularly diving into different theatrical styles and subject matter.

The audience gets the rug yanked out from under them within each of my shows, but also from one show to the next. The most extreme example was when we followed *Untitled Feminist Show*,[26] which is a celebratory, feminist, all-nude, weird, dancing-singing entertainment, with *Straight White Men*,[27] which is this completely naturalistic three-act play about straight male identity. We made the title *Straight White Men* so that people would come in to the show expecting a condemnation or satire with straight white men acting like entitled dicks. The characters are stereotypical in some ways, but, while they skirt right on the edge of becoming caricature, they never actually cross that line. In fact, they are very politically correct and self-aware, and one of them reads more like a minority female than a male. That was something that we played with through the entire play. The audience was just waiting for somebody to say something racist or sexist or homophobic, or for the naturalistic

---

[26]Young Jean Lee's Theater Company, 2011.
[27]Young Jean Lee's Theater Company, 2014.

structure of the play to collapse, but these things just never happen. The twists and turns in the play are just plot twists—dramatic events that you're not expecting to occur.

Diane Rodriguez

Once they're hooked in, then you can take them anywhere

When I direct, I want to make sure there is a definite point of entry at the top of the play. The most important question to me is, "What is so important about this story now?" Once the audience understands why they're there, they're hooked. Obviously that's partially script, but it's also the way that you open it up. How do you bring that first character down stage to be close to the audience (or not)? How are you lighting the very beginning? It's within those first few moments of the play that you develop tone, set up why you're there, and invite the audience in. Once they're hooked in, then you can take them anywhere.

Rodriguez emphasizes that you can start the process of hooking in audience members even before they enter the auditorium.

In the Kirk Douglas Theatre, we're really into lobby experiences. We have concierges that help you answer questions, we have these games that we create for each show, we have events where people do an activity to conceptualize the play beforehand, then stay after to have a drink and talk about the play. Some are fun, like when we did *How to be a Rock Critic*, which is about the rock critic Lester Bangs and is set in the 1970s.[28] Before the show, people wrote on these cards which song they remembered most from the 1970s and we posted them. We also had photos from that era and audiences tried to identify the people. On the other end of the spectrum, we did Dael Orlandersmith's *Forever*, which was very harrowing to watch.[29] In the lobby, we created a place for a little ritual before you entered. People would answer the question, "As a child, who was your champion?" and then they'd put these little cards on the table that was like an altar as a tribute to this person who

---

[28]Center Theatre Group, 2015.
[29]Center Theatre Group, 2014.

was your champion. It was so successful that now wherever Dael does that show, they build an altar in the lobby and the audience participates in that ritual. It's a real communal experience.

Kimberly Senior
The power of an engaged talkback

Senior describes audience reactions during a talkback for a staged reading of Ayad Akhtar's The Who & The What *at La Jolla Playhouse.*[30] *The play is about a Muslim American family grappling with their divergent views on Islam.*

There was an Imam who was very aggressive toward Ayad about what he was putting forth in the play about the Prophet. Ayad said to him, "Come on, you studied this, you know that there are many interpretations." He said, "Well, I know that," and he turned to the woman sitting next to him, "but I'm afraid of what she thinks." The woman (who later told us that she happened to be Jewish) replied, "You don't know what I think. I saw this as a story of a family. It didn't make me think badly about Islam. It made me see it as just as far ranging and complex as my own religion." And then it launched into this lively discussion where the audience was talking to each other and artists and audience alike were on equal footing. It was really dynamic. Afterward, the artistic director pulled Ayad and me into his office and was like, "What's the next step with this play?" That was on a Saturday, and then on Monday, we got the offer to do a full production of it. Because he saw what was happening with his audience. This is what we're after.

Leigh Silverman
Tuning out the audience, then listening to them

I try and tune out the audience in my head for as long as I can. Because all you can do is do the work. Everything else is noise. There can be

---

[30]La Jolla Playhouse, 2013.

a lot of noise in a rehearsal process. You can be writing the reviews in your head every day. Or you can be thinking, "Oh my god, my friend so-and-so is going to hate this" and putting words into other people's mouths in your head. You can make yourself crazy and also distract yourself from what's really in front of you. You have to trust in your (and your collaborators') vision, experience, and instincts. I try not to think about the audience, whoever that audience is, until they're with me in the room.

Then, at previews, you bring in the audience. I've spent the rehearsal process trying to tune them out, and then during the preview period, it becomes my job to listen to them. When do people lean forward? When do they lean back? When do they fidget? When are they reading the program? When are they clearly uncomfortable? When are they confused? That is a really critical time in the process. Because you have to be brave enough to really look around a roomful of people— whether it's ten people, twenty people, a hundred people, or a thousand people—and say, "They're not getting it, they're not following it," or say, "Okay they thought that was really funny." I often feel like people dismiss an audience's reaction because "they're so old" or whatever. I just think people want the play to be good. They put in their money and their time to come to theater because they're getting something from being in that room and communing with other people that they're not getting anywhere else. Whatever their response is, it's useful information.

One of the things that's crazy about directing is you think a play is one kind of play, then you put it in front of an audience and they get on board a different kind of ride than you thought you were making. Then you have to decide if that's a more interesting ride or a less interesting ride. For example, I did a play recently where the lines that got the biggest laughs weren't funny in the rehearsal room. The audience was experiencing those moments in a way that we hadn't anticipated, and, in that way, the audience was teaching us something about the play. So, if we like that they're laughing, we can work toward how to keep that. If we don't want people to laugh at that, we have to make adjustments to make sure that it's not funny, either in the writing or the direction or the acting.

3

CONCEPTUALIZING THE VISUAL AND ACOUSTIC

Since audiences experience theater primarily through their eyes and ears, the visual and acoustic elements of a production are central concerns for every director. Directors integrate these elements into all aspects of their process—from initial conceptual thoughts about the script through the design phase and rehearsals—in order to carefully curate the audiences' experience. Examples of this integration abound in this chapter. For instance, it is striking how much the directors use the word "story" when talking about spectacle and sound, underscoring the fact that these are the media through which theater tells its stories and conveys its ideas. That is not to suggest that spectacle and sound are just delivery systems for the ideas of the playwright and director; in fact, they profoundly influence those ideas. The design process informs the development of a director's concept, the aesthetics of the stage environment shape the actors' interpretation of their characters, and a director's and designer's conceptions of spectacle and sound can even influence a playwright's choices about plot structure for a new play. The comments in this chapter illustrate how deeply the visual and acoustic elements of theater are embedded into a director's consciousness throughout the production process.

Discovery in the Design Process

Sarah Benson

Finding the play through the design process

The design process is often where I really find a play. Obviously, there's already been something that's made me want to work on this play; but through the design process, I get more specific about why I'm doing this and what approach I'm going to take. It's where I try to really put myself into the work, which for me is one of the adventures of directing. Some shows I'm constantly photographing stuff and sending it to my designers and saying, "This is what it should be." Then on other shows I'll say to them, "I have no idea what it should look like but this is the feeling I want to generate." For Lucas Hnath's play *A Public Reading of an Unproduced Screenplay about the Death of Walt Disney*, I wanted to create a space that felt claustrophobic, airless, a space that was totally controlled in the same way Disney would create these completely controlled environments where he would even make it snow in the winter.[1] It is a death chamber too, we see him die during the process of the play, so it wanted to be funereal and have a formal quality to it. I was working with Mimi on how we could generate this feeling and I randomly visited someone in a strange building over by the United Nations. The lobby was carpeted in bright red and everything was wood paneled. I got that same unsettling feeling of a controlled, muted environment where it feels like nothing bad could ever happen! We ended up using those same colors and materials in our set.

Blanche McIntyre

Serving the play

McIntyre describes the kind of questions she poses to designers.

"What's the nature of the play? What's the meat of it? What are the problems of it? How are we going to make it in the clearest and most exciting way?" Because we've got to serve it. Normally the designer and I aim to find a visual way of expressing the concerns of the play—for example, the *As You Like It* I did sprouted leaves from the pillars and gave them roots that sank down into the audience, because the play brings most of its energy from the experience of being alive and ordinary.[2] The first scenes are stiff and hierarchical, and as the play

---

[1] Soho Rep, 2013.
[2] National Theatre, 2015.

goes on, all the boundaries blur, so we realized we had to find a way of messing with the lines between audience and actors, and that blurring was literally our Forest of Arden. Once we had that central idea, the other things—how to create the court where one's identity is literally worn on one's sleeve, and specific things like how to render the God Hymen—worked themselves out more easily, and then the tiny details took no time at all.

KJ Sanchez

The designer was such a leader

Sanchez gives an example of how discussions with a designer can shape both the mise-en-scene and the casting for a production.

The sound designer, Jane Shaw, was such a leader in our production of *Jane Eyre*.[3] From our first meeting, we talked about the emotion of the piece. We both felt that it was about breathing in constricted clothing and constricted environments. So we decided that we wanted breathing instruments—accordion, whistles. We then decided to counter this breath with percussion—we both instinctually went to the "cajón"—which is a box that's hollowed-out and has lots of resonance. You sit on it and you play it with your hands. It's very sensual, very sexy, and aggressive. So those were out counterpoints: breathing and pounding. With Rochester's arrival, Jane hears his horse's hooves, which kicks her heart rate up.

We killed two birds with one stone because we needed objects for people to drum but also places for people to sit. The cajónes became the benches, beds, stools—all the furniture in the play. When they were offstage, the actors played them live. Once we knew what instruments we were going to use, we went into auditions looking for actors who could play particular instruments and be able to embody a horse or a dog without any kind of costuming or props, just with their bodies.

---

[3]Cincinnati Playhouse in the Park, 2017.

Anne Kauffman

Designers are the best dramaturgs

When I'm in a design meeting, I have to get honest with the play, and my attachments to the play, and what I think the play is about. Designers are the best dramaturgs, in my opinion, and my design collaboration is really my most in-depth preproduction process. Good designers ask tough questions about character, tone, and the world of the play. They also ask seemingly simple questions, like "Well, is the bathroom here, or is the bathroom there?" which, more often than not, can be quite provocative. For example, in *Belleville*, we finally figured out that the front door to the apartment was way, way up center.[4] The play is a thriller, and we discovered that when someone enters way up center, they can be backlit and framed in the doorway while facing the audience head on. That creates a very different visceral experience than if a character enters from stage left or right in profile. That decision to place the front door upstage center at the end of a long hall was sort of the crowning piece to the design. The play was about perception and Amy Herzog was playing with the characters' and audience's assumptions of events versus what was really happening. She included a lot of offstage business that could be heard but not seen. We wanted to push this a little further and give the audience a partial view of the offstage activity. Each seat in the house had access to a different portion of a room onstage. So, audience members were exposed to varying pieces of information which allowed for a multiplicity of interpretation.

Young Jean Lee

Helping me articulate what I want

I've worked with the set designer David Evans Morris for a really long time. I usually have a pretty strong idea of what I want, but I don't always know how to articulate it, and he is really good at helping me with that. We were having a really hard time with the *Straight White Men* set. I kept using adjectives like "realistic" and "middle class" and

---

[4]New York Theater Workshop, 2013.

"Midwestern," and he would submit designs and I wouldn't like them.[5] At one point, he told me the design he was showing me was exactly like the house he grew up in; he said to me, "It's perfectly realistic." Then it dawned on me that I wanted it to look like *my* family room when *I* was growing up. I had my mom send the diagram, and I described what kind of furniture was in it, and so he then perfectly recreated my childhood family room.

Nadia Fall

Tone: Sometimes clear, sometimes elusive

Sometimes I take the tone of a play for granted because it feels clear beyond any doubt. Either the play has been done a hundred times or the writing makes what's needed with regard to the design and approach explicit—like Akhtar's *Disgraced*, which was clearly naturalistic.[6] With that play, I felt like we ought to be in the characters' lives, we're voyeurs. So the design was immersive, and the audience literally walked in through the front door of the protagonist's apartment and into his living room.

Other times the tone is much more elusive. For instance, Shahid Nadeem's *Dara* was heightened and epic, almost Greek in parts, but at the same time it included smaller scenes which were intimate and conversational.[7] The audience needed to be able to access both the humanity of the characters but also be struck by the awesome history of an Asian dynasty centuries ago. Working with my designer Katrina Lindsay, we realized that called for scale and grandeur, but what do you do when your play is about the Mughal Empire? These dudes built the Taj Mahal, one of the wonders of the world. How do you show that onstage? That beauty and opulence which took decades to build? As soon as you attempt to show the Taj Mahal onstage you're going to look like an idiot because it's never going to be as beautiful. Instead, Katrina managed to suggest the Taj Mahal: the marble, that weight, and the beauty. And she used screens to allow intimate scenes for the lovers on this huge stage. Neil Austin did the lighting and it was deliciously

---

[5]Young Jean Lee's Theater Company, 2014.
[6]Bush Theatre, 2013.
[7]National Theatre, 2015.

cinematic. The design shaped the epic tone. It blows my mind how talented designers are.

Lyndsey Turner

Developing the script with the designer and playwright

Some of the most rewarding projects I've worked on have involved a collaboration with a writer over a number of years. Laura Wade and I spent around three years working on her play *Posh*,[8] and Lucy Kirkwood and I spent eighteen months working on *Chimerica*[9] before it received its premiere (although it's worth saying that she had been writing the play for a number of years before I became involved). One of the things I enjoy most about being at the writer's side throughout the development process is the fact that the production and the play evolve at the same time. I am never prouder of a piece of work than when an audience struggle to determine whether a particular idea, moment, image or experience was initiated by the director, the writer, or the designer. When I was working with Lucy Kirkwood and the designer Es Devlin on *Chimerica*, we hit upon a design before the final draft of the play was complete, so we had a set model to play with for the last six months of the writing period. The set design inspired a reordering of scenes, while a new scene allowed us to open up a new possibility in the design. It was one of the most collaborative projects I've ever worked on where, to this day, I would be hard-pressed to trace back any particular idea definitively to Lucy, Es, or myself. And as a theatergoer, I am much less interested in seeing the individual personalities of the creative team on stage than experiencing a complete and three-dimensional piece of work.

Paulette Randall

Getting a sense of environment

Because my own personal geography is pretty bad, I have to have the designer explain exactly what is outside of each door and what is down

---

[8]Royal Court Theatre, 2010.
[9]Headlong/Almeida Theatre, 2013.

which street or around which corner. They have to spend a lot of time telling me about those things that the audience will never see but that I have to understand in order that I can do the intimate or the small. Then I bring that into rehearsal for the actors. They have to know geographically what they might be able to see or smell just down the road or around the corner from where we discover them. It's about placing yourself, really.

Randall describes the value of site-specific environmental research with a designer.

Once when I was working with designer Libby Watson, I was fortunate enough to get some money from the Arts Council and I took us on a research and development trip to the Deep South in the United States. That meant we could talk about what it felt like to stand in a field under the expanse of sky. Geography and climate play a big part in the way that people move and for a lot of people here in the UK, the scale of America is incomprehensible. That trip really gave us a sense of scale.

Rachel Chavkin
Discovering the world with designers and actors

Chavkin emphasizes the role that both designers and actors play in discovering and shaping the three-dimensional world of the play. She refers to two different projects—Hadestown,[10] a folk opera about the mythological figure of Orpheus based on Anais Mitchell's concept album, and Preludes,[11] a musical by Dave Malloy that delves into the mind of composer Sergei Rachmaninoff.

I try to have as many group design meetings as possible, which I think has really fallen by the wayside. It has become common for people to Skype for forty-five minutes and make really fast decisions; but during the preproduction process for *Hadestown*, for example, the design team spent no less than thirty hours together spread over two and a

---

[10]New York Theatre Workshop, 2015.
[11]Lincoln Center Theater 3, 2015.

half months. We gathered in Rachel Hauck's studio, pouring over the model and staging through the entire libretto.

You continue to build the specific world of the play in rehearsals with the actors. Early in rehearsals for *Preludes*, the actor playing Rach entered through a door this certain way, which made the door feel very important. Then we had to decide, Should Rach's wife should also come through the door? Or does she already live in his mind? If this space is Rach's mind, does his wife live in the kitchen where she makes tea or the music room where she teaches students? She should enter there. We begin to set up the rules of world together as the actors think about what the play is. That's what a director does—builds a world that produces the action of the play and the lines that have to be spoken. Actors are my closest and smartest collaborators in piecing together the moment-by-moment rules of that world.

Liesl Tommy

Integrating design and tech into rehearsal

Tommy has directed a number of shows with complex multimedia design elements.

At some theaters, you're pushing them out of their comfort zone when you use multimedia elements that they haven't yet integrated into their technical toolkit. It's really challenging for you and the actors if you don't get those elements until tech, so I've learned to just ask for things as early as possible. For example, I did this show a few years back in Canada for the Luminato Festival, which is an international creative arts festival. One character gave another a gift and I wanted that gift to kind of take on a life of its own, become a character of its own, so we hid a video camera inside it and the video projected on the back wall. Basically the poor actress who was given the gift had to become a cinematographer as well as an actress. While she was working away at a scene, she also had to be angling the camera in the gift so we could, for example, get the face of her husband and then the face of the male guest behind her husband over his shoulder. Everybody wanted to kill me at various stages. There was a point when the actors were like, "What are we doing? This is crazy." But then they started working with the camera and seeing what we were after and creating these beautiful compositions. Sometimes the camera would capture what was happening between actors but at other times it would be on the table, amplifying an empty wine glass or a broken crayon on the ground from their child. It was a really grueling, weird process but had a huge payoff. I was really afraid that people were going to tell me no or that they were going to pull the plug on it halfway through. But they never did. And that taught me going forward to just ask. You just don't know what your power is, how much you can get away with. If they don't have the capacity, then they'll tell you no, but most times if the idea is exciting, they're going to work really hard to make it happen for you.

Visual Storytelling

Blanche McIntyre

The stage picture tells half the story

One of the few ways theater resembles film is that the stage picture tells half the story. For example, something they taught me in drama school was, because people in the West read from left to right, audiences have the sense that that's the direction power flows onstage. So if you have your protagonist stage right and the person they're trying to change stage left, momentum is with them; the other way round, the opposite applies because they have to push back against the current. Of course, that only works in proscenium theater. As soon as a play is on a thrust or in-the-round stage, then the picture becomes democratic—it's different depending on where you sit. The distances between characters also tell a lot of the story. When we were doing *The Seagull*, I blocked it so that the distances between the people onstage were expressing an emotional or intellectual distance or closeness rather than a physical one.[12]

---

[12]Headlong, 2013.

Anne Kauffman

The central metaphor of the play is encapsulated in the space

The central metaphor of the play, for me, is usually encapsulated in the space. That means the design really has to be an expression of that metaphor. For *Stunning*, the characters prized their house above all other things.[13] They were descended from recent immigrants, but they were in no way, nor had they the desire to be, connected to their past. The definition of their identity was to have no past and to be the purveyors and consumers of American culture. They lived in a pristine white house whose walls were tended to by a maid so that not a single mark marred a surface. For me, their home was a mausoleum. A crypt where the severing of ties from the past destroyed any potential for growth. And so the set reflected that infertile space.

Your Mother's Copy of the Kama Sutra was a play about how the past haunts the present.[14] The set resembled a basement, a space where items from the past get stashed haphazardly. A kind of sub-conscious writ concrete. The beige carpeting had evidence of previous furniture configurations—shadows from another time, residue from the past. And there were several entrances from hallways that connected the doorways, or led nowhere. The slightly misleading architecture reflected the cul-de-sacs where our thoughts can get trapped when trying to work out how a certain event played out in memory. I liked the way the basement was a blank space with history. That oxymoron felt like the right contradictory environment to house the events of the play.

Rachel Chavkin

The text doesn't mean anything

When I used to teach directing, the very first thing that I taught was "the text doesn't mean anything until you decide what it means." I'm not saying that's a monomaniacal decision—I'm saying that meaning is created by all the different elements together. Take the line, "To be or not to be. That

---

[13]Woolly Mammoth, 2008.
[14]Playwrights Horizons, 2014.

is the question." There are a million different choices that you have to make. Is Hamlet happy or sad articulating that question? Has he been thinking about that question a long time or does it occur to him in that split second before he starts that speech? If it occurs the second before he starts that speech, then he's never thought about suicide. So what does his bedroom look like? What does he dress like? What music does he listen to? You begin to extrapolate from choice to choice to choice, and one choice leads to five others. Every single one of those choices has visual ramifications because we live in a three-dimensional world.

Humans behave the way they do because of the three-dimensional world. Right now, I'm wearing jeans, sitting on a couch, drinking coffee, so my voice sounds a certain way and I'm talking fast. It's the same for characters in a play. I can't think about how an actor would play a moment separate from what the space feels like. So one of the first things I have to do when I start working on a play is imagine how the set would function. That's true even in the most highly stylized or poetically staged pieces. The elements are not extricable. In his book, *The Actor and the Target*, Declan Donnellan says that when people talk about bad acting, they are saying that the actor seems lost. And he doesn't mean that metaphorically; he means they literally don't know where they are because they haven't filled in the details of their imaginary world, like "I'm sitting on a couch. The fabric is slightly scratchy. It's early afternoon and is raining outside. I don't dye my hair, but am thinking about it." All of these things comprise the emotional latitude and longitude of where we are in any given moment in time. That's work that an actor needs to do, but that work definitely begins with the director saying, "This is the world of this play." That world is visual. And acoustic. And tactile.

Maria Aberg

Illustrative design is being asphyxiated

My generation of designers are so interesting and so intelligent when it comes to thinking about what performance is and can be. They approach the relationships between performance and text and performance and audience in a completely different way than designers did when I came to England sixteen years ago. It feels like the illustrative "this is the location in which the play takes place" approach to design is being asphyxiated, which is lovely to see. Designers have become a lot bolder about interpreting text in a way that isn't as bound to space, time, and location as the tradition has always been here. There's some properly brilliant, brilliant talent among designers. We just need to keep up as directors!

Aberg has worked extensively with designer Naomi Dawson. To illustrate their process, she traces the evolution of the design for the painted backcloth that featured in their RSC production of The White Devil.[15]

The painted backcloth was something that we wrestled with quite a while. The conflation of the Catholic Church with an oppressively patriarchal society is what gives the play its fundamental brutality. So we wanted an image that fused those two things—the sexualization of a female figure and Catholicism—so we chose the central female figure of Catholicism, the Virgin Mary. We knew we wanted it to be an image that was somewhat sexualized or represented a commodification of the female body, some version of male construction of a feminine identity. So we looked at lots and lots of different images of the Virgin Mary (of which there are very, very, very many!) to find what we were looking for.

Initially, we debated where on the stage we should put it. There was a time when we wanted to put it on the floor because we were quite interested in the idea of it being walked on, but I don't think it would have had quite the same impact. Once we decided to put it behind the set as a backdrop, we debated which bits of her face the audience should see through the set pieces. Should they have visual access to the eyes? The mouth? Also, by putting it at the back, the Virgin Mary could watch the action much in the same way as we were watching, which added another layer to the idea of contextualizing the spectator's gaze.

Tina Satter

The authenticity of rehearsal objects

Satter gives an example of an often overlooked way to create authenticity onstage.

---

[15]Royal Shakespeare Company, 2014.

Elevator Repair Service has toured the world. They're very well funded at this point. Yet you'll still see props in their shows that came from the rehearsals. In their play *The Select*, which is based on *The Sun Also Rises*, they had these amazing bullfight sequences where they used a table.[16] Because when they rehearsed, they just had a table to work with. A prop is always a stand in for an object—we pretend that it's the thing it represents. But when you've created a moment with an object in rehearsal and you continue using that actual object in performance—the actual object that was present at the genesis—you have a degree of authenticity that you don't usually get. It's very subtle and totally organic.

Lear deBessonet

Storyboarding

One challenge of directing for the stage is that you don't get to actually see the full visual picture until the end of the rehearsal process. To mitigate this, deBessonet uses a film-directing staple when working on huge-cast, musical Public Works productions for the Public Theatre.

With Public Works productions, I storyboard the entire piece before it happens. Sometimes it's literal blocking, but it's also capturing what the feeling of a moment should be. There's real rigor that goes into that, and I love the precision of lighting cues and sound cues and these things that are helping to craft focus and to really just be as thoughtful and clear as possible about, moment to moment, what the event onstage is. It's a tool for me and the choreographer.

Acoustic Storytelling

Anne Kauffman

Language creates the space

I had this eureka moment once with a friend of mine, who's a commercial producer. He said to me, "You know, the problem with Downtown

---

[16]Edinburgh Festival Fringe, 2010.

theater is that you guys don't have any money for the physical production, you don't have any money to produce. So you can't really indulge
in spectacle. It's all dependent on language." I was like, "You're right,
you're absolutely right, and that is exactly what I love about it." The
plays I'm attracted to, and the collaborators I'm attracted to, are those
who use language in a way that actually defines the world, because
that's what makes theater theater, and not television or film. Theater
is the medium of language and metaphor. Since you're limited in what
you can do physically (in comparison with television and film), language
creates the space. And that's thrilling.

In *God's Ear*, the language is long runs of streams of consciousness
composed of a kind of absurdist poetry that vacillates between deep,
simple truths and clichés.[17] And on top of that, there's repetition. The
language reflects the protagonist's state of being, her deep grief, her
mourning, and how that state affects her perception. And how that perception becomes her world. Mel is simultaneously stuck and floating in
space; she is untethered and between worlds. So, the space became
that as well. It was a stark blue platform that existed between an under-
world (characters popped up through the blue surface) and the world as
we know it above (a character climbed through a trapdoor from above
the platform; when the trapdoor was opened we heard the sounds of
New York City traffic). The protagonist existed on the platform between
the two worlds as though she were both stuck and floating.

Rachel Chavkin

Music isn't that different from text

*Chavkin emphasizes the importance of casting actors who are a fit for
the text.*

Text is mysterious, which is both frustrating and a joy. A writer hears a
rhythm and a texture when they're writing, but those aren't on the page
when you're reading the play. The page is neutral. The writer made a
whole ton of decisions about rhythm and texture—many that they didn't

---

[17]New Georges, 2007.

even know they were making—so when an actor pronounces their text wrong it's like nails on a chalkboard to the writer. Sitting in the room with any new writer in auditions, you go through incredible actors who just may not be the right people to speak those texts. I think that's a reason that playwrights tend to collect actors because there is something about that person's natural rhythm and weight that fits that writer's voice. And directors have to not get in the way of that, because that would be the hardest thing to correct in an actor. You just need to cast a show with actors who get how the text wants to be spoken.

Chavkin describes how music differs from text—and how it's similar.

With music, there's much less space to make those choices. So much more of it is filled in—the rhythm is filled in, the pitches are filled in. Maybe even the texture of voices is filled in if the artist has written it for folk versus R&B versus Rogers and Hammerstein operatic purity. So, in some ways, music does a lot of your work for you. Of course, then it makes up for it with a whole bunch of other work because you have a choreographer and instruments and so on. At its core, music isn't that different from text; it's just a whole lot more dictatorial.

Nadia Fall

You can achieve liftoff with song

When a character sings, you can achieve liftoff much quicker than with dialogue alone. The book for musical theater pieces is very thin because the songs can speak a thousand words. That's why I find myself shoehorning music into straight plays all the time. That worked beautifully for *Our Country's Good*.[18] We needed to take this much-loved play, which was originally written for a small black box at Royal Court in the 1980s, and fit it onto the giant Olivier stage at the National Theatre. It was a Travelex-sponsored show, which meant ticket prices were low and so the budget was relatively small too, so we couldn't have lots of furniture and "stuff." The designer Peter Mackintosh created a beautiful, bare, epic stage that felt vast and hot like Australia. Then we added

---

[18]National Theatre, 2015.

music and song that really helped further fill that void. We did need to be careful not to put in too much music though, because it would have unraveled the rhythm of the piece (which goes at juggernaut speed). Added music stops the natural rhythm of a play, so in the case of *Our Country's Good*, too much would have made the production more reflective than the play actually is. As we rehearsed, Timberlake Wertenbaker actually said that if she wrote it again, she would leave much more room for music. I wish I could get in there earlier with writers and go, "Can we make some more room for music and singing?" It's such a powerful tool.

Karin Coonrod

Listening and silence

Coonrod uses silence in the rehearsal hall to encourage the actors—and, by extension, the audience—to listen attentively to the characters.

Typically one begins the work around the table digging into the text and talking about the scenes and the events of the scenes. Along with these I like incorporating physical "exercises" that get the actors up from the table so that the words swirl inside of them . . . and so they can find how the words work with silence. There is an exercise I love to do in all the plays during an intense scene when the actors have read through the scene several times and we have talked about it: when one actor feels incensed by what the other is saying, to simply get up from the table and begin to walk around and look at the other character or characters. During this time that the silent character is up and moving, the one talking must stop immediately and wait until the silent one has taken back the chair. Then the speaker can continue. When the exercise finishes, the air in the room has changed. An example of this is the first public court-room scene in *King Lear*. The father-king poses his profane question, thus setting up an outrageous rivalry, "Which of you shall we say doth love us most?" In the exercise I ask the three daughters—when they are outraged or pained by anything that is spoken aloud—to move in the space. In the exercise, whoever is speaking must stop speaking until the silent mover has stopped moving. To use an often-used word these days, the exercise "empowers" the silent movers but, most importantly, draws visceral attention to the transgressive danger in the scene on a cosmic plane and the irresponsibility of power. Words mean. If the characters are listening to the words spoken, so will the audience. This is the magic of the wordplay in the theater. Because I feel that *King Lear* is a play sculpted out of the silence, we begin to experience together the ineffable.

This physical exercise about silence and power from the table work puts a layer into the work unforgotten in the performance. Opening scenes in Shakespeare are important because often audiences are a little fearful of an evening of listening to a Shakespeare play. So we have to be very careful to bring our audience in right away. The complete commitment of all to any action on stage is absolutely required of the company. If there is a weak link (someone who is not present, who is not listening to the other characters), I can smell this right away as an audience member and lean back in my chair, unengaged; however, when all are viscerally involved, I lean into the scene from my chair, wanting to catch everything the actors say.

Tina Satter

Listening to the rhythm

I'm really interested in words, text, and rhythm—to hear the way people articulate things theatrically. Not just in service of moving a plot forward, but also to let things land the right way. When I was directing *In the Pony Palace*, someone said to me, "Some of the time you aren't even watching the actors."[19] I replied, "I can tell so much about if it's working by listening." Rhythmically, I know that a line needs to come in sooner because the character would say that sooner. They would speak up sooner if someone said that. So I try to really hear each piece.

It's not only what the "realistic" time is a character would respond to that I'm listening for. It's often not that at all. It's also the formal shape of the whole piece that I am very much figuring out by listening. The formal shape is made up of the energy between actors and where

---

[19]Half Straddle, 2011.

they stand on stage, when they look at each other, when they are not looking at each other, when their gaze takes in the audience, and so on, and one of the starkest definers of the space is what we can hear— so the language—but how it is said, the pace of each line and the space between lines—that really fuels not just the energy of a piece but to me feels like a huge aesthetic informer. So, as much as I'm listening perhaps for a line to come in sooner or later based on a character's character, I'm more often less interested in crafting "character" that way, but in listening to know if more space should be between lines so we can hear the language fully before our brains need to move to the next thing.

I've also gotten kind of obsessed in the last several shows with movements happening *not* when an actor speaks. Say the line, take a beat, then move. That is using the sound of the language to frame gesture and vice versa. And these are not usually abstract dance movements that are being framed out, but the character turning to look at the other character or bending down to scratch their arm—these kind of "regular movements" are often very highly directed in my work, and in that sense I am looking to "hear" both the actual line and the movements. The piece becomes a delicate and loaded canvas at that point, when each thing is fully seen and/or heard—start to finish, but that's often how I'm figuring out all the parts for myself—they need to be delineated out, and for many pieces it ends up making sense to keep all the elements delineated out for the audience as well. When I made *House of Dance*, which is a show set in a tap dance studio where all of the characters were walking around in tap shoes, it was a whole other amazing rhythm to then contend with and control any time they moved across the floor.[20] That's like directorial candy to me. Not only was I getting to think about how long it made organic sense in the feel of the piece before they should wait before saying the next line, but if they moved across the floor, we got this incredible texture of the clop of the tap shoes moving across the space . . . and that is something formal that then literally adds in the dramatic and emotional landscape of the kind of plays I make.

---

[20]Half Straddle, 2013.

Polly Findlay
Subliminal cues

The most powerful thing about sound is that you can produce a set of cues that people process in a subliminal way. In *As You Like It*, the characters find the court oppressive and restricting and break out of it.[21] They flee to the forest, which is an imaginative space where there is creative room for self-reinvention. So we knew the court had to be the opposite of that creative, imaginative forest space. Sound was a very useful way of engineering that contrast. We decided that the sound in the court had to be about electronica and bleeps. There are a certain set of notification sounds—the email failed to send, a text message was received, the printer jammed—that go into our spines and translate, without us even thinking about it, to stress, panic, and failure. We filled the court with those kinds of sounds—sounds that were being imposed upon individuals rather than created by those individuals. In contrast, the sounds of the forest—birds, animals, and so on—were created by the actors. This contrast in sounds between the two settings replicated the basic split in the play between an environment in which you are modified and controlled and an environment in which you are free to act.

Lear deBessonet
The meeting of perfect order and complete chaos

The most interesting art is at the meeting of perfect order and complete chaos. Like Nietzsche says, the Apollonian and the Dionysian. I could go through pieces of visual art or music and point out the ways that, for me, those two things intersect. And in the Public Works projects they intersect in a much more overt manner. The Public Works form embraces a very playful relationship between messiness and precision. On the one hand, we exercise extreme precision both in the cutting of the text and in the decision of where a song comes and how a song comes. The story would be completely lost if it were not if it were not attended to so specifically and carefully. And, because we are organizing two hundred

---

[21]National Theatre, 2015.

bodies entering and exiting the stage, we choreograph down to the millisecond what needs to happen. On the other hand, because of that number of people and the wide variety of experience on stage, the aesthetic needs to embrace a looseness too. In *The Tempest*, the group of taxi cab workers accidentally entered from the wrong spot almost every performance, but the audience was completely enraptured by them, and the small amount of what you might call Dionysian chaos that ensued from their unexpected entrance point was balanced by the great structure around the moment that gave the audience a sense of safety and that they were taken care of and in on the joke.[22]

DeBessonet describes the role composed music can play in shaping emotional discovery in rehearsal.

Incorporating the performance music into rehearsal really helps. You put on a certain piece of music and you say, "Here's the story moment we're inhabiting, this music is on. Go." And already it sets people in a direction. I work very diligently with the composer (Todd Almond has been my cocreator for all of my Public Works shows) to score the emotional moments of the show in a way that will help both the actors and the audience find their way into the imagined world of the piece.

Body and Movement as Spectacle

Rachel Chavkin

I love being lied to, but I don't like faking

As an audience member, I love knowing I'm being lied to, but I don't like faking. Lying is the spiritual act of saying "we're being playful," whereas faking is trying to look like you're doing something without actually doing it. I love seeing an actor really doing something. Twice I've directed Michael Ramirez's *The Royale*, which is about the boxer Jack Johnson.[23] The boxing sequences are staged really athletically

---

[22]Public Theater, 2013.
[23]Old Globe, 2014, and Lincoln Center Theater, 2016.

and physically, but in an abstract way. The fight is constantly revolving and the actors are constantly moving, so they are really sweating and breathing heavily, but they aren't pretending to have a fight. To me that's lying, but not faking. Another example is *The Lion King*, one of the most artistically and commercially accessible works of art of all time. Audiences are being lied to constantly in that show and they love it. They're in on the bargain. Because obviously we're not looking at lions; we're looking at performers with these stunning masks and choreography that is drenched in both folk dance and modern dance. If you asked an audience member about that layering and used the language I've just used, they would probably have no idea what you were taking about because only arts professionals think about that shit, but they would say, "Oh, it's so imaginative!"

Patricia McGregor

The physical life pallet of the production

McGregor, who is known for the physicality and rhythmic nature of her productions, describes how she found the concept for two of them: The House That Will Not Stand,[24] Marcus Gardley's play about a Creole woman in mid-nineteenth-century New Orleans; and Spunk,[25] George C. Wolfe's adaptation of three Zora Neale Hurston stories.

Just like there is a color pallet for the piece, I feel like there is a physical life pallet that I need to find. In *The House That Will Not Stand*, the corset really helped to tell that story. My costume designer Katie O'Neill and I talked a lot about the physical cage of the corset—how it limited where and when they can look, forced them to present themselves in this upper body kind of way, and hid what was actually going on underneath both sexually and emotionally. They could only express themselves in this very limited physical pallet.

With *Spunk*, I talked about the physical world in terms of dimensions. It set in three different time periods. In the first one, people's bodies and

---

[24]Berkeley Repertory Theatre, 2014.
[25]California Shakespeare Theater, 2012.

humanity were being flattened, so we looked at a lot of Kara Walker cutouts for inspiration and the rule became that everyone had to walk in a very flattened way, turning at right angles (we did a lot of work up against the walls to figure out what that meant). Then for the second time period, we moved to a Harlem full of zoot suits, and that world to me was diagonal. I worked with my sister Paloma, who is a choreographer, to create a world where people's postures were diagonal and there was a lot of negative space they were trying to take up as they walked the streets of Harlem. Then the third section was set in a time where people were allowed to be themselves and live in the fullness of their humanity. They weren't being flattened and were trained to take up more space so they were able to be three-dimensional and move fluently through the world.

The body doesn't lie. We can lie with words but the body doesn't lie. I sometimes will shut my ears and just look at what the bodies are doing onstage, and if I can't tell what's going on because of what the bodies are doing, then something hasn't been calibrated correctly. I'm always looking for the truth that lives in a person's body.

Tina Satter

Sculpting the stage picture

Satter adapted Chekhov's writing to create an experimental piece called Seagull (Thinking of You).[26] *She directed it with her company, Half Straddle.*

We very carefully sculpted the actors' movement and energy. One of my main ideas I wanted to try was to very tightly frame and push emotional moments—to physically put actors very, very close to each other when they said these often fraught and/or romantic or heartbreaking lines to each other. In the first rehearsals, I'd have them say these lines literally centimeters from each other's faces, or clutching each other and standing practically nose to nose, they'd just have to stay there that close, locking eyes as they ran scenes, while putting very little emotion on the lines themselves. We eventually broke out of doing that for entire

---

[26]Half Straddle, 2013.

scenes and played with more dynamic staging, but it became clear to me that what seems to be the "antithesis" of the natural way people (or characters) would respond in emotional conversations by looking away when upset, or coming together when feeling safe and romantic, became loaded in unexpected and strong ways when we had the lines said in oppositional ways—like try, say, this throwaway line looking directly into their eyes. Say this very vulnerable line, sitting right next to them, but both looking directly forward at the audience . . . and so on. And, once we began working this way, it became necessary to rigorously set the whole piece that way to keep the very specific energy we'd been harnessing moving throughout the piece. What we also did to cut against that very precise controlling of how emotion physically passed between the actors was using this roiling metal-infused music between and sometimes in scenes that felt super raw and openly emotional, so once we knew we were using that music score, it allowed us to work against that with the physical and line delivery control—one of the heartbeats of the play in a way was that tension between that physical control of the actors and this body-rattling emotional music.

Each actor brought something really specific—Jess Barbagallo's weird charisma, potency, and simmering-ness; Suzie Sokol's halting relationship to her body; and so on. I was constantly pairing up their energies and sculpting what needed to be held physically at each moment so it could then be released in the next part. We figured out exactly what to do second by second, in some instances down to the eyeballs. In one of the very first stage pictures after all the actors enter at the top of the show and do this choreographed and synchronized arm-lift/snap gesture—two performers, Eliza Bent, who plays Masha, and Julia Sirna-Frest, who plays Polina, come and stand downstage left on the very edge of the stage. They do several lines in Russian, so most American audiences have no idea what they are saying anyway, but I directed them to stand shoulder to shoulder looking out toward the audience—not directly at anyone; it was not supposed to be playing with any coy audience eye contact thing there, but in my mind it was the setup of characters in the original *Seagull* looking out over the lake. Julia and Eliza never look at each other until the very end of the scene, so you get this sense something has passed between them—which is also a setup of the idea I'm interested in in Chekhov, of all these nothing conversations between characters actually loaded with subtext only the two of them could ever understand, and getting to watch characters share a moment that we don't totally know what it is is very exciting to me—and would have been diluted if they'd had some banal fight in English, or even if it stayed in Russian, but we used prescribed gestures to indicate some prescribed idea of "tension." Also in that small scene, before they look at each other at the very end, I directed them to both look straight ahead as I said, but Julia had to then put her eyes very slightly like she was looking off to the side—so since that stage picture was so stark, you also get the slightest intimation and idea that perhaps one should and could look to the side. What else does she know? What else could we know? By framing out this opaque scene at the top, you're not only getting clues of how to watch the play, but to me they are totally dramatic clues of the opaque dynamics between any characters at any time. They are standing shoulder to shoulder so they know each other, but how do they know each other really? That's a great important layer of any human dynamic to see onstage, and I love to stage it in this at once direct and then totally mysterious way using bodies, eye angles, and specific looks.

Later in the play is a scene taken from Chekhov's original *Seagull*, where Arkadina and her son Treplev have this horrible fight—she says horrible things to him about him being a loser. We put Jess as Treplev in this chair center stage, and he's wearing a bandage on his head as a nod to his attempted and then successful suicide attempts by gun-shot, and Susie as Arkadina stands behind him, with her hands on his shoulders in a fully embodied way as she says these awful things to him—it's really intense to watch these mother/son characters as she touches him—not pushing it in any acting way, but because we've pulled back on so much physicality and it's all been so controlled up to this point, the actor playing the mother character actually placing both her hands on the body of the actor playing her son as she says she always knew he was a loser takes on this really heartbreaking depravity and tenderness that, to me—although *so* staged also it's then so lightly and naturally done—it's just an actor touching another actor but saying certain words—that it *actually* is what allows the amazing contradictions with love, familial love, familial hatred, pride, and des-peration to be captured in one thirty-second scene. And because these are live actors who are not "playing" a part but carrying out certain movements and saying text within their own charisma, there's also an inherent looseness within it actually.

There's a real excitement to looseness, where actors don't know exactly what they'll do and then hit stuff in the moment. I love that, too. But for this piece, I was trying to push it as far as we could the other way. We got to a point where they were in it in a core way, able to be totally present in this fabric that was inching forward.

Anne Kauffman

A blank envelope for the actors to write on

I am more and more trying to keep the design as open and flexible as I possibly can because ultimately I want to have room for discovering how space works in rehearsals. So, instead of bringing on and off stuff for scene changes, I ask how we can put the onus on the actors to define space and time. How can we give the stage just enough to create an envelope that means something for the play, but leave it blank enough for us to write on it?

Blanche McIntyre

Spectacle amplifies

Spectacle should amplify something interesting or well observed about the human experience. In my production of *Comedy of Errors*, two of the actors bungee-jumped from the roof.[27] The characters were trying to scare a crowd with their entrance. They could have run on, but the bungee made their idea bigger, wilder, and more dramatic. It pointed up the absurdity of what the characters wanted to achieve—they were doing something with too much bravado, because they were scared themselves—and it gave the audience a sense of what it would have felt like to be in that situation, which is to say like a terrifying drop in your stomach. In my production of *Arcadia*, one of the central metaphors is about heat going to cold in the universe, usable energy becoming

---

[27]Shakespeare's Globe, 2014.

unusable, which connects to the waste of several of the young lives in the play.[28] We had a permeable set—actors could walk through it like atoms—and in the last scene, while Thomasina and Septimus were dancing, several of the characters, some we hadn't seen since the beginning of the show, moved through the space and came to rest. That was a moment of picture-building that amplified the sadness of the final scene.

McIntyre gives an example of how a set can help create the right blocking for a production.

I directed Dawn King's *Foxfinder* a couple of years ago, which is set in England's West Country in a possibly sci-fi landscape, but told like a Greek tragedy.[29] It's a brilliant play where a farmer and his wife are investigated for collaborating with foxes (the equivalent of witches in this world) by a teenage government agent. It's incredibly spare, stark, but it has all these scenes in different places—in their farmhouse, in someone else's farmhouse, in the yard, in the field . . . I thought, "I cannot represent these naturalistically. It'll be hideous. It simply won't work." So, on the one hand, the play has this terrific virtue that it is muscular and practically skeletal in its leanness; on the other hand, it creates this terrible staging problem. So I thought I was just going to have to do it with total simplicity. Possibly just a chair. But then our designer James Perkins came up with a wedge-shaped platform on which the actors stood. There were two joyful things about that. One, people's eyelines went up into the darkness behind the actors, as opposed to across the stage to the other audience members, which created a sense of space even though the Finborough is a fifty-seat theater. Two, it forced the actors into powerful three-dimensional blocking. On a tiny triangular space like that, every move is charged. A turn of the head becomes significant and a shrug or a sit down is huge, and a turnaround is like somebody's left the stage. So the design allowed the blocking to be still and the stage pictures to be simple, which is exactly what the play needed.

---

[28]English Touring Theatre, 2015.
[29]Finborough Theatre, 2011.

Performer–Audience Relationships

Caroline Steinbeis

Come with us, we've got you

Steinbeis directs a lot of nonrealistic, concept-led plays that eschew typical dramatic conventions. When a play lacks these familiar cues that tell audiences what to expect and how they should react, directors need to find ways to communicate the piece's particular theatrical contract to their audiences.

You need to teach the audience the rules at the beginning and then they'll be willing to go with you. My first production for the Royal Court was of a Polish play called *A Time to Reap* by Anna Wakulik.[30] The play is about the emotional corruption of a young woman through her relationship to two men under the yolk of Polish Catholicism. The rules of the game were that the actors would continuously break the fourth wall to implicate the audience, making them complicit in this corruption. The prologue enabled us to meet the audience straight down the middle; the actors took us on a whirlwind twenty-year synopsis of their lives in context of Polish history. All we were asking for was for people to keep up with the rhythm we were setting. To complement this, we staged the show in the thrust, audience was all around the playing space and you were never further than three meters away from an actor. Through big, brash calls on lights, music, and sound as well as props (like a christening cake in the life-sized shape of a baby), we gave the audience to understand: "Okay, this is the level of engagement we are asking from you but come with us, we've got you." If your intentions come from a place of generosity and warmth, then I think your audience will feel that and respond by coming along for the ride with you, even if the subject matter is challenging. But, of course, you never know.

---

[30]Royal Court Theatre, 2013.

Blanche McIntyre

A human-sized art form

Theater is a human-sized art form, and that's at the heart of the contract between a piece of theater and the people watching it. If you are interested in impressing your audiences with the money you spent, or the scale of the effects, or even the quality of the ideas, but don't bother to check out whether people would actually behave like the characters, then that contract isn't being honored. There is something unsatisfying about those productions because you feel, at the end of the day, as though you've been sold an untruth about human experience. In all cases, when you're working on a piece, everything you use onstage should help to tell the story, or ask the question, or address the issue.

Diane Rodriguez

Surprising the audience

I give the audience breadcrumbs all along the journey because I want them to be able to follow the story clearly, but then I also have to figure out where and how to undermine their expectations. So I always look for little surprises I can unearth in the script and the staging. I did *Bordertown* in this beautiful jewel box of a theater in Arizona.[31] We pulled out all the masking and put a mound of dirt on the stage. I used the mound in only one way through most of the piece, and then three-quarters of the way through, somebody came in through a trapdoor under the mound. They climbed through and planted a flag, which was a big story point and also a big visual surprise because the audience didn't know we could do that. It was a beautiful, memorable moment that helped tell the story but was also really entertaining. The playwright will have built in surprises, but as a director, you can add your own little twists too.

---

[31]Actors Theatre, 2004.

Anne Kauffman

Busting out of the box

Directors are trying to always bust out of the box of theater. I know I am. I don't mean in a rebellious way, necessarily; more that the challenge is to defy the actual space of the theater. You have to create thirty different locations in one box, so you have to constantly try to defy the laws of physics through theater magic. People cut angles to create an illusion of depth, or do things like put the audience on the stage and the actors in the house or extend the playing space into the lobby, but you can also break out of the box through the imagination of the audience. And that's what I'm interested in . . . engaging an audience's imagination. I did a play called *You Got Older*, which is constantly shifting in place and time, but nothing on the stage moved.[32] Are we in a bedroom or a living room right now? Instead of clarifying that through moving new furniture on, we created a contract with the audience where they projected their imaginations onto the stage to create a bedroom/living room space. We invited them to make the piece with us and to break out of the box through their imagination. Of course, that's nothing new. It's similar to Shakespeare's theater. I would argue that through the ages, most of what we theater makers have wanted to do is somehow fight the box. There's a tension in that, right? An exciting tension.

I also like to mess with what an audience has come to expect from the theater. I'm talking about tiny expectations, expectations they don't even really detect having. I'm amazed at how much we respect the ritual of the theater as audience members—how it's kind of in our DNA. I remember reading a production report for Amy Herzog's *Belleville*.[33] The stage manager had reported that in the middle of the climactic scene, where all hell's breaking loose and the two characters are in the middle of an emotional and physical fight, a kind of quiet but steady alarm was sounding in the audience and continued for a few minutes. The actress couldn't bear another second and stopped the action, looked out into the audience and asked if somebody was having a medical issue. Was there somebody in the audience who needed help?

---

[32]Page 73/HERE, 2014.
[33]New York Theater Workshop, 2013.

Well, that shocked the *hell* out of the audience and shocked the *pants* off of me! It was then that I realized what a crazy contract we've struck between audience and performer—that my actress violated that contract and something pretty incredible happened because of it. But what I'm talking about is much subtler and will now sound rather insignificant when compared to breaking the fourth wall by accident or rearranging audience seating. I like to have somebody walk on another person's line. Or have somebody start to move and then have somebody else move slightly afterwards. I like to disrupt internal rhythms an audience has gotten used to when watching a play. It's tiny subterfuge, which I think awakens something that makes an audience take notice in a slightly different way, without even really clocking it, maybe? It's a theory.

Sarah Benson

I don't care what the set looks like, I care what it does

What's special about theater is that we're all gathering in a room together—performers and audience—for a time-based event. I'm always trying to figure out how to translate that specific relationship into space, so that what an audience member is experiencing is changing what's happening on stage and changing how other audience members are experiencing the piece. It doesn't make any sense to me to just put scenery around the stage, because it somehow negates the marvelous, amazing things about that actor/audience relationship.

Ultimately, I don't care what the set looks like, I care what it does. How it's going to make people feel, how it's going to function. In *An Octoroon*, we had layers of walls actually falling toward people throughout the show, which was us trying to disrupt how people were perceiving what they were looking at.[34] At first, we wanted to people to think, "Oh, I guess the room is really shallow. This is it. I'm in a black box. This is a one-man show. That's what I'm here to see." Then the back wall fell forward to reveal another set behind and people would think, "Oh, now I'm in this weird light box seeing this melodrama." Disrupting perceptions is a big part of what the play is trying to do.

---

[34]Soho Rep, 2014.

Those walls falling forward made air and dust and cotton balls hit people. It was actually affecting their bodies, which is what I want to do with scenic elements—create an actual, physical reaction rather than just changing what people are looking at. When you go to the theater, you show up with your body, so we should be trying to figure out how we can literally affect people's bodies in that space. When the first wall came down in *Octoroon*, it was frightening because it felt like something was going wrong architecturally with the building. We had to have an usher stand in the front rows to make sure no one bolted because when this wall they trusted to be solid came down, some had a flight or fight reaction.

With Sarah Kane's *Blasted*, we were also trying to very prominently acknowledge the civic nature of the event.[35] The first half we made a deliberately very conventional set of a hotel room. The stage was built up and there was literally a frame around it in a typical proscenium relationship. The audience were voyeurs, watching what was happening through a fourth wall. Then the room exploded. All the curtains dropped out, all the walls dropped out. You could see the truss and the sandbags and all the mechanics of how we had created that hotel illusion. You could see the actual architecture of the building. The lighting changed to incorporate the actual industrial and emergency lights of the theater. And the floor and ceiling of the hotel tracked back, so that everything that was on the stage floor dropped onto the real floor. Some of it broke every night, people in the front row had ice cubes in their handbag, that kind of thing. It felt like the events that had happened in that hotel room (Ian's rape of Cate) were too big to be contained by the play, so the whole play (and the whole form of theater as we know it) broke apart.

Karin Coonrod

The closed door leaving us all together

At the start of *The Tempest* at La Mama Annex in New York City, the company of actors all entered the space through a door from the back of the house, passing through the audience to the front.[36] When

---

[35]Soho Rep, 2008.
[36]La MaMa, 2014.

the door slammed and they all turned around and looked at the audience, it was as if to say, "Are you ready? We're going on a journey now together." Then Prospero (played by Reg E. Cathey) began by calling Ariel (played by Joseph Harrington) into action. This idea of the closed door, leaving us all together in the dark for a journey, comes from my friend and collaborator—András Visky—whose seminal prison experience at an early age inspired him to create "Barracks Dramaturgy." As a one-year-old prisoner of state in Southwest Romania with his mother and six siblings, he developed this theater of being closed in, to hear the whispered truth together as in a prison cell. With *The Tempest*, this dramaturgy matched the extreme isolation of the characters on Prospero's island. With the set designer, Riccardo Hernandez, we radically changed the typical "proscenium" setup in the vast room to surround the action in three quarters. Thus, the actors could take control of the entire room. I was lucky also on this occasion to work with the late composer and musician Liz Swados, who created uncommon sounds emanating from the island in response to Prospero's tyrannical spirit. These sounds came from the actors, not from recorded music, so the actors were always present moving throughout the audience. Sometimes the actors sat and watched the action. I am very struck in Shakespeare's texts by his creation of "an audience inside an audience," as if he is always giving us lessons on how to listen.

Kimberly Senior

The play found its right home

When a director is given the opportunity to transfer a play or mount a new production of a play in a bigger theater, their feelings can be mixed. While the chance to reach a larger audience is exciting, there is always the risk of losing vital intimacy in a larger space.

We first did *Disgraced* at American Theatre Company in Chicago where there were 120 seats.[37] It's this really cool space but it's intimate. Then

---

[37] American Theater Company, 2012.

we did it at LCT3 at Lincoln Center with 110 seats.[38] Then we were going to Broadway and I was terrified.[39] I remember talking with John Lee Beatty, my scenic designer, and saying, "John Lee, I directed this play so that someone blinks their eye and it's meaningful. How is that going to happen with 940 seats? How is this not just going to become presentational? What am I going to do?" We talked a lot about how to focus the action and worked a lot with the lighting designer about how to make that clear. I worked with the costume designer about ways the costumes could help me tell a story in a broader way. Then when we got into the theater the very first day, I turned to Ayad with tears in my eyes, and said, "The play found its right home." The scale of that play is Greek. What happens in the play is that enormous, and so, retrospectively, I realized that something about the play felt a little unbelievable in those tiny spaces. Granted, big things happen in plays and plays are heightened moments, but suddenly in the historic Lyceum Theatre—it's the oldest Broadway theater—this play in a larger sense was taking its place along the continuum of theater. The events that happen in it fit there. The play takes place over a short period of time so we see these drastic changes immediately. When 940 people laugh at a joke and when 940 people gasp at the violence, you're like, this is right. This is the impact it's supposed to have.

Rachel Chavkin

Space between the actor and character

I love when there's space between the actor and the character and I'm aware of both of them simultaneously. *Natasha, Pierre, and the Great Comet of 1812* lies constantly. There's one lyric where Pierre says, "I put my fur coat on my shoulders unable to find the sleeves." As he says that, I have the performer putting on his coat and easily flipping his arms into the sleeves. It gets a huge laugh because there's such pleasure when things don't align exactly. When we cast that show, we articulated to our casting directors that we were looking less for

---

[38]Lincoln Center Theater, 2012.
[39]Lyceum Theatre, 2014.

actors than performers—people who can live in that duality and do that layering.

Natasha, Pierre, and the Great Comet of 1812 *was first produced in Downtown New York and eventually moved to Broadway.*[40]

I think one real division between Downtown and Uptown aesthetics is that Downtown is much more interested in personalities—what I call performers—whereas Uptown seems to more so value the actors' total transformation and invisibility. That's not putting a value judgment on either one; each has their place.

The Broadway run of Natasha, Pierre, and the Great Comet of 1812 was nominated for several Tony Awards, including a nomination for Best Direction of a Musical for Chavkin—an instance where Downtown aesthetics were well received by Uptown audiences.

---

[40]Ars Nova, 2012, and Imperial Theatre, 2016.

4

COLLABORATING IN REHEARSAL

Many directors say their love of rehearsal is what first drew them to directing. The rehearsal room offers the joy of discovery, the exciting challenge of collective problem-solving, and the satisfaction of sustained focus on a shared goal. Of course, these pleasures do not just magically materialize—directors must actively shape a process and environment in which the actors and other members of the creative team can do good work together. Then they must synergize that work into a cohesive production. In order to accomplish these objectives in rehearsal, directors must nurture individual relationships and group dynamics, create structure for the process while retaining flexibility so they can be responsive to new discoveries and shifting needs, and provide their collaborators with the information and tools they need to succeed. In this chapter, directors describe how they approach these responsibilities, starting with casting and moving through the rehearsal process.

Casting

Caroline Steinbeis

Opening a dialogue in auditions

Steinbeis emphasizes how important it is to take intentional steps to shape the atmosphere and social dynamic of the rehearsal room. Here she describes the first of those steps.

It begins with casting. It's very important to put together the right companies and match the right chemistries. I look for independent thought, an openness, and accessibility. We have such amazing actors in the UK who think and feel about character with huge empathy and sophistication. And it is so fantastic to be surprised by an actor's choice in an audition process, when someone walks through the door and shows you something you hadn't considered. From here on in, the dialogue remains open right the way through rehearsals and to performance, and it is this openness that is key to enabling the actor to take ownership of the work. I often catch myself assuming that we all think the same way about the world, when in reality we really don't. I see it as my role to establish the common denominators in the room to help demystify and create a shared frame of reference.

Kimberly Senior

Auditions should feel like the first day of rehearsal

I'm not looking for someone to turn in an opening night performance at auditions. I'm looking for someone who is going to be my partner. What raw material are they bringing in? What's our conversation like? I don't know what opening night looks like, so I want somebody who is going to get on board with me in that way. I don't actually *say* that because I think that's a weird thing to say to someone who doesn't know you. I'll say, "OK, that was great. Here's what I loved about what you did. What about if you throw this ingredient into it?" I'll start a conversation. When we did auditions in New York for the character of Jory in one of my productions of *Disgraced*, the actor who is playing Isaac came in to be my reader. Afterward he said to me, "It was so amazing because I feel like every woman who walked out of here thought they got the part." I asked why and he said, "Well, you just create a place where they were working already." Auditions should actually feel like the first day of rehearsal. You're familiar with the play, you come in with some ideas, and you're ready to get to work.

Patricia McGregor

Both the facility and the appetite

Some people hate auditions; I am riveted by them. So much of my work is done in finding that right person and giving them the best opportunity to be the best person in the audition. If people are fidgety at the audition table, I get really aggravated. That actor is out there trying to help us solve a problem, so please pay them all the attention you can.

One of my favorite acting teachers, Ron Van Lieu, would often say, "What do people have an appetite for?" I look for that in auditions. You can have a fabulous actor but they might just at that time in their life not have an appetite to go into the place you need them to go. Or they may have an appetite but not have the facility to go there at that time in their career. What I'm always looking for is somebody who has both the facility and the appetite to go where the piece demands.

I am most drawn to people whose physical life seems really open. Head-up acting, or what I call voice acting, makes me crazy. I always want to see them physicalizing. For *The House That Will Not Stand* auditions, we called back several groupings of women for the three sisters.[1] I remember the three women we ended up casting came bursting into the scene with this bubbly physical life, then constrained themselves immediately when they saw their mom. I needed actors who had an appetite and an ability to tap into this innocent, bubbly, sister-filled movement vocabulary and then to cut that off and go abruptly into something very contained.

Young Jean Lee

Charisma

I look for charisma—for somebody who is good with cold readings but also has a very winning personality. Cold readings are important; since I write during the rehearsal process, I'm giving them new text constantly, and I want to be able to determine as quickly as possible whether it

---

[1] Berkeley Repertory Theatre, 2014.

works or not without having to go through some big rigamarole to get the actor to feel comfortable. Charisma is important because the audience has to like them immediately. I tend to make ensemble pieces, and charisma is what gets the audience to stay on the ride. Also, I've found that charismatic actors tend to be good at cold readings. They come in and charm you and knock their audition out of the park right off the bat.

I'll have a team of people evaluating, and our rule is that if they leave the room and we feel afraid that we won't be able to get them, then those are the people we cast. We don't want to cast people where we're considering if they're right or not. We only cast people when we're just so sure they're right that we'll feel lucky if we could get them.

Leah Gardiner

Shaping the cast dynamic

I think you do need to cast some leaders, some people that you know could manage leading a bunch of people. It's important because when you leave the project, the stage manager manages the stage, right? But who manages the warm ups? Who sets the tone for the actors? How dreadful is it to go to work every day from 5:00 until 10:00 p.m., surrender who you are and become someone else, and hate it because no one is taking charge of creating a joyful environment? When I did a production of *Antony and Cleopatra*, I had to cast a Cleopatra who had extreme confidence as a person and could carry a show.[2] So, in the audition process, when people walked into the room, I started watching the dynamics. How did the women auditioning for the role work within the context of the group of actors in the room? I think of a cast as a family and the woman playing Cleopatra really needed to be the mother of the group.

Over time, you kind of learn how a personality sits in a cast dynamic. Out of interest for the actors, knowing that they need to live with each other for three months, I take into consideration how people talk to each other during auditions, how it seems they would treat each other, and the level of respect for one another that I think they would bring to work. I ask, Who's going to be the problem child of the family? That sort

---

[2]Houston Shakespeare Festival, 2014.

of thing. It's not like I'm trying to create a love fest, but I want to go to work every day knowing that I'm having fun, and I want people who are around me to come to feel the same.

Maria Aberg
Cross-gender casting

Aberg has cast numerous women in major male roles, particularly in her Shakespeare productions.

I feel very strongly that there aren't enough women on our stages, which is the source of my impulse to interrogate my choices around gender in the casting process; but that isn't the only reason I will decide to change the gender of a character. The main factor to consider is obviously what impact it will have on the story, so I investigate if it might reveal anything interesting about the relationships in the play, if it helps me highlight a particular theme that I'm exploring, and if it encourages the audience to view events in the play differently. There might also be a particular actress I've got in mind that I'd like to work with, and who I know would bring something interesting to the story. The only unique challenge cross-gender casting poses in rehearsal is that it means I have to clearly and comprehensively communicate to the actors my reasons for the casting, so that they can understand and own it on stage.

Lear deBessonet
Casting unconventional casts

For the Public Works program at the Public Theatre, deBessonet has directed complex, high-production value, large-cast productions in Central Park's open air theater that include a mix of professional and nonprofessional performers.

One of our arch goals is that the piece as a whole rings with excellence, meaning that the presence of nonprofessional performers does not mean that the integrity of the storytelling will be sacrificed or that an audience is going to be put in a charitable position. When you attend your godchild's second-grade violin recital, that's a joyful experience as well, but as an audience member, you are there to give, not to receive— it's an act of generosity. For the Public Works shows, my intent is for the audience to both give and receive, for it to be a resonant and clear and magical experience that completely stands on its own without any kind of sympathy points. Because of that, we always try to find the moments of the story that seem to require some sort of large theatrical gesture, then think about what group would most illuminate that moment. In *The Tempest*, for example, there's the storm, there are the invisible hounds that chase Caliban and the clowns—these are moments of theatricality and magic that have to be solved.[3] So when we think about groups or types of groups to cast for that moment, we never want them to be extraneous. We want that casting to create that solution and be in conversation with that moment in the play. So for the storm in *The Tempest*, we were very interested in big elements of sound, so we ended up working with a fabulous Taiko drumming group led by Kaoru Watanabe. And there are other moments in the plays we've produced for Public Works that just invite something in. Within *Winter's Tale*, when we're in Bohemia at the festival, there are a number of performances called for in the text, like a dance of the shepherds and shepherdesses.[4] That is an invitation to do something that doesn't feel extraneous.

Sometimes the *process* of casting these shows is pretty crazy. Like, when I directed *The Odyssey* in a similar way in San Diego, we had a lot of difficulty casting the Cyclops.[5] Originally I thought it was going to be this San Diego icon, Chunky Sanchez, but he was having health issues, so then we assembled this crazy list of other people that we thought could do it. We wanted it to be somebody who would be recognizable to San Diegans. So one day we were at a very serious moment in rehearsal when my assistant Sarah Grossman passed a Post-it Note to me that said, "The San Diego Chicken just called." The San Diego

---

[3]Public Theater, 2013.
[4]Public Theater, 2014.
[5]Old Globe, 2011.

Chicken is one of the people we had contacted about playing the Cyclops, so the message made sense, but I was like, this Post-it Note is too outrageous for words!

Paulette Randall

Now we can play

When I'm casting a play that's already written (rather than a devised piece), I know I've got the casting spot on when I think, "Ah, I can't imagine anybody else doing that part". And then I'm like, "Yeah, now we can play! Now we can really push this thing further and further."

Setting the Tone for Rehearsals

Nadia Fall

Fear management

We want raw humanity to resonate between the actor onstage and the person sitting in the audience; when it happens, we know the power of that spiritual exchange. Without it there really is no point. That's why actors have to show vulnerability and inhabit painful spaces. I think if we're asking the actors to cope with this kind of exposure at points, then we directors ought to bloody do it too. That's why I sometimes share relevant personal stories in the rehearsal room. I know some directors don't, but I find it helps develop a camaraderie and create a free space where it's okay to open up about the time you were in this or that situation or you had this violence or pain inflicted on you. I'm very clear that the room is not a therapy session, however—that would be dangerous and indulgent. I think a director needs to lead, there needs to be a vision, and the actors need to know that you've got their back. Fear is in the room, and, as a director, I'm trying to face it and say, "We're all right. Let's work our way through the inevitable fear of putting this in front of people and sharing our souls by concentrating on the work itself." Fear management is definitely part of the job!

Sarah Benson

We're here to fail big

I try to create a process where everyone feels we're here to fail big, try stuff together, and make stuff together. So in the early stages of rehearsal, I need to build company and build trust. That's more important than any other work I'm achieving then.

I don't do a ton of table work—usually one day at the beginning. I can get lost in talking and talking about ideas. I just want to start. Then, during the process, when we encounter a particular problem, we can have a conversation about what is going on in that moment and try different ways of doing the scene. That often sparks bigger conversations about: "Why are we doing this play? Why are *you* doing this play? Why do we care?" Those are always better conversations for me to have during the work rather than at the beginning. Later in the process, those conversations help everyone figure out why they care about what they are doing, which is something I'm very interested in being palpable in the work. I'm interested in the characters people are creating, but I'm as interested in why these particular actors are showing up to do the play as, ultimately, that is what the audience will feel more than anything.

Maria Aberg

Infecting everyone with your love of ideas

I prioritize creating an environment for actors and creatives to be excited about engaging with the ideas of the play. You do have to infect everyone in the room with your love of those ideas. It can sometimes seem like a bit of an overwhelming task to try and win people over, but actually, as long as you love it and know why you love it and why you think it matters, all you usually need to do is tell them. Enthusiasm is after all deeply infectious.

Roxana Silbert

A playful, anarchic atmosphere

I see my role in the rehearsal room as creating the conditions where the actors and other members of the creative team can do their best work. I like a happy, playful, anarchic atmosphere in which everybody feels safe enough to try things out and open enough to throw some of their ideas out. I do this by trying to remain very open myself as well as watching and listening to what actors are offering as carefully as I can and reflecting what they're sending out back to them. I ask lots of questions and try lots of approaches, physical and text-based, to unlock the truth of the text. I don't consider there to ever be a right or wrong, just the way we are choosing to do it . . . for today.

Erica Whyman
Doing something that matters

Although Whyman has undergraduate and postgraduate degrees in philosophy and is very interested in plays that explore big ideas, she doesn't spend an atypical amount of rehearsal time discussing those ideas with the actors.

In rehearsals, my connection to the ideas is very important in persuading the actors that we are part of something that matters. But once we've done that, the work is in making the drama live, getting up and communicating with an audience, really listening intently to the text and what it wants to say, how it wants us to feel. I don't think of myself as a particularly intellectual director in the rehearsal room, but rather as someone who's really passionate about why we're doing the play.

Caroline Steinbeis
Doing is always better

I try to create an environment in which we experience and interact with our work on our feet as soon possible. That means diving in at the deep end, so while there may be some table work at the start of a rehearsal period, I look to enable actors to stand up, take the attention off themselves and start playing, get the thing inside their bodies and not overthink anything. Doing is always better than talking about doing,

because ultimately—and irrespective of what the play is or how rev-
erent you feel towards the author—the experience you are creating for
an audience should be emotionally and physically present. And for this
to start happening, I feel a playful rehearsal room is the most energized
and enjoyable environment. Playing with the material, looking at it from
different angles, breaking it apart, and putting it together again. And
there is a huge satisfaction in working something out together, thereby
breaking down hierarchies and freeing actors to feel equal in voice
and input so they can intuit the most interesting choices for the piece.
Through playing, I can enable a strong communal feeling that will flow
into the work, and we share equally in the creative process, which is
elemental. Anyway, playing by yourself is boring. Playing with others is
much more fun.

Anne Kauffman

The rhythm of language combined with the rhythm of human activity

I often do what I call "table work on our feet." I'll do maybe one day at
the table, then get people up and moving. It puts them at sea, which
I find helpful. When we're exploring movement at the same time as the
language, we're not really thinking very deeply about the words, which
lets them be absorbed in a different way. They kind of wash over us,
which allows us to discover things we wouldn't at the table.

With a language play, you can do a great reading of it and it all
sounds amazing: but what that reading discounts is the fact that we're
three-dimensional human beings. It's different when the play is going to
be produced. You can't sit at the rehearsal table making this beautiful
language sound perfect because then when you get up the rhythm of
the language doesn't fit with the rhythm of human activity. We're not
cartoons. If a character is going to take something out of her pocket it
doesn't just appear, the actor has to actually reach into the pocket and
get it out. That flesh and blood action breaks up the rhythm of the language. So I get the play on its feet right away, so we can see how the
rhythm changes in an interesting way once we combine language with
human behavior.

Kimberly Senior

Informing the work by drawing from the world around us

Sometimes directors set the tone for rehearsal in a way that may feel counter-intuitive, like when Kimberly Senior dedicates an hour at the top of rehearsal just to talking with the actors.

I talk about directing in 360 degrees so that it's not just about the text. How are we drawing from the world around us as a constant resource? To someone else it might look like we're wasting time, but I will spend an hour at the top of rehearsal talking about current events, playing each other music we heard, and telling anecdotes. You might not even be sure how it directly relates, but it is informing the work. I once had a stage manager tell me, "It's amazing because the time that other directors spend getting stressed out about stuff is time you spend fucking around and you still get the same amount of work done."

Leah Gardiner

Just go to work

While working with new, fresh voices can be exhilarating, Gardiner describes one of the benefits of working with more experienced playwrights.

A lot of young playwrights like to have extensive discussions about what it will be like when you get into the room, what their expectations are, what they hope you will do for them, and so on. It's so refreshing to be at a level now where I'm working with experienced playwrights and that conversation doesn't have to take place. You get into a room and just go to work.

Empowering Actors

Anne Kauffman

Give space for the actors' ideas

Actors are terrified, and they should be because they're so vulnerable. There have been a few times where I've had to sit down in a dressing room with an actor and say, "I am not going to let you fail. I have you. Do not question that." Sometimes this makes me think maybe they need me to be more of a dictator so they feel certain I know what I'm doing. But that's not who I am. There's a kind of paternalistic relationship between a director and actor, in a hierarchic way, but that doesn't mean the director has to be authoritarian. I'm collaborative and experimental in the rehearsal room and like to give space for the actors' ideas. I don't come in saying, "This is how it's gonna be," because I don't know what it is until we find it.

Blanche McIntyre

Elasticity and ownership

You can't make a piece of work that is derived from fear or is inflexible. I know some directors who say, "Take two steps forward. Raise your hand to there. Then say the line. Stress this word." If you do that, the actors can't respond to an audience because they're going to be thinking about the feet, the hand, the word. If you do that in rehearsal, there's no time to look at what underpins the moment—the shock of a piece of news, or the change when an argument becomes public, or the reason the man burgles the house or whatever. If actors know what they're doing and why, they can adjust it in response to the audience. You give them something more elastic. So the shape of the play can change, but the truth of what's happening in the moment doesn't change because you've spent rehearsals talking about that truth as opposed to the external attributes of it.

The lucky thing for me (it didn't feel lucky at the time) was that I had to do enormous amounts of work on the fringe before anyone would trust me to do a paid job. Nobody on the fringe was getting paid and everyone was hoping to get good reviews and some profile (which was eventually what happened to me). I realized quickly that I had to learn how to create collective ownership of a piece. Because if the actors don't like it, they'll walk. And rightly because they're not getting anything. But if they like it, if they own it, if they value it and invest in it and have created it themselves, then they will do it beautifully with every ounce of heart that they have. The piece will be better and more valuable. So, it's important that everyone makes it together. I had to learn it through necessity, but I think it's an important principle. You can't have a steep hierarchy at the fringe and I came out of it going, "Why should you have a steep hierarchy anywhere?"

If you're saying to actors, "Ultimately, my creative vision is more important than yours," you're turning them into puppets. But if what you're saying is, "You're making it, I can see it and you can't, I think this is what you're going for, it will be more successful if you do it this way," it will work better because they built it themselves. Theater is made by a bunch of people for another bunch who are watching it in the same moment. And if the people who are acting it are disempowered, then ultimately all you see are some disempowered people on stage. You don't see any kind of collective exploring of a question or raising of an issue. One of the things that interests me about Greek tragedies and comedies is that they were put on for a small community, by people and using people from that community. They were articulating the issues that were concerning them and using each other to do it—it was political in the Greek sense of the "polis." It was a magnifying glass put over a theme or an issue for the collective and by the collective, and that's the way I think theater can best work.

Diane Rodriguez

Helping the actors be storytellers

A lot of actors—especially in TV but also in theater—will say, "I'm just doing this part," and don't focus on trying to see the whole. I tell them, "No, you're doing your part but you're also helping tell the story." It's like a relay race. One actor takes it to a certain point, then the next character comes in and builds on that and so on until we build to the end. To do that well, they all need to understand the shape of the play, so I take the time to map it out for them and describe for everyone what every single character's role is in unveiling the story. This makes it much clearer what they need to accentuate to realize each moment; it helps them understand where they need to intensify, it helps them with pacing, and it helps them realize how they need to affect another character at a given moment in order to better build the story. Letting them know *how* they're important really empowers them to help me tell the story.

Caroline Steinbeis

Opening up the right channels

When I make a production, I am most interested in what feels alive and present now. The wonderful thing about actors is their ability to receive and channel emotionally, from the gut, unlike many directors who tend to intellectualize. Tapping into this flow of expression seems to be key, so I am becoming increasingly more reactive in my direction. There needs to be space for an actor to make an offer. It is really only once this offer has been made that the work begins. It's a very delicate moment, and it is important to shed any expectation of what it might feel like before it has happened. By keeping things light and open, we can break through together, just start and be bold. A big part of this for me is about letting go of needing to know the answer. It is useful to have a plan B up your sleeve but stepping in too soon can be the death of something potentially very interesting. An openness can show you doors that you didn't know were there to begin with.

Openness alone is not always enough to coax an actor to make an offer in the rehearsal room—they also need to feel safe knowing that their offer will be accepted.

The prospect of walking into a room full of strangers, your heart on your sleeve, ready to push to the far reaches of the emotional spectrum? That is a tough job. As is the case with any relationship, actors need to trust that the work will be worth opening up for, so a healthy dose of guards up is absolutely fair enough, as all too frequently directors do not handle the expectation to "give it, show me, drop everything" very sensitively. But sometimes you may just find the right question to put to an actor, or allow them space to follow an instinct, and suddenly a door is open. Then it is up to me to say, "Well, if that is where it takes you then that's where I'd like to go with you." This is the moment when you have established trust; a path is clear that feels accessible because it's honest, which also means that it can be found again and again in performance.

Even when a director works to create an open, collaborative rehearsal room, some actors can still be resistant.

If I encounter an actor who challenges, the task is to work out what is at the core of that, and equally what can be done to resolve the issue. The majority of people in the industry are up against huge competition, always vying for jobs. This puts on a lot of pressure. But actors also have individual circumstances. Everyone needs different things, and in my experience, there is a certain time frame in which to establish the parameters before a collaboration has potential to become complicated. At that point, it's a question of how much room to allow and establishing where the boundaries are so that the work can continue and everyone else in the room feels unrestricted.

I have learned that I need to love something in order to invest in it, and that the most satisfying work emerges when I find a way of bringing that out of the people I work with as well. This goes for all members of the creative team. The challenge lies in opening up the right channels to engage an actor to invest in the work personally, to work out the distinction between the actor and the person underneath. It's at this stage that the work becomes interesting: because it is personal.

Young Jean Lee

Every actor's self-awareness is different

As a director, you need to have an aesthetic point of view and then be able to communicate that with your collaborators. Every actor is different in terms of how much explanation they need from you. There are some actors who are so sensitive that if you just tell them something didn't work, they'll be like, "I know exactly what went wrong. I did this, this and this," and then they'll adjust it. That's the extreme end of the spectrum. At the other extreme end is the actor who has no sense of what it is they just did, and so you need to be very explicit with them. I would say that most experienced strong actors are at the more self-aware end of the spectrum.

Kimberly Senior

"What do you want to do?"

As she describes in the "Shaping the Process" section of this chapter, Senior avoids giving actors specific instructions about blocking or character choices. Instead, she guides them through deep explorations of the characters and the play.

Actors are the most disempowered people in our field and it breaks my heart. When they look at me and say, "Tell me what to do," I reply, "What do you want to do?" I've had actors get frustrated with me because they just want me to tell them what I want. I will have to say, "Okay, I think in order for this actor to walk out of the room I need you to drive them out of the room. You can do that in your way." That's as far as I'll go. For too long, I watched actors crossing stage left because I told them to. I can't do that anymore.

Older actors find this the most challenging. Actors over sixty often say, "I'll give you what you want." I'm like, "What do *you* want? Gosh, it breaks my heart that the machine has made you that way." Younger actors have a much easier time with my "try something" approach, but they don't have the tools to do it like older actors do. What's amazing is when you get those two groups in a room together and a younger actor is inspiring an older actor to be a little bit freer and an older actor is teaching the younger actor the tools of the craft. At those moments, my job is to just step back.

Maria Aberg

Approaching difficult sequences

In her production of John Webster's The White Devil *at the Royal Shakespeare Company, Aberg focused on the misogyny inherent in this tale of Renaissance court corruption.*[6] *To highlight the play's misogynistic undertones, Aberg made bold staging choices that could have put the actors in some potentially uncomfortable situations. In order to avoid this, she solicited the input of the actors in her decisions.*

In week two, I sat everyone down and said, "Right, we need to have a conversation about how we do this because I don't want to get it wrong." I wanted to make sure we didn't tell a story that we didn't want to tell, but I also wanted to make sure that I didn't make any of the women or men feel uncomfortable portraying any of the things that we were about to portray. I just wanted to make sure that everyone could really stand for what we were going to do.

The part that was worrying me most was the Shibari bondage club where we set Camillo's murder in our production. In that scene, we had six actresses in full body stockings with their faces completely covered, so they were seen only as anonymous bodies in sexually provocative postures in a big, clear box. We knew we had to be careful there, so we decided to have them egg on Camillo's murderer by singing, which gave them some agency to affect the story, and take off their wigs when she started to kill him, which turned them back into individuals rather than just being objects or bodies.

Karin Coonrod

Owning the vision and deliberately derailing actors

There's a growing hunger among actors for making something together, for crossing boundaries and creating presence. Lately, I like the actors to be very present throughout, not only when in the scene, but also when "offstage." To do this, the actors have to be on board and there must be tremendous trust and commitment. The relationship with the actor is one that I cherish and continuously work on. It is the actor who must own the vision of the play and carry this vision to the audience.

"Give actors ownership" can sometimes be misunderstood to mean "don't push actors in a direction they don't want to go." Coonrod

[6]Royal Shakespeare Company, 2014.

emphasizes that it's important occasionally to challenge even the most experienced, confident actors.

Sometimes very confident actors need to be derailed from their agenda. They have to go through what they know so well to get to something deeper and more vulnerable. Once I worked with a fabulous actress, a powerful person in her own right. I needed to bring her to a place of being more vulnerable, of not anticipating the action, not thinking about what "to do" but rather just breathing into the present moment. As she was playing a love scene, I wanted the words and the action to be heard in a new way, as if the audience were experiencing their own renewed love vows. I remember talking with her on the telephone a few times and just saying: "breathe, just *be*." It was hard for her to let herself go, but as we came into performance she did just that and the scene played stunningly.

Paulette Randall

Understanding who and where you are

Randall emphasizes the importance of giving the actors time early in the rehearsal process to explore their character's identity and environment.

They need to understand who these characters are and the space that they inhabit. Because once they know who they are and where they are, they know how to move. It's just the same as if you moved into a new apartment, you'd take a bit of time to get your bearings and then before you know it, you don't have to think about, "Oh, I've got to go down to the left to go to the kitchen, I've got to go right to go to the phone." It just becomes instinctual. So, it's about making sure that the actors know who they are and therefore know how to inhabit their space.

Nadia Fall

Through repetition, actors are released

I think repetition is so important in rehearsal. Through repetition, actors are released; free to go beyond worrying about words and moves they can begin to tap into the spirit of a play. Only then can they really find a sense of ownership and put their own detail into it. Especially intelligent actors—I love intelligent actors. I don't necessarily mean academically, but emotionally intelligent people that surprise me by the way they say a line or do something that I hadn't thought of. I want a collaboration, where both parties offer things up. That's what a lot of rehearsal is about; I'm not interested in directing marionettes.

Erica Whyman

What matters about the play

I'm a devil for needing longer with actors in auditions and that's because I want to see if they can hear what matters about the play rather than just whether they're right for the role. I want collaborators—coconspirators. And then of course we also talk about why we're doing the play in early rehearsals. I don't have tables, which is the only mildly radical thing about my process. I like just being in a circle. There's something about desks that immediately makes people feel we're in a classroom or a library and there's somebody who's supposed to know all the answers and everybody else feels a little stupid. I'm really interested in how afraid quite a lot of very smart actors are of ideas and of exegesis of a text. There is something in what they do that persuades them that they aren't suited to a certain kind of thinking or that they don't do it well. I want my room to feel like everybody is truly equal in the contribution that they may choose to bring when we sit down and talk about the play. Then sometimes, restating why you're doing the play strikes the perfect note just as you open. Particularly with new work, if you've commissioned the play or if someone has written the play because something really matters and needs saying, it can be very releasing to say "let's just remember why we're doing this" in that moment before opening where everyone's in terrible fear about whether it works. You mostly have to put down "why it matters" in between those early rehearsals and opening, I think, and concentrate on telling the most compelling story available to you.

Tina Satter

You can operate in a deeply coded way

Satter, a playwright/director, talks about how her long-term relationship with actors in her company, Half Straddle, shapes their process.

When you've worked with actors a lot, you can operate in a deeply coded way. I've been making shows with the core group of actors in my company for years. Sometimes I can literally say, "Do that thing," and they will know what I mean. Before the script for *Seagull (Thinking of You)* was cleaned up, it said stuff like, "Jess does her weird eyeball thing. Eliza does the hair twirl."[7] Because I know them so well, I'm always drawing on what they do when we're not in a moment. Like the way they sit when they talk just offstage. Or something they do when they are playing around in a moment they aren't needed. At one point in *Seagull*, Jess [Barbagallo] guided Eliza [Bent] across the stage on a skateboard. That came from a time they were playing around in rehearsal when they were bored. The choreographer I was working with saw that and said, "That's kind of dumb, what they're doing, but there's something about it . . ." So we put it into the show. I love to layer in what the actors instinctually do, not necessarily related at all to the play itself. It brings a stylized realness because it comes from something only they would do.

Liesl Tommy

Clarity, specificity, and ferocity

Specificity is the beginning, middle, and end for me. We need to excavate everything with such clarity and specificity that everyone knows what we're careening toward and the actors are free to pursue their objective with the height of ferocity. That applies to quiet, nuanced storytelling as well. I did *Melancholy Play*, written by Sarah Ruhl and music by Todd Almond, who, to me, are the two forerunners in the

---

[7]Half Straddle, 2013.

American theater in terms of delicacy.[8] They both have such a beautiful, delicate, nuanced hand. The reason I wanted to work on that play is because I wanted to explore that and live in that world. I feel like I didn't do a single thing differently in my approach. It is a really emotional, quiet play; but it has this heartbeat of wildness underneath it that comes from the actors being really clear about what their task is, what their job is. I used to be an actor and I moved into directing because I just felt like there were a lot of directors who weren't clear. They didn't know what they wanted and didn't know how to communicate it. That's why I feel like, in a way, my first responsibility to the actors I work with is clarity and specificity so that they can really flourish and be free on the stage.

Shaping the Process

Karin Coonrod

Baptizing the space

When I go into the performance space for the first time with a company, we do a holy exercise. I tell them to throw everything we've done in the rehearsal hall out the window and do all the words of the play in order, but do whatever they want to do as they say them. I tell them, "We have to baptize the space for the audience's appearance and so I want you to occupy the whole space with the words." At first, they're kind of polite, but by the end the wildest things are going on. It's incredible what happens and what we find. The space teaches us. And it makes the actors feel so free. When we did this in the La MaMa space for *The Tempest*, at the end the actors were standing there and then everybody who was there watching just stood up and we all put our hands on our hearts.[9]

KJ Sanchez

Spreading out table work

I used to do three days of table work and then start staging on either the third or the fourth day, but kept finding that those first few days

---

[8]Trinity Repertory Company, 2015.
[9]La MaMa, 2014.

of table work would get really problematic, because we didn't know each other yet. We would get into a weird place where people were trying to defend their homework or to make judgments about their characters, or other characters, before any of us really knew the play together. A random comment from the guy playing Rochester about who he thinks Jane is to him could really throw the actor playing Jane off her axis because we're all just shooting in the dark before we know the play. Once we've had a chance to work on the play a little bit on its feet and get to know it a bit more and get to know each other a little more, then it's a much more comfortable environment to start talking about what characters want and where we're going in terms of arc.

Now, on the first day, I do a read through and a design presentation, and cover the general things of the world of the play, then I start staging on the second day. After we've staged the first chunk, we do table work on that and I just call in the people that are working on that chunk. Then we do more staging, more table work, run-throughs, more table work . . . Even during tech, I try to get ahead of schedule and so I can spend a couple hours with the actors in the green room doing another round of table work. By then, we know what the whole play feels like. We understand the arc and are in the world. We can identify the trouble spots where the story is getting lost, grab our scripts, go back to the page and talk about what those moments are about. (You also become everybody's favorite director when you can offer the production manager two hours of tech time to do work notes!) So now a part of my process before we go into rehearsal is figuring out when these little loop de loops back to table work will happen and which thread of research we'll follow in each one.

Liesl Tommy

If it's not in the play, it doesn't exist

From the beginning, when we sit down to do table work, I make it very clear to the actors that if it's not in the play, it doesn't exist. We have to make really clear delineations between the rules of the play established by the writer and the rules that we, as an ensemble, are creating for ourselves for this production. We have a hundred million choices that we could make at every moment—that's what artists do, we make imaginative choices. We cannot get attached to the things we imagine because they are not real. They are not laid down in the script, so we can't get precious about them. You have to establish that the script is the bible.

This also helps the playwright refine the script when you're working on a new play. An actor will say, "I feel like my character does *x*," and then I'll say, "Well that's fine, but let's just be clear that that is something your imagination is coming up with because it's not in the text." Then the playwright can decide, "I absolutely want every single human being who does this play to make that choice and therefore I have to put it in the text" or "I don't mind if this is a grey area left up to the artists on each production, so I won't prescribe it in the text."

Nadia Fall

Starting small and building up

Directors have got such different approaches in the rehearsal room, and I've been very lucky to have been in the rehearsal rooms of directors with very varied personalities back when I was an assistant. In my rehearsals, I suspect I myself am rather careful and controlled and sometimes a little "over tidy." I have to start with really small details and then build up, up, up—like with an oil painting—whereas other people splash the paint on and rub it out and blend it in. Rufus Norris, Artistic Director at the National, teases me, saying, "Nadia, get up from your chair!" It's true I like to start around the table with the text. The first phase for me is about being forensic with the words, back story, and world of the play, and I think it's very important to lay that foundation. If this isn't done at the start, I feel it's hard to go back to it later. Though it's not a good idea to put off getting up too long, or else it feels like putting off the inevitable. I do like to break up that table work at the start of the process by carrying out some carefully designed improvisations, which can help get to the jugular of a play.

Anne Kauffman

Throwing spaghetti at the wall

I do a lot of throwing spaghetti at the wall to see what sticks. Like in the early rehearsals for *God's Ear*, I would have the actors try a moment twelve different ways in a minute.[10] If you're open enough and connected enough to the play, you'll recognize "ah, this is it" when you see it. That's a great way to discover the rules of the play's world. Doing that for *God's Ear*, we actually discovered that the rules of the world shifted constantly. The only way we figured that out was by me saying, "Walk over there and straighten his tie even though you guys are in two different places" and finding that was right for one scene of the play even though it was wrong for another.

Oftentimes, I ask actors to do the exact opposite of what we think we should be doing in a scene. Because when I'm going after something I can get sort of myopic about it; I become a dog with a bone and I have to shake myself out of that in order to see the play again. So I ask us to perform the opposite action and I would say about 50 percent of the time, it turns out to be the right thing. It's like letting your peripheral vision find it. What I'm looking for, it often turns out, is actually that thing over there that I'm not looking at.

Patricia McGregor

Finding the physical vocabulary

To find the physical life of the production, I often tell actors the goal, then give them assignments. For *The House That Will Not Stand*, the goal was to find the physical vocabulary of a life lived in a cage.[11] I brought in my sister to work on what it would be like to live in your body in that constrained, Victorian period. We did some of the social dances the characters would know and worked on some things just to get them into their characters' bodies. Then I told them to "go away and come back with ten different ways you might touch when you first greet each other" and "show me three different ways you use your fans to alert each other when you're surprised" and so on. Then we would choose

---

[10]Vineyard Theatre, 2007.
[11]Berkeley Repertory Theatre, 2014.

two of those ideas and add them to the physical vocabulary of the piece. I identify the bull's eye and then we all shoot to find that bull's eye.

Young Jean Lee
Creating the piece with a choreographer

Lee describes the role choreographers play in the collaborative process of creating her shows.

I've used a choreographer on pretty much every show I've made. They come in, we improvise with the performers and see what they can do, and then the choreographer, with input from me, builds a dance for them. Usually, there are lots of dance numbers in my shows. *Untitled Feminist Show* was all dance.[12] That was a real collaboration between me and the choreographer, Faye Driscoll, and my associate director, Morgan Gould. I would usually come in with a song and a concept and ask the performers to improvise something. That would give me a sense of what I was interested in, and then Morgan would come in and shape it or Faye would come in and choreograph it with high input from me. For example, I brought in a Mozart piece and I gave the performers a fairy tale-like scenario, which they acted out to the music. Then Morgan did a lot of work to actually time out all the movements very precisely. There was also another song that I brought where I wanted everybody to be very, very sensual. I asked them to all to shake, which they were doing, trying different things, when Faye came in and said, "Keep doing what you're doing but form different shapes with your bodies. Shake your way into different formations of everyone's bodies."

Lear deBessonet
Bringing large casts into the imaginative world

The rehearsal process for large-cast shows can feel chaotic, particularly in a unique situation like Public Works where the cast includes professional

---

[12]Young Jean Lee's Theater Company, 2011.

and nonprofessional performers, as well as community groups. But deBessonet explains that, at its root, the process is the same as any other.

We bring a Public Works cast together in a way that's similar to the way you bring any ensemble into a shared vision of the world you're creating together. There's a real lightning-in-a-bottle thing about turning a hundred people onstage. Unleashing that chaos and messy, imperfect, imprecise humanity is one of the great strengths of a Public Works show. But within that chaos, the work is organized by the action of this scene and what we're doing in this scene moment to moment, all hundred of us.

There is a moment in *Winter's Tale* when the shepherd brings in baby Perdita, who he has just found on the Bohemian coast.[13] We staged it so that, within that same sequence, we had the Bohemians—played by our hundred-person community ensemble—dancing in a separate space. Bohemia is a festival culture and this was a festive day within that festive culture, so everyone was dancing. Then one of the Bohemians, played by an unbelievable actor from the Fortune Society, named Donald Gray, saw the shepherd and his son enter and screamed, "It's a baby!!" Everyone turned, and Sebastian, the man playing the shepherd, brought the baby up onto this sort of step and the whole community gathered around. He passed the baby off to the community and they held it and passed it through all the hands. Once they passed it around, they brought it back into the center and they sort of folded down over it. Then the play skipped forward sixteen years, with the time monologue, and when they opened back up, they revealed the sixteen-year-old Perdita. When we staged that sequence in rehearsal, the community understood it so beautifully and implicitly: there's a new life being brought into this community and we're all gonna touch it and support it and send our blessing to it. I think there's something so human in that impulse that they all just got.

When we stage those kind of moments in rehearsal, I guide the process by impressing upon everyone how important this moment is in the play and how much we want the audience to feel it and understand it. So, they all know the moment that they're a part of. They knew

---

[13]Public Theater, 2014.

the image that they're creating. They knew the story that we're trying to tell. I'm not manipulating them without them even realizing what's happening; we're together telling this story.

Kimberly Senior
Making actors feel unsafe

The work of rehearsal is not cumulative. It's not pretty good on Tuesday and then by Wednesday it's better. We're not looking for better. We're actually orbiting the material and deepening our experience of the material and going, "What if we came at it from over here? What if we threw this away and tried this?" Once the play is on its feet, I run the whole show every day. I'll say, "For today's goal, all I want you to do is connect with your scene partner. Forget everything else that we're doing. If you have to change the blocking, if you have to do whatever, just get in that scene and your scene partner's face. Great, what did we learn from that? What worked? What didn't work? How did this teach us about the play? OK, tomorrow, throw that away. Tomorrow I want you only to drive your agenda." I start out pretty early on talking about the need to always be beginning and to be in a place of constant and active discovery together for four weeks of rehearsal, then to continue to discover in my absence in performance.

We identify the things that are true about the character no matter what—Hedda is married to Tesman, Hamlet is a prince, and so on. The actors get those bones, learn them, inhabit them, and then forget about them because they're true. The audience knows they're true. They're in the text. You don't have to act them. They're there. Then there are moments that the playwright has packed the drama into: the kiss, the punch, the door slam. Everything that the actors do has to earn those moments. I don't really care how they get there—there are many ways. I love the Jory speech in *Disgraced* because she could be scolding him or trying to liberate him with the truth, and I don't care that it's different night to night because both can work as long as the actor earns the moment when she slams the door at the end. Really, all I'm asking is that they're present in the moment.

I joke that I've been making actors feel unsafe since 1995. Because I say, "Nothing is set. There's nothing in stone. Rely on nothing.

Surprise the other actor on stage." I don't believe in formal blocking at all. Because eventually the actors are just going to go where it makes sense, but that might not be until fifth preview (I'm a stage managers' and lighting designers' nightmare!) I think if you're feeling terrified and vulnerable as an actor you're probably doing your best work. In no other field do we want that. I do not want my surgeon saying, "I'm feeling really vulnerable today." I'll reschedule. But I feel like in art that's when we're at our best. So I think it's about time to create a space where we say, "I don't know, guys, this might suck."

Sarah Benson

Individual actor preferences

The process I use really depends on the actors. Different actors work differently. Some actors like talking about the ideas of the play and then trying stuff. But a lot of them don't respond to sitting and talking—they're doers, they're makers, they feel things in their bodies. So they'll say, "I just want to show you stuff and then you tell me what you like," and then give me three different versions to respond to. Or others say, "Tell me what to do and I'll push into it." It really varies person to person.

Leigh Silverman

Dress rehearsals and previews

The thing that tests a director's mettle is that day after the dress rehearsal, before the first preview. It's always the day where people are feeling the most freaked out. Usually, the producer saw it for the first time at the dress rehearsal, your friends were there, and you watched them see all the things that don't work. You have a ginormous work list and generally four or so hours to try and do it all. I have redesigned all the sound of a show in one day. I've put in thirty new pages of material. I've said, "Okay, we have four hours, I'm going to completely restage the end because it doesn't make any sense." That's the walking-into-a-fire moment for a director because you have to be the most on your game and the least precious. You don't have any time to doubt. It's one of the most important times for any play director.

Using Research in Rehearsals

Maria Aberg

Keeping the themes present in the room

I feel like my job is to make sure that the themes or ideas of the play are always present in every scene and in the rehearsal environment and then they will naturally pervade the work.

At the beginning of the rehearsal process for *The White Devil*,[14] we talked a lot about the themes of the play and read a lot of theory, like Laura Mulvey's 1974 essay about the male gaze, "Visual Pleasure and the Narrative Cinema." We also read about objectification and discussed various ideas of how to put misogyny on the stage without objectifying the women you portray. And we collected images and research and put it up on the walls of the rehearsal room. So that conversation was very much on the table from the beginning and it became impossible after a little while to not see the themes in every scene and everything we did. After a while it just kind of becomes part of the oxygen in the room, you know? And we didn't stop doing research. Someone would come in with a book in week four and say, "You've got to read this chapter!" And we'd photocopy it out. It's not like we shelved the theory and said, "That was research, now let's deal with the play"—they were constantly in dialogue with each other, which was really rewarding.

Paulette Randall

Experiential research

Randall gives an example of how experiential research outside of the rehearsal hall can enrich an actor's understanding of a character's experience.

If there was a character that had been in prison, I might send that actor off to a prison to sit in a cell and speak to prisoners about the emotional effect of being locked up. Even if it's a historical play, you can still go to a

---

[14]Royal Shakespeare Company, 2014.

contemporary prison and get the feeling of being incarcerated and what that can do to you. The environment itself might have changed but loss of liberty is still loss of liberty. You can still sense what nighttime does to you when you're in that cell on your own or with someone else and how that affects you in the morning. It's that kind of detail that I'm interested in.

Kimberly Senior

Talking about it in their language

For *Disgraced* rehearsals, we'll take a field trip to a museum to see Bonnard and Constable, artists that are referred to in the play.[15] We'll meet with a corporate lawyer from mergers and acquisitions. I don't just want to read about it. I want to go be in it. I want to be in it and I want my actors to be in it. I want them to be talking about it and talking about what they see and why in their language, not just the language of the playwright.

Liesl Tommy

You have to have context for depth

To get the depth of performance I like, actors have to have context from me. I spend the first week doing table work, whether it's Shakespeare or a musical or a new play. That is, just going from the beginning moment to moment, doing really intense scene work so that every decision that a character makes has been excavated. I share a lot of research and show a lot of video. Actors have to be intellectually rigorous that first week because there's going to be a point where it's going to be all emotional, all in the body, and we have to be building upon something so that there's depth under that emotion. Of course, there are wonderful actors who don't have a particularly intellectual process but are more gut-driven. Those actors can be capable of incredibly profound performances; I just have to figure out how to get that depth from them. That's also part of why I do rigorous table work—to learn how the actors are thinking, how they're processing information, because that's going to teach me how to talk to them in the rest of the process.

---

[15]American Theater Company, 2012, and several subsequent productions.

KJ Sanchez

Misunderstanding of "leave your homework at the door"

I'm surprised how many young directors have a misunderstanding of that great phrase, "leave your homework at the door." Some young directors now think that the work only happens in the rehearsal room. That's partly because they watch great directors like Les Waters or Anne Bogart or Anne Kauffman, who make it seem absolutely effortless in the rehearsal room—they don't look down at their notes on the script but sit and watch the actors and bounce off of what's happening and respond to it. Young directors see that and think, "Oh, to be a director is to walk into a room and be responsive." That's not the case, because Annie and Les and Anne do so much homework and preparation. They've just done it so long that it's second nature. I think these young directors' impulse is great, because they're thinking, "I don't want to be prescriptive. I don't want to be a dictator who's done all of my blocking with little stick figures, little miniatures on my model, and then I come in and tell people what to do." But the key is you have to do all of that preparation, and then you have to be willing to throw it away when you get in the room.

Leigh Silverman

Dramaturgs hold the big picture

In the best-case scenario, a dramaturg is able to look at a picture in a really macro way and stay macro. The job of the director can often be macro/micro, macro/micro. That kind of back and forth is really great, but on a day when you're really focused on why a scene doesn't work, or a moment doesn't work, or a beat doesn't work, or one line doesn't work, it's really helpful that there's someone constantly staying big picture. John Dias worked with Lisa Kron and I for five years developing *Well*.[16] It was an unusual dynamic because Lisa was the playwright but was also in the play, so she didn't have the experience of what it was like to watch it. Sometimes I would say to her, "Lisa you have to stop

---

writing the play while you are onstage. Perform, because the other actors can't do anything without you being present for them. I'm seeing you rewriting as the words are coming out of their mouths. Stop." It was really helpful in that case to have a dramaturg, because Lisa was on stage and John was in the audience looking at the big picture.

5
BUILDING A CAREER

By its very definition, a career covers a long time span and progresses through various phases. The directors in this book have mostly followed a similar career trajectory: discovering their interest in directing, getting established in the field, maintaining a pattern of steady work, and stepping into positions of leadership in theater companies, trade organizations, and/or communities. That said, their individual paths on this journey have diverged significantly. Some trained in undergraduate and postgraduate programs, others dove into the profession with little formal training. Some became artistic directors in their twenties, others have remained freelancers into their fifties. Some have maintained close ties to a particular company for the bulk of their career, others regularly work with numerous theaters. Most of the directors said that they had no clear career advancement template to follow, so they each had to find their own path forward. In this chapter, they describe their paths and how they forged them.

A career path runs concurrent with all other aspects of life's journey, so this chapter also includes discussion of how the directors balance their career aspirations with other concerns, such as financial security, community, quality of life, and relationships.

Discovering Directing

Patricia McGregor

Curating the audience experience

We moved around a lot growing up. I was born in Saint Croix in the Virgin Islands and performed in the Caribbean Dance Company there as a kid. Then I ended up going to a performing arts magnet high school in Orlando, Florida. There were a lot of performance opportunities at that time in Orlando, so I worked as an actor for Nickelodeon and other things. That helped me understand this could actually be a career. Then I went to Southern Methodist University in Dallas. That was the place where I turned from a performer to a director. I was reading Fugard's *My Children! My Africa!* and thought, "Well, there's not a part in it for me so let me direct it." Big light bulb moment on opening night. I just remember thinking earlier, "Okay, I'm glad to have done this but nothing will be as satisfying as performing." But when I saw the production, I realized, "Oh, I was able to help craft all of these moments and then curate this experience where the audience is having a dialogue with what's going on onstage." I found it thrilling in a way that I had never anticipated.

Lear deBessonet

An eleven-year-old's vision

DeBessonet grew up in a Fundamentalist Christian family in Louisiana.

Starting at age five, I was directing shows at my house with whoever could be persuaded to be part of them. By the time I was eleven, I wanted to be a theater director. I have a journal entry from around then where my vision was to start and run a Christian theater company in Russia. Why does a ten-year-old choose that? It's very bizarre, but this is 1990, Perestroika. The channels of information that were coming to me, filtered through really specific Fundamentalist sources in Baton Rouge, were all about religious oppression in Russia and the fact that people weren't allowed to have bibles. So what is contained within that casing of a dream is an idea of theater for social change, which is ultimately what became my focus.

Lucy Kerbel

I thought actors just got up there and did their thing

I didn't really know that directing was a job that one could do. As a teenager, I really liked drama but knew I didn't want to act. I'd seen there were stage managers and I assumed someone was designing the costumes, so I thought maybe I wanted to do something like that. I studied Technical Theatre and Stage Management in college from the ages of sixteen to eighteen. It was being in the rehearsal room and watching the directors coming in to direct the acting students that made me realize, "Oh, that's what I want to do." It was a world I had no idea even existed. I thought that the actors just got up there and did their thing and that was it.

Leigh Silverman

"You're a terrible actress"

Silverman grew up in Washington, DC.

Growing up, I was a total theater nerd. When I was fifteen, the summer between my sophomore and my junior year in high school, I went to this UCLA Theatre Abroad, kind of summer-campy thing, in Cambridge, England. It was a really intense time of my life, my mother had just died and theater was in my life in a major way. I got to Cambridge, and on the first day of the semester, we all had to perform monologues and then talk about the plays they came from. Afterward, the teacher, who was an incredible, old, angry British lady, said to me, "You're terrible, you're terrible, you're a terrible actress." It was so crushing. Then she said, "You're really smart and you said really smart things about the plays. It seems like you understand a lot about theater. I think maybe you're a director, not an actor. I think for the summer you should be my assistant. Read all the plays and help me go scene to scene and work with the actors." Like so many things in the theater, it was simultaneously massively disappointing and completely amazing. She steered me in a direction that I hadn't even really totally understood or imagined. I spent the summer reading Shaw and Chekhov and Ibsen and watching her work with the other students. I simultaneously felt really special and kind of like the one who got held back a grade.

Then in my senior year, my high school had a one-act play festival. You were allowed to submit proposals for shows that you wanted to direct. I submitted a play that I had found in a bookstore in London from the Gay Sweat Shop. I had no idea what the Gay Sweat Shop was and had just I picked up this play called *Compromised Immunity*, which was about the AIDS crisis. This was the early 1990s and AIDS felt like such an important topic, so I felt passionately about doing this play; but I had no idea what I was doing. I was picked to direct and was put on a double bill with *Really Rosie*, which was crazy. Let's just say people loved *Really Rosie* and they were horrified by my play (in fact, people were a little afraid of me after). But my high school invited some local theater people in for a critics' night. Howard Shalwitz, who is Artistic Director of the Woolly Mammoth Theatre in Washington DC, was one of the critics. After the play, he said to me, "This was really ambitious that you picked this play. I feel like you make really interesting choices. I'm going to hire you someday to work at my theater." Ten years later, he did. He was one of the first artistic directors to ever hire me. Those words from him were so important to me at the time. He probably doesn't even remember it, but I took it very seriously. I so appreciated that there was somebody who understood why I would choose this play.

May Adrales
A little push in the right direction

After college, Adrales volunteered in Cameroon and eventually took a job in New York City at the prestigious foreign policy think tank the Council on Foreign Relations. She was inexorably pulled toward theatre though, and spent her free time in New York seeing, directing, and writing plays.

Since I was very young, I wanted to use stories as a channel for social justice. I wrote many plays that were passionate, political, and so glaringly obvious in their messaging. I directed my own plays with a playfulness, inventiveness, and also naiveté. At the NY Fringe Festival, I directed and wrote a feminist expressionist drama (which was by all means pretty terrible writing). A frank, but very wise, reviewer wrote, "Where Adrales lacks as a dramatist, she makes up triple fold as a director." This (and also getting fired from my day job at the Council on Foreign Relations) helped push me onto the path of directing. I knew I painted stories in visuals rather than text, and I just needed a little push in the right direction.

Caroline Steinbeis

The atmosphere in a rehearsal room

I must have been about sixteen when I realized that I wanted to work in theater. I had absolutely no clarity on what that would entail or how I might go about doing it, but my family was very supportive and it felt right. At that time, I didn't understand what directing was, but I was fascinated by the atmosphere in a rehearsal room. How a group of people can get together and make something; suddenly something exists that wasn't there before. Something that could only have been made by those people present, something that has a piece of everyone inside of it. This is what I put most emphasis on in the rehearsal room now—how the actors and the creative team can support each other mutually to get the best possible work out of each other. This doesn't always have to be a harmonious process; conflict and friction are just as necessary.

Karin Coonrod

"Where have you been?"

I was an English major in college. In my last year, this little group I was in did a radio play and I realized I was sort of directing it. We did it for the convocation, and I remember the theater guy came up to me and said, "Where have you been?" Then, after college, I was teaching English at a Catholic boys' school and the principal asked me if I would direct the musical. I said yes without even hesitating. I threw out *Shenandoah* for a title and we did it. I had no idea what I was doing, but it was fantastic. We had a blast. I went on to do several others as well—all the big classics like *Fiddler on the Roof*, *My Fair Lady*, and *Guys and Dolls*. Then we did *Joseph and the Amazing Technicolor Dreamcoat*. The basketball team was the school's pride and joy, so I decided to start the play in the circle in the middle of the basketball court, with nothing for a set but a rotating carpet and a really great camel. That's when I realized how much space interests me and I realized I had to leave and go to New York. So I did.

Erica Whyman
Directing is everything

Whyman describes her circuitous path from secondary school to directing.

Before university, I thought I wanted to be a performer but I absolutely couldn't persuade my family or myself that I wanted to go straight to drama school. I had a French teacher who taught me Sartre and Camus and the Existentialists, so I became fascinated with philosophy. Which is significant, not just because it's what I did first, but because I think, actually, it's still what I do. Something about the complexity of ideas, the ambivalence of ideas . . . I was always interested in something that wasn't just black and white or as simply confrontational or oppositional as I perceived quite a lot of Anglo-Saxon ideas to be. There was something about French thinking that appealed to me. So I was offered a place at Oxford and set about taking a French and Philosophy degree very seriously, and acting very seriously, trying to figure out which one it was going to be.

I loved acting and it was a very important part of my life, but I think while at university, surrounded by all sorts of people who wanted to do it for a career, I started to think, "I'm not sure I'm cut out for it." And I wasn't. I sometimes flippantly say, "I wasn't good enough," but that's not completely true. I think I knew I couldn't survive what it asked of you as a person—to surrender yourself in such a way that you were not in control of the broader picture, the production itself, or which productions make it to the stage. I think now, with retrospect, that I couldn't imagine not being able to take an idea all the way to an audience, but only to participate in part of that process. Then I went to Paris for a year as part of my French and Philosophy degree and, while I was there, did two courses with the acting teacher Philippe Gaulier. I found, the second time, that I was resisting getting up. And that's not how an actor should feel—you should want to be on stage all the time. I was watching Philippe instead and was more intrigued by seeing him find a way to change wholly how a performer approached something. That was a really key moment.

But I went back to Oxford and put my head down and finished my degree and became convinced I was a philosopher. So I went to University College London to do a Master of Philosophy degree and then began a PhD. I was studying there with an inspiring philosopher, Professor Ted Honderich, but I then found myself in a play again. And he saw me in it and said, "You looked really happy at the end of the play." Which I'm not sure is how you should look at the end of *Caligula*, but it was a very interesting moment. Then a fellow PhD student (Tassos Stevens, now a very innovative theater maker) asked me to direct Frank McGuinness's *Someone Who'll Watch Over Me*. And I asked, "Why are you asking me?" and he said, "I just have an instinct that you would be great." So I got into that rehearsal room and I thought, "Hmm. Directing is everything. It's acting and philosophy. It's bringing ideas alive." And my brilliant professor suggested I take a year off, so I did and ended up at Bristol Old Vic, training as a director.

Getting Established

Lear deBessonet

Assisting directors who can teach you something specific

After training at Anne Bogart's SITI Company after college but not working directly with Bogart, deBessonet serendipitously ran into her in an airport and asked if she could assist her on a future production. Bogart said yes and helped deBessonet launch her career.

When I assisted Anne Bogart, she was very clear that she felt assisting is one supplementary way to learn about being a director, but there's no substitute for making your own work. That is the best way to learn. And so she said, "You're gonna assist me on this one and then you need to make something on your own." So then I moved to New York and did site-specific devised work, but also ended up assisting a few more people: Martha Clarke, Bart Sher, and Marianne Weems. I spaced out those assisting gigs over the course of five or six years. I tried to learn what I could with each director, then tried to apply that as fully as I could in making my own work. When I would hit a road block, I would think "Oh, there's something else I don't know how to do. Let me try to work with a director that I think I can learn from."

The assisting job with Marianne Weems is the only one that found me that I didn't find. There was a job open as a video assistant with the Builders Association on a show they were doing at BAM, *Alladeen*.[1] I thought, "I don't know anything about video. I don't even know if I'm interested in using video in my own work, but this seems like a great opportunity to learn." So I took that position for a workshop they were doing, and then when the show went into full production Marianne brought me on as her assistant director. That was my first investigation into multimedia and how that mode of storytelling functions.

I was interested in working with Martha Clarke because she's so successful at creating these wholly realized yet unique theatrical worlds. She's a theater artist—like Tim Burton in film—who brings such holistic visual and aural integrity to whatever piece they're doing. If you're doing a piece grounded in one naturalistic sociological reality—like an apartment in Pittsburgh in 1978—you know how to research that; but if it's an imagined world, how do you get it to be fully realized? I was really curious about just how she did that.

Then with Bart Sher, Anne Cattaneo from Lincoln Center introduced us. This was after years of devising and I had just done *St. Joan of the Stockyards*, my first Brecht, which I loved.[2] I felt like, "Oh my gosh, a piece in which the story is already set and the language is already set, this is fabulous!" Also, I had been integrating music very holistically into my pieces for a while, but I had not transitioned to doing musicals. I said to Anne, "I want to do Shakespeare and I want to do musicals and I have no idea how to step into those. First of all, I actually don't know how to direct a musical, and, secondly, I don't know how to get

[1]Builders Association, 2003.
[2]P.S. 122, 2007.

the opportunities that would allow me to do that." And she said, "I think Bart is the person that you need."

Blanche McIntyre

Fringe as training ground

I made the choice to go professional at age twenty-three (terrifying!), did unpaid fringe work until twenty-nine (by which point I knew what I was doing), won an award, had a couple more years of slight bleakness on the fringe, then finally got two shows that critics went very, very keen for, and suddenly people started paying me. So it has gone passion-endurance-oasis. And the turning points tended to be when somebody who's already in establishment or in the loop has taken a chance on me. For example, Gareth Machin, who gave me my first main house show at Salisbury Playhouse, and Max Stafford-Clark, who took me on as Associate for Out of Joint and then gave me *Ciphers*.[3]

McIntyre describes how working on the fringe has changed since she started her career in the early 2000s.

When I started out, it wasn't unusual to work your way up through the fringe, but it is now. Back then, you could do a play on the fringe for £4,000—half your student overdraft—hoping that people would buy tickets and cover the cost. Now it costs £15,000 or more. So what's happening now I think is that young directors are taking the assisting route. Assistant directing is often paid or at least you're not gambling your own money. And you get more quickly into houses and you learn under experienced directors and see how they work, then at a certain point somebody gives you your own show; but you do much less actual directing.

She describes what young people miss out on by not directing their own work on the fringe.

---

[3]Out of Joint, 2013.

I'm a believer in the Malcolm Gladwell ten thousand hours rule and I think it's increasingly difficult to get your ten thousand hours in. Directing and assistant directing are different skills. When you take the assisting route, you've more experience of how to run the tech, how a building works, how other people direct; but you don't experience the responsibility. For some people who have assisted, the moment where they get their first show is terrifying because running it yourself is so different, and because it's an official paid show, the stakes are higher. So that's a scary new thing that the generation behind me are having to cope with.

Nadia Fall

A catalyst for amazing things

One of my first jobs was as a trainee producer in a small to mid-scale touring theater company. It's there that I began to understand the mechanics of theater making and because it was a small operation, I turned my hand to a lot of different areas, such as participation work. I began directing little scenes and dramas and I was more and more intrigued by the creative side of things; I just wanted to be in the rehearsal room itself. At an expense and a risk, I gave up my job, and two weeks later I was doing an MA at Goldsmiths University in theater directing. I really shouldn't have been allowed onto the course, without such little knowledge about directing but I talked my way in. We learned some theory, but most of the course was having a go at directing, which was so brilliant. School is a lovely, intense cocoon. You have these few years of intense work and prep. What an opportunity. It's so precious. Sometimes I think, "God, what I wouldn't give to go back to university and bask in the reading and talking and seminars. Oh what a lovely life!"

Our final exam consisted of essays and directing a play in a fringe venue. The first night of the very first play I ever directed was coincidently seen by someone from the Young Vic theatre and another person from the National Theatre. That was a catalyst for all these amazing things that followed. I've been very fortunate that certain things have happened that have allowed me to seize an opportunity, then seize the next one, and the next one. Nothing came magically; it was about taking risks and working hard, but you also need people to give you a chance.

And you need stamina. So many of my peers that started at the same time as me gave up because it was so difficult to earn a living and sometimes it becomes just too hard to justify the endeavor. It sounds unromantic, but I think it is a long game. You keep going because you're determined to say something and you are compelled to make theater because you cannot live without it.

Patricia McGregor
The benefits of an MFA program

McGregor earned her MFA in Directing from Yale.

The MFA did three things for me. One, it's just like an Olympic training ground in that there are few distractions. You're not focused on anything but the work for three years. So you can really pack in your ten thousand Malcolm Gladwell tipping point hours.

Two, they ask you to do a whole range of things—commedia dell'arte, a devised piece, Shakespeare, and so on—so you're exploring all kinds of ways into a play and constantly training new muscles. It's like athletic training where you change up your training routine to make your whole body stronger. You can't just run marathons all the time—you have to change it up. As you take on these leadership roles in different kinds of productions as a graduate student, you're constantly training new muscles.

Three, the MFA program acts as your producer for three years, so you don't have to worry about finding rehearsal space or actors or collaborators. The economics of being a director can be really challenging when you're starting out freelance because you have to do the work of producing and get the money together, but I had the time and resources to do about fifteen shows while I was at Yale.

Leigh Silverman
Learning to keep all the plates spinning in a conservatory

I knew when I was in my senior year in high school that I was going to Carnegie Mellon for a BFA in Directing. I had gotten in early, after doing a pre-college program there. It was intense conservatory training.

I worked on fifty-three plays in four years: directing, stage managing, run crew, sound crew, light board op. All on top of school work and independent projects. One of the great things that it taught you was how hard you have to work. How disciplined you have to be. How many things you have to have going all at the same time. How well you have to handle it. Now I say to directors who assist me, "What else are you doing?" And any time an assistant says to me, "Oh, I'm just going to be assisting you, we have really long days." I'll say, "That's not enough. You need to be making your own work. You need to be making money, because I know you're not making any money as my assistant. You have to have all those plates spinning at the same time." That's what it is to direct. It's being able to manage actors, tech people, creative teams, *and* producers. It's being able to constantly multitask in a very sophisticated way. I feel that that was one of the great things about being at Carnegie Mellon.

When I was at Carnegie Mellon, I wanted to work with a writer, but there was no curriculum to support that and we did not have access to any playwrights. So in my junior year, I applied for the playwriting program and two years later graduated with a double degree in directing and playwriting. That was my only way to sit around the table with writers. I feel like I learned at least equal, if not more, about directing during those writing classes. I learned about story and character. I learned how to talk to writers. I learned about what goes into making a play. What it is to have your ego on the line. What it is to struggle in that way. It was so helpful to me. That time was invaluable.

Roxana Silbert

Finding a niche in new writing

After earning an undergraduate degree in English Literature, Silbert worked in a community arts outreach program and found herself drawn to drama. At age thirty, she decided to retrain and received her diploma in directing from Drama Studio London. Here she describes how she came to specialize in directing new plays.

In drama school, I fell in with a group of people who did a lot of devising work. And at that time, in the mid-1990s, all the energy in British theater was in devised work. Companies like the The Kosh and Complicite had emerged and there was an enormous influence of Le Coq here. So, I was just following the trend at the time, really. New writing was kind of dead in this country. There was the Royal Court Theatre, but they'd closed their studio theater upstairs because it wasn't funded, and there was very little going on in terms of playwriting. The great work was in visual work—what was called at that time total theater. So I started like everybody else did then, devising with a small company (which is now Told by an Idiot).

I had a brilliant time making devised theater, but I had a better time than the audience. My experience of devising theater—and this is *my* experience because obviously I'm not Simon McBurney who is brilliant at devising theater—my experience was that there were moments of brilliance that devised work produces which no other form of theater can really capture, but that it was very uneven. So I started to get very interested in dramatic structure because I felt that that's what I was lacking. I started to read plays. I became a reader at the National, the Hampstead, and the Royal Court. And when you're a new reader you tend to read a lot of very, very bad plays. You then have to write a letter and explain why that play is not good, which means you have to be really precise and articulate and understand what that play is trying to do and understand where it succeeds and fails. It was fantastic training. So then I got a job as an assistant director at Paines Plough (which is a touring theater that specializes in new plays). At that time, Paines Plough was run by Anna Furse, who was an interesting artistic director for me because she had come from a dance background and was trying to bring words and physical action together. Then I went to the Royal Court, which I would say was my formation. Stephen Daldry was artistic director and I started as assistant director and left as an associate. Once I left there in 2000, I was basically established.

Silbert ruminates on why several women of her generation specialized in new play directing.

When I started, there were very few women directors. And the women of my generation—who were the first to come through without having to kill someone en route—almost all were doing new plays. Most men of my generation took what I would call a traditional route. They started doing some fringe work and then they got some bigger shows and then they got some classical work and so on. But women's careers didn't do that then. Katie Mitchell and Deborah Warner were a bit further on than me, and they had to set up their own companies and produce their own work. They got there doing that. We didn't have the stepping stones, we had to find our own paths. New writing allowed my peers and me to be more maverick, you know? There were new writing festivals, you could just grab a playwright and you didn't need the support of a theater organization because you didn't have to go through the whole issue of rights. You could just be enterprising and do it on your own. Also, new writing was a dead area then, so it wasn't the glamorous thing to do. People were doing visual theater or taking classics and tearing them apart and making them into something else. Because new plays weren't that fashionable, there was an entrance for us into organizations like Paines Plough and Royal Court. There were a lot of people who wanted to *write* plays, but the time-consuming love and support and dialogue that's required from a director to coax a play out of a new writer? When I work on a new play I wear two hats: I am a dramaturg as well as a director, but that role is not publicly recognized. As dramaturg, I see myself as a sounding board for the writer: reading drafts and talking about them, workshopping early drafts and generally being a shoulder to lean on. I love it and it really helps me with directing the play because I have the opportunity to get right inside the writers' head. Maybe I was more willing to give that than some of my male counterparts who wanted to be facilitated rather than facilitate. So, I was very lucky because I went into the profession via a side route and then the temperature changed. And the person who changed that temperature was Stephen Daldry. He took over the Royal Court and it suddenly became really cool to direct new plays.

Indhu Rubasingham

I accidentally fell into it

The traineeship I received at Theatre Royal Stratford East after university was funded by an Arts Council bursary and that bursary was specifically about directing new writing. I think that was a very strong influence. But you can always pull away from that if you want to—I've done my *Romeo and Juliet*,[4] Moliere,[5] and other existing plays—but I still get drawn to new writing. So even though I accidentally fell into it, my passion was ignited.

Lucy Kerbel
It's much, much harder now

Kerbel's organization, Tonic Theatre, has conducted extensive research on employment in and training for professional theater in the UK.

Under the Labour government in the 1990s and early 2000s, there was a lot of money put into the arts. In particular, there was a focus on supporting emerging talent. I personally benefited massively, from just happening to leave university in 2003. An economic boom was going on and there was funding from the government for the arts. I benefited from bursaries and awards and all those things that supported me as a young director. With the current government, we're in austerity and a lot of that financial support is gone.

In that same period under the last Labor government, there was a massive growth in the number of higher education courses teaching directing. As a result, in the last few years there's been an explosion in the number of people coming out of those courses and wanting to get into it. When I started out ten years ago, you could get unpaid assisting gigs. It took a while to get in, but you could do it if you met the right people. Whereas now, apparently, from speaking to young people, it's now much, much harder to get even unpaid assisting work, which is your first step.

Now it's really hard to get in without an MA. Obviously that has a massive impact on diversity, because you are narrowing significantly the type of young person who can access that. There's a two-year Directing MA that Birkbeck College runs, which is considered to be one of the best, and it's £14,000 per year. I was speaking to the current first years and there was one kid whose parents had re-mortgaged their house to

---

[4]Chichester Festival Theatre, 2002.
[5]Minerva Theatre, 2002.

send him on it. They've all taken out loans. A lot of them are getting help from parents. But the difficult thing about being a director is it's not like training to be a doctor where you go, "I'll train for seven years and it'll cost me a hell of a lot, but I know at the end I have guaranteed work. I will always be a doctor if I want to be, and I'll earn a decent amount of money." You can invest a huge amount in training to be a director, come out, and earn peanuts. It's an overly saturated marketplace. There's a huge holding bay of emerging directors, and "emerging" can now extend to describe anyone up to their late thirties because there's this huge bottleneck.

At the same time as the number of directors coming in to the field is increasing, there is a reduction in the number of directing opportunities available. For the Advance Project, Tonic looked at how many freelance directors the theaters in our cohort employed in 2013. (We excluded the Royal Shakespeare Company [RSC], because they just produce so much more work than anyone else it would have skewed the sample.) I think, it averaged out at two freelance directors per theater for the whole year. The arts are not nearly as healthy as they were, so theaters more and more often have someone in-house direct—an artistic director or associate director already on the payroll—to avoid shelling out £5,000 to pay for a freelancer to come in. And when they do hire freelancers, it's often established directors in their forties or fifties.

Caroline Steinbeis

Cutting your teeth in London

I don't think there is a specific path to follow to become a director— there are so many ways into this job. But having said that, many of my peers went to university, produced plays at festivals, and assisted other directors, so there is a correlation there. And really there is nothing quite like the baptism of fire of taking a show to the Edinburgh Festival, getting rained on for a month, and playing to houses of four. Extremely character building. What I do find interesting is that many of us seem to have launched our careers in London, while until relatively recently, directors cut their teeth in regional theaters where they learned to direct on large stages and built a relationship with their audiences. I missed that apprenticeship, but sadly the UK is so London-centric and there seems to be a fear of being forgotten about if you stay away too long.

Steinbeis describes some realities about the work of directing.

I do believe that a healthy balance of graft, tact, and confidence goes a long way. You are your own maker, no one owes you anything in this game; this discovery was a huge revelation to me. And I am only just beginning to taste what excites me, what I burn for. With every project you make, you start again from zero. You know nothing at all. And once you accept that this is the case, the creative process becomes more and more liberating. It's a wonderful feeling not to know.

Young Jean Lee
Hustling

Midway through writing her dissertation for an English PhD, Lee realized she wanted to be a playwright. With little theater experience under her belt, she moved to New York and started her career through an intern-ship with the experimental company Radiohole. In recent years, she herself has mentored interns and assistants in her own company, where she both writes and directs.

For me and for the people I've mentored who have been successful, it's all come down to one thing—hustling. You find the people you want to work with, and then just hustle your ass off to give them everything you've got. Making a career in theater is making people want to work with you again, so make sure you're working with people you respect and who respect you, then give 200 percent so that they want to work with you again.

We get so many requests every week from people who want to intern. I started this policy where, instead of looking at their resumes and interviewing them, I just give them assignments and see how they do with them. It's amazing, I'll get an impassioned three-page email from somebody saying how much my work has inspired them and how badly they want to work for me; then I respond by sending them a spreadsheet and asking them to proofread it, and I never hear back. To me, that's hustle. Turning the spreadsheet around in twenty-four hours, that's what hustle is, and I feel that's what makes people successful, sometimes even when they're not very talented. And if you have both artistic brilliance and the willingness to hustle, there's absolutely no way you're not going to succeed. I believe that absolutely.

Mentorship

Young Jean Lee

Assistants should be asked what they think

Lee has worked with numerous assistant directors.

I think assistants should always be asked what they think, from early on in the process. You should only have people in the room where their opinion actually means something. Otherwise it's just a waste of time. I've had brilliant assistants who actually ended up almost codirecting my shows because they were so good and I saw they had strengths where I was weak. They've told me that they've assisted on so many other productions where nobody once asked their opinion about anything. They would see a simple technical fix to a problem in a scene and just have to sit there in silence. I think that's such a waste. I think it comes from this misguided arrogance where people think that once they're an established director, there's nothing a young person could contribute. That's absolutely untrue, because no matter how experienced you are, you're always going to have blind spots.

I don't like when assistants come in the room and just start presumptuously telling me stuff, but I always ask. After an audition, I say, "Give me your notes. What did you think of the people?" After a run through, I say, "Give me your notes. What did you think of the performance?" If I'm working on a DVD of a show, I send them the DVD and say, "Give me your artistic feedback on this." That's how you know that the person has aesthetic judgment. It just becomes really clear right away.

KJ Sanchez
Director training

Many directors find important mentors among their professors. In 2016, Sanchez joined the faculty at the University of Texas at Austin as head of the Master of Fine Arts in Directing program. The department invited her to redesign the program as she saw fit.

I think that the best way to make your way in the field now is to be as diverse as possible. So here at University of Texas at Austin (UT), we're giving our directing students exposure to many things. For example, we have a program where I work side by side with Sven Ortel, who's an incredible media designer. We put our directors and our media designers together in a composition class, and they build compositions together with a group of actors and other designers so that our directors can leave and have the skills to direct, say, a half-time show at a football game. And I'm working with a couple of my students right now who are directing the freshmen student orientation presentation for the university. I'm trying to find avenues for all of my students to make a living as a director in a lot of different ways.

To complement this focus on developing diverse skills, Sanchez has also carved out significant space in the MFA program for deep, individualized study.

I have no interest in teaching anybody how to direct like I direct. I don't want any of my students to be making work that looks like mine. No teacher intends to create acolytes, but it does happen naturally and we're very, very conscious of working against it in both the Directing and Playwriting programs at UT. When each student comes in, we design their experience around what they are interested in working on. What they want to learn. For example, right now I have one student who really wants to make theater that has the same immediate impact on the audience as a rock concert. My colleagues and I got out our Rolodexes and got guest artists in that she could interact with to work on that focus. Every time we're in a methods and practice class, that's what she's working on specifically. Another student is very interested in the documentary style of theater making. Since I've done that type of work, I'm teaching him those skills as he builds his own show based on interviews. It's a very different program for every single director.

Diane Rodriguez

Sharing your experience

Not everyone will have a champion—I've never had one. But I've had people who have opened doors for me. I started performing with El Teatro Campesino when I was nineteen years old. I made a living with them and got training from Luis Valdez, and that kind of experience when you're young is really valuable. That's why I think companies like that are really important. Later Gordon Davidson opened the door for me at Center Theater Group (CTG) and gave me a home where I could have a job, soak things up, and make theater. Neither Luis nor Gordon were my personal mentors, but they gave me opportunities and supported me in that way.

During her years at CTG, Rodriguez has taken her turn opening doors for many young artists.

I'm always open to talking to people and trying to help them. It's not even about giving advice, it's about sharing your experience and listening deeply. I have a lot of young women who call me their mentor, but I would say that there are maybe three women that I feel I really, really have a mentorship relationship with. I think that to be a good, close mentor, the relationship has to be long term and has to be very honest—brutally honest, in some cases.

Kimberly Senior

Finding mentors outside of school

I went to Connecticut College, a small private liberal arts college where there were only eight majors in my year. The faculty were terrific and loving and wonderful, but not professionals working in the field; so it was kind of like a playground (which you need and was amazing), but it was not a place where you would find a professional mentor. Then I didn't end up going to graduate school for a variety of reasons. I feel like those are typical places to find that mentor. So Chicago became my graduate school instead. Most of my mentors are leaders of institutions in Chicago and often are not directors, so they can advise me on free-lance directing but don't necessarily know how to do it. Most of them have been men with the exception of Martha Lavey (former Artistic Director of Steppenwolf Theatre Company), who's probably been my most influential mentor. She taught me how to assert myself. Anytime someone complements me on being articulate, I say, "Martha Lavey is my mentor, have you ever heard her speak?" She taught me a kind of economy of language and intention in speaking and how to address a group and inspire a group with intellect, not just with good cheer and enthusiasm (of which I have boatloads).

Getting Work

Diane Rodriguez

Become a spherical artist

As a theater artist, it's good to be able to do a bunch of different things, but you need to do things that fit together. I started out as a performer and costume designer, but realized those wouldn't work together, so I let costuming go. After leaving El Teatro Campesino in the 1980s, I came to Los Angeles and performed for many years, including as part of the four-person company Latins Anonymous. We were all actors, but we also challenged ourselves to write our own pieces. That's how I started writing. In a small company, we all had to do other things also. Somebody did publicity, somebody did such-and-such, and I produced because I had all these contacts from my years of touring. That's how I started producing. Writing, performing, and producing all sit so closely that it was like a ball of skills that I could just roll forward with.

Then, as I got older and the reality of being an aging actor in Hollywood and Los Angeles set in, I realized that, even though I was a working actor, I had to do something else to make an income. People started asking me to direct the work that I had written five to six years before for myself to perform. That's how I started directing — with work that I knew very, very well, because it was my own. When everything fits closely like that, you naturally become a ball, a sphere. It allows you to focus on different things at different phases of your life, which helps you sustain a career. Now I'm doing more writing, whereas ten years ago I was doing more directing, and in a few years I could be doing more acting because as you get older you enter new casting categories. That's why it's so important to become a spherical artist.

Roxana Silbert

It's a slower burn

When I was young, there was a perception that you couldn't be visionary unless you came in and shouted, "This is my vision, thank you very much, and you will follow my vision!" Directors were often bullying in the rehearsal rooms and just behaved appallingly. And that's still what some people think confidence is, but it isn't a real measure of the confidence or ability of the person. I remember being told I would not be a director because I was too nice, too pleasant. But the reality is that you have to work with people. It's a slower burn and you have to accept that. You have to come to some kind of agreement with yourself about how you're willing to behave and not behave. It damages your work if you don't. To be a good theater director, you have to expose yourself and put yourself in your work. If you don't know who you are, that is really, really hard and there can be a brittleness there. You see a lot of work that doesn't really move you because it's as defended as the person who made it.

Blanche McIntyre

Self-starting

The joy of being a freelance director is that you can self-start. So, you're always talking to people about potential projects, but in the meantime—when the phone isn't ringing—you're busy developing your own things. You're workshopping a new play or getting together with two actors to do a reading—you're always keeping your artistic energy going.

Anne Kauffman
Juggling a freelance schedule

When you're a freelance director, no one cares about your schedule except for you. Even my agent once wanted me to fly to Philadelphia to start the production process during preview week for a show in Chicago. I wanted to do both projects, but I couldn't and just had to say no. And no one who hires you thinks about how long it takes to prepare for a project. If you do plays back to back to back, when do you audition people? When do you have design meetings? Theaters don't ask, "How's your schedule? Do you have enough time?" And they shouldn't. That's incumbent upon you. So you have to perform that juggling act. I've just now reached the point in my career where I feel I can ask for and demand certain things, like shifting a rehearsal process to fit my schedule. I can finally say, "If you want me, then these are the things that we need to discuss." I actually feel a little embarrassed by it, but it's really necessary.

Lucy Kerbel
You're outside of the decision-making process

When you're a freelancer, you're outside of the decision-making process so you don't really know why things are or aren't going your way. You sit at home, waiting for the phone to ring. You try and generate projects, you go and meet artistic directors, and pitch ideas. Occasionally they say yes, but in the main they say no, and that no might come from a whole range of reasons. It might be "well we did something by Noel Coward last season so we can't do another Noel Coward," or "we like your idea but we're talking to this big box-office actor about doing stuff and I can't see a role for them in this," or "'we think we've been a bit comedy-heavy recently." There are so many factors, but generally you're less likely as a freelancer to be told those factors. You're more likely to go to the meeting, pitch your ideas, hear, "Great, that's brilliant, leave it with me and let me have a think," and then not hear anything more or just get a courtesy message saying, "We're not going to go with any of your ideas, but do keep in touch." At that moment it's easy, especially if you're feeling a bit insecure anyway, to think "It's about me," rather than, "It's about the system that I'm in."

Erica Whyman

Have confidence in your idea

Whyman, who has been on the leadership team for four theaters, emphasizes that directors have to sell their ideas in pitch sessions.

It's not exactly that directors have to convince me an idea will "work." A lot of what I do now and what I've always done is research and development, creating space to fail, so I don't believe everything you try has to be a success. But a director does have to begin with tremendous confidence that what they're pitching is an idea worth exploring. Because if I accept their idea, next thing they've got to do is persuade someone else: a designer, an actor, somebody in marketing. So they mustn't be apologetic. And I do still encounter a lot of "you won't think this is interesting, but I do" from women directors. And I want to say, "That's a shame because it would be great if you had confidence that I might think it is interesting!"

Vicky Featherstone

Conviction

As an artistic director, Featherstone frequently interviews potential directors for Royal Court productions.

When I meet with a director, I'm looking for conviction. That they understand the project and believe it needs to exist and believe it is going to make the world a different place in some way. And they don't need to communicate that conviction to me in a confident, "lean in" way. They could also communicate it in a "somebody who feels so strongly about it they can't look me in the eye" way. But I have to sense their feverishness—their fiery need to make the production exist. And often there's a humility around that, which isn't necessarily how one would ordinarily read confidence.

Indhu Rubasingham
What I look for in a pitch

Like at many small theaters in the UK today, the Kiln (formerly Tricycle) only produces a few plays per year and coproduces or presents the rest of their season; thus, Rubasingham has few opportunities to hire freelance directors. When she does hear pitches, she looks for a few specific things.

I want to see that they have an understanding of what the venue might want. I have had young directors come in and not know anything about the Kiln or its mission and I've gone, "Right, you don't know anything about the organization and you've not seen any shows here so why do you want to work here apart from your own career?" If someone wants to do their version of *Waiting for Godot*, it's got to be pretty extraordinary for me to want to do it here. Or if someone wants to do a new play that's all about straight white men and their neuroses, this isn't the theater to bring that play to. So, when hiring directors, I look for (1) an understanding of the organization and (2) passion. I want to smell passion on someone. And passion doesn't always equal high risk. With a more experienced director, I want to see a willingness to take risks; but with a less experienced director, I want them to take risks that match their experience.

Leigh Silverman
Be proactive

You have to be so proactive all the time. You have to make your own projects, particularly starting out as a young person. If you fundamentally believe, like I do, that directing is about creating a world and a vision and saying, "You guys, it's that way, let's go there," then you have to be able to do that in your own life. You have to be able to manifest opportunities for yourself like you manifest art in a rehearsal room or manifest a world for an audience.

Silverman gives an example of how persistence helped her manifest a crucial opportunity in her career.

Well was what someone might refer to as my "big break." I got to know Lisa Kron because she was one of the Five Lesbian Brothers, and I assisted Molly Smith on their play *Brides of the Moon*,[6] then helped them remount on old play of theirs, *Brave Smiles*,[7] at P.S. 122. Lisa had just gotten a commission from Baltimore Center Stage to work on a new play. She said to me, "I burn through directors, so there's no way you're going to end up being the director on this play. But do you want to start to work on it with me?" I said, "Sure." We ended up working on it together for five years. Pretty much every time we'd do a reading of it for the first four years, she would say to me, "This is the last time you're going to direct it." I would say, "No problem, Lisa." Then George Wolfe, who was the artistic director of the Public Theater at the time, saw the work that Lisa and I were doing together and said, "Okay, you can direct this play at the Public." It would have been a perfectly acceptable for him or Lisa to replace me at that point. I was so early in my career. Then the amazing producer Liz McCann had a wild kind of kamikaze vision for how the play could speak to people on Broadway. She took this crazy big chance on me and let me direct the Broadway production. It was an absolute commercial flop (lost every penny) but the critics loved it and it changed my life and Lisa's and Jane Houdyshell's (who played Lisa's mother).

Silverman observes that new media platforms are shifting the landscape of opportunities for young directors.

There used to be this way of working your way up in a natural order. Like, "I'm going to sweep the floors for a while in that theater and then

---

[6]Five Lesbian Brothers, 1997.
[7]P.S. 122, 1999.

I'm going to usher. If I'm really lucky I'll get to be run crew. Then if I'm really lucky I'll get to sew costumes." There was a lot of pride in doing summer stock and putting in the hours to learn your craft. Today I think young people have much more of a sense that it needs to happen *now*. They don't think "I'm going to make sure that that person gets to know me and my work" because they can get to know other people through social media and there are all these other platforms where they can work, like web series.

Lear deBessonet
Building a new department at the Public Theater

DeBessonet's visionary approach to large-cast, community-based the-ater productions got the attention of one of the most influential art-istic directors in the United States, who then hired her to found a new department at his theater.

My productions of *Don Quixote*[8] in Philadelphia and *The Odyssey*[9] at the Old Globe in San Diego led to the starting of Public Works. Prior to that, I had relationships with a number of different people at the Public Theater, like Barry Edelstein and Maria Goyanes, and had done readings and shows at Joe's Pub. So while I was in the germinating process of conceiving the Old Globe *Odyssey* and pulling the groups together, [Public Theater Artistic Director] Oskar Eustis keyed in to what was happening and said, "I want you to keep me updated on everything that happens with this project." Then as I moved through it, he asked if I thought something like this could work in New York. That was really exciting because the projects in both Philadelphia and San Diego—each of which was about two years' germinating—felt in some ways like such missed opportunities because I didn't live in either city. Closing night felt like the end of something when I wanted it to feel like just the beginning. So Oskar and I got very excited about the idea that it would not just be one project-specific collaboration but that we would be building a new

---

[8]Broad Street Ministry, 2009.
[9]Old Globe Theatre, 2011.

department of this theater that would do this work in an ongoing, longitudinal way. We wanted to make a commitment to community partners that would extend beyond one show into a multiyear commitment in which doing these shows together would be one of many points of contact we have with each other. And that is what has happened.

KJ Sanchez

Tell your story in a positive light

If I were a better strategist when it comes to my career, I would probably simplify things when I start to talk about who I am. I like complexity, but we humans aren't really geared for it. My biggest rule as a documentary play maker is only tell one story at a time. An actor can only play one thing at a time and audiences want to understand one story at a time. So, when I talk about myself and my work to people, I should do a better job of telling one story at a time. And I should choose words that have a positive patina, like describing my career as "eclectic" or "Renaissance" rather than "schizophrenic." So, my story in a positive light: I run my own theater company, it's devoted to making work that chronicles our time, work that serves as a bridge between people. We tour shows across the country and around the world. I direct plays of many different styles and genres: I direct plays in the cannon of classic American plays, I direct contemporary plays like *The Elaborate Entrance of Chad Deity*[10] by Kris Diaz, and direct world premieres like *Seven Spots on the Sun*[11] by Martin Zimmerman. I write documentary plays and my plays have been produced at many theaters including Berkeley Rep, Baltimore's Center Stage, and Actors Theatre of Louisville. I direct in large spaces in the League of Resident Theatres (LORT) A and B theaters and I also direct plays in tiny, scrappy, grubby spaces off of Broadway. My directing and playwriting tends to toggle between very physical, fluid and choreographed, and cerebral work, based on tons and tons of research. I love my job—How's that for positive light?

---

[10]Actors Theatre of Louisville, 2012.
[11]Cincinnati Playhouse in the Park, 2013.

Work–Life Balance

Nadia Fall

Our job is to portray life so we ought to live it

Directing is such all-consuming work; if you're not in rehearsal, you're prepping a play or conjuring up the next project. It becomes increasing hard to physically get away or mentally switch off from it all. I would say that being a mother has actually helped me have to actively engage in real life outside of the theater and at least strive to achieve a better balance. It is always hard to park work but it is also invaluable to reboot the imagination, our job is to portray life so we ought to live it!

May Adrales

Look at your life as a whole

Adrales is based in New York City, but works extensively in regional theater. She also teaches a course titled "Bridge to the Profession" to directing students at her alma mater, Yale School of Drama.

It's important to take time for self-reflection, to think about what kind of artist you really want to be, and how you can find balance in your life. When I teach directors at Yale, I let them know it's okay to really look at your life as a whole. To ask yourself, "When I look back on my life, what will I point to and say, 'This is what I did right'?" I find, particularly with young women directors, that it can be hard to get them to admit they want a family, or a partner, or financial stability. We are taught that there's nobility in being an artist that doesn't make any money, is alone, and feels tortured. In reality, all work and nothing else—no family, no friends—is too great a cost. If you want something different than that, you have to articulate that for yourself and then create choices that are going to make that life worth living.

Leah Gardiner

Parenting and directing

Gardiner describes how the industry has become more family-friendly for directors.

A woman director from an older generation was telling me that when she was starting out she had to hide the fact that she had children. No one knew. Thank god it has been better for me, but it's still hard. When I had my son ten years ago, none of the women directors of my generation were really having kids. When I was pregnant, Louisa Thompson, the set designer, was also pregnant and an assistant director on Broadway. I proposed to *American Theatre* that I write an article about what it's like to be pregnant and working in the American theater as a freelance artist, because we were all freelance artists. The magazine said no, because no one would be interested in that article. That was in 2005. Luckily it has changed since. It's a different world now. Back then, there were certain theaters, like South Coast Rep, that worked with you when you had kids; now, many, many more theaters are becoming much more family-friendly.

Parenting does still place some career limitations on directors.

As a parent, you have to book jobs well in advance. I can't, at the last minute, say "Sure, I'd love to come," because I'm not single and I have my husband's and son's schedules to work with. I've been asked to go to the Sundance Directors Lab a lot, but I've always had something else already booked, usually something where I can take my child.

Theater is not my entire life. I don't have nights to go to dress rehearsals and hobnob and meet playwrights. A lot of the work that I've done has been based on recommendations or connections to people I know because I can't chase. With my son, I just don't have the time to do that marketing part of the job. Maybe that competitive side of me should be the more dominant and should be chasing, but that's not the path that I chose. For me, making art is not about that. I'm not interested in burning myself out, because I feel like then I will have nothing to give and I can't make great art. The great thing about the circles of life is that, if you're doing what you're meant to do, things come back. You'll get the opportunity when you are meant to. I have not directed on Broadway yet, but I will and when that happens, fantastic. You just have to be truly grateful for what is. My husband Seth and I are in a position where we can support each other and love our work as much as we love our kid. I feel very, very grateful and blessed.

Gardiner emphasizes that parenting has also brought benefits to her career.

As soon as I became parent, I became a much better director. You become more organized. You become much more focused and your priorities are made very clear. You know how much time you have allocated for certain things and you don't have time to play around— you have to get it done.

Kimberly Senior

I'm a better artist since becoming a parent

Senior is the mother of two children who were elementary school age at the time of the interview.

There is no separation for me between family and work because these are the bones of my life. I'm a mother. I'm a director. I'm a sister. I'm a daughter. I'm a friend. I'm a yogi. These are the things that I am and they are all a factor in everything that I do. If I were a doctor it might be different, but I'm in a field where I have to be personal in my work and I can't be personal without my children being a part of it and accepting the fact that I'm a mother.

My children are an asset, not a liability. For instance, my son is a rabid perfectionist and I am, too. I see him beat his head against the wall because something isn't perfect and it's a thing that's in me, and so I get worked up and I can't help him when I'm worked up. I was talking to my friend about this and she said, "Oh, you don't know? Our children inherit our flaws in order that we solve them in ourselves so that we can help them." I thought that was genius. We have to help them and we can't help them until we've figured it out. I have relaxed so much since examining the question, "What is perfection?" You know what it is? It's about working to the best of my ability. That's a better way to talk about perfection. If I did the fullest exploration of myself in this task, if I worked to my fullest potential in that moment, then it is perfect. All I can be is me. Now I try to teach and live that value instead of perfection. I am such a better artist since becoming a parent. I am so much more present in my work.

Being a mother, being a teacher, and being a director, I'm often the person who is in charge in those three places. I want to create boundaries for my actors—whether through elements of design or through the facts of the play's world—but I also want to create a safe space for them to explore and experiment. Similarly, children need boundaries—our values and family rules—but they also need to boldly dare and imagine. I'm always asking, "How do we create enough rules that we're safe enough to play?"

Lucy Kerbel

The loop of visibility

It's really hard to get someone to give you a show if they've not seen something you've done really recently. You might have directed a brilliant show four years ago, but that's almost irrelevant. If you directed a brilliant show four weeks ago, four months ago, that's current. So successful freelance directors go from show to show to show to show to show. It's quite exhausting, but if you stop going flat-out, it can be really hard to get anything because you risk dropping off that loop of visibility.

The implications of this for women who want to have children through natural conception are huge because if you leave that loop for a while to have children, it can be really hard to get back in. That pressure is even greater on young women now than it was ten to fifteen years ago because directing is such a saturated marketplace. There are so many directors out there that people are getting established later than they used to. Women who have been able to get themselves established by their thirties and get shows lined up for after their maternity leave have reentered the loop. But if you're still at the assisting level when you have children, it's much harder to then progress your career afterward. The astronomical boost in the cost of childcare, the unsociable hours of theater, and the fact that you're essentially on call at least twelve hours a day when you're directing make it very hard to balance that work with parenting if you're not already commanding a certain rate and holding certain seniority before you have children.

Men feel less pressure. When I was running director focus groups for the Advance Project, I would ask, "Family, parenthood, is that something you're thinking about?" Generally, young male directors would respond with things like "Oh my God. Not until I'm at least in my mid-forties" or "I haven't even thought about that yet." It was such a distant thing for them, but for a lot of the women it was soon. They would have plans, like, "Oh yeah, by the time I'm thirty, I need to have done this and gotten to there so that I can take two years out and have something set up for when I come back . . ." It was so present in their thoughts. I'm interested in the impact that has on their relationship to success and failure. If you're twenty-seven and get bad reviews and think, "Well, that's just one show of an endless number of shows—I can pick myself up and move onto the next one," does that make you more comfortable with artistic risk than if you get that bad review and think, "I haven't had enough shows to hit a certain level and I have to get that to level before I need to step out for maternity. Oh my God, I can't believe I got really bad reviews"?

Blanche McIntyre

Getting squeezed out

McIntyre foresees that the ever-increasing cost of living and cost of fringe production will have a damaging effect on the directing profession.

It's especially difficult for working-class directors. I was lucky, I'm from a middle-class family and my parents live in London. And although there were times when I had literally not enough money to buy a pack of eggs, I always knew that I could, in a nightmare, go home and be looked after. That I would ultimately be okay. But there are people who come from out of London or who need to pay rent to their families to make it work financially. For them, the new situation is infinitely harder. And I have a terrible fear that we're going to see a middle-classification of directing as people from alternative backgrounds find themselves squeezed out.

Roxana Silbert

People who leave directing behind

Many people who train to be directors leave the field over time. Silbert describes where some of them go.

When I started out, there was a big old group of us and suddenly I remember turning around and that group was very small. I think it happens at the point where you can't bear to live in someone's spare room anymore and you think you might want to have a family and a holiday and a car. I'd say typically early thirties. A lot of the people that I knew went into academia, which now would be much harder. Or they went into running a youth theater. Or they went into television and radio at the BBC, particularly script development and producing. Or they moved into things like opera, where it's really properly paid. So, they went into related fields. Or they've diversified, like David Farr, who was at the RSC with me. He's a freelance director but started to write a lot as well, and now he's mainly writing.

Leigh Silverman

You can't do it only a little bit

A freelance director, Silverman is based in New York City but works in cities across the United States.

There is an unrelenting demand on directors—freelance directors in particular—in terms of the amount of time you have to put in. Because you can't do it only a little bit. You have to be all in to make a living. I've done between five and seven shows a year for ten years. It's a lot, but that's what I have to do to afford my life.

I've now been in New York for twenty years. Among my theater colleagues, there were people who moved out after the first year, then after the first five years, then at the ten-year mark, and now there's just been another wave of people who have left. When everyone turned thirty, there were people who said, "That was good, that was a good run. Now I'm going to go do something real." Now for a lot of us who have turned forty, you start to feel like, "Wow, I've really clocked in some time. I don't know quite where it's left me. I'm still young enough to change." So people leave to have kids, or move to somewhere else, or shift from freelance to working in an institution, or focus on teaching, or go into opera, or transition into TV or film.

Expensive cities like New York can be particularly challenging places to live on a freelancer's income.

When I leave New York to work somewhere else, I usually spend the first two weeks thinking, "Why don't I live in this place? This place is incredible. I could live in a house and have so much room. I could have a dog." Then in week three, I start to realize there's nowhere to eat at night after nine o'clock. By week four I'm going stir crazy. That happens everywhere I go. I think New York theater is just a demanding, demanding mistress. If it's your passion, then you suffer it out. There are days where I think I can't bear it one second longer, but the truth is it's absolutely the only place I've really been able to imagine building my life.

Success

Vicky Featherstone

Giving an audience an exceptional experience

To me, a successful director is somebody who's creating an interesting body of work, where you can see a journey and a certain fearlessness in their approach. They're pushing the boundaries of what theater is as well as the needs of each production. It's also somebody who gains some critical success but isn't always chasing that. Who has the confidence to create work that has integrity but might not necessarily push all the buttons of the people who put the stars in place in the press. And it's also somebody who feels thrilled by theater magic and stagecraft and is striving to give an audience an exceptional experience. Because a lot of people aren't. A lot of people just put plays on and do really well but they're not actually striving to give the audience an exceptional experience. That kind of thing really doesn't interest me. I'd rather do a different job.

Leigh Silverman
This is what you've signed up for

Uncertainty about the future is a recurring theme in the life of freelance directors. Some directors manage to get established in the profession, some do not. Even those who have established themselves aren't guaranteed steady work.

Why someone's career happens and not another? That's just part of the crazy randomness of the theater. You didn't choose theater because you thought it was safe. You chose it for some other reason, so why are you mad when it turns out to not be reliable? It's not a reliable job. I was just complaining and complaining to a friend of mine about how I was so broke. Then I was like, "Did I think I was going to end up a millionaire? It's just not that kind of field. This is what you've signed up for."
I worked really hard, I was good at it, and I got really lucky. I think those three things have to be in play in order to move on and advance in this field. You can't have one without the other because you can't get lucky if you're not good, you can't work hard if you don't get lucky, and you can't be good if you haven't worked hard and you don't get lucky. You need all three to happen. I worked really hard and I got lucky early and I feel like I wasn't punished too harshly for too long in the ever-punishing world of theater.

Leah Gardiner
Admiration for other directors

The definition of "success" is highly subjective, as illustrated in this anecdote from Gardiner.

Leigh Silverman and I were both at an awards night somewhere and she said, "I just have to say to you, I am in such admiration because you've been able to do it all." I looked at her and was like, "Do it all?" She said, "You have a family. You have a great career," and I'm thinking to myself, "I haven't even been on Broadway yet. What are you talking about? You've gotten three shows on Broadway!"

Blanche McIntyre

You're excited about the piece and pushing yourself

McIntyre elucidates common statements that one director might make about another's success.

"She's doing really well," means she's making rent. She's got projects coming in, she's booked up until next July, she has more work than she can eat. "She's making great work," means she's got something interesting that to say and she's expressing it with skill and she's being given the resources that allow her to make the most of her expression of it.

Of course, space and money help and collaborators are crucial; but some of the work I've been proudest of has happened in tiny spaces with no budget and not much experience. And sometimes I've made a well-made well-resourced piece and loved it with all my heart and it still hasn't worked for audiences or critics. Increasingly I find time is the valuable thing—I used to be able to knock out a piece in three weeks and now I find that hard. (The big theaters give you twelve—I've never had that!) But, however it's received I think you can only be proud of your work if you're excited about the piece and pushing yourself and the other people working on it. That's the bare minimum.

Paulette Randall

It's like a heat change

I love the challenge of trying to emotionally move somebody with someone else's words and with all of the other stuff that you fling at a play—the lights and the sound and all of that. Can I take the audience on this journey, whatever it is, and actually get people to feel? You know you've done it when you feel it yourself. First you feel it in the rehearsal room—the feeling of the room changes, almost like a heat change. Then if you're in the audience, you can feel it there too. If you can move people in that little rehearsal room with almost nothing in it and then put the play onstage and fling all the other stuff on top of it and still manage it, then there's got to be some truth that's being portrayed in order for that emotion to travel. How do we make that happen? That for me is the most exciting bit about directing.

Nadia Fall

You get better with practice and time

You do get better and better the more you direct. You're not just born with the ability; some people have a knack for it, sure, but you definitely get better with age. I think that's one of the great things about it—when you get older you can be thought of as a has-been in other jobs, but with directing it's the opposite. Of course, there's still the cult of youth that makes me mad. In every interview they ask, "How old are you?" Youth and brilliance are somehow linked, wrongly. You get better with practice and time.

Polly Findlay

The problem with star-based reviews

The practice of assigning theater productions one-to-five stars in a review is ubiquitous in the UK. The star system is also used in the United States, though not as widely.

The star-based culture of critical reviews in the UK is really absurd. It's one of the things that I envy directors working in most of the rest of Europe. There is none of the sense of play as product that I would argue dominates the theater scene in the UK. The whole idea of reviews giving star ratings could after all only happen in a culture where the audience feels that they are customers, that they are buying something which can be scored out of five in the same way as the things they buy on

Amazon. I'm not sure that dynamic is conducive to making the best kind of work.

Indhu Rubasingham

Your artistic journey

Rubasingham describes what she sees as the most important criteria for judging a director's success.

"Success" for a director is about peer approval, because we can be the toughest judges. There are reviews, but reviews often don't match how the community of peers is talking about someone's work, so a mixture of those opinions are important. It's also about whether it sells — whether audiences want to come and see their work and are talking about it. Whether it moves and provokes audiences. And, of course, it's also about whether they are doing something really interesting. Good directors make you inquisitive. They are being themselves and showing you a way of working or presenting work that's different from what you've seen before and that makes you curious. And there's a rigor to their work and therefore integrity — it's not flash in the pan or lazy or just "I want success." The directors I really respect have an authenticity to their work, which means . . . What does that mean? That means there's an honesty and a vulnerability, and an exposure to risk, which means they may fail. So you might see something and go, "Oh, that didn't quite work, but I can see the intention behind it. And the value and the aspiration."

Rubasingham explains how focusing on a following a career path can damage a director's chance of success.

I'm not really interested in a career path because I've never seen one for myself. I've tried to look for one, but couldn't find a person to follow or aspire to because there weren't many people like me in terms of gender or race. So when I tried to find a career path everything would go quite higgledy-piggledy. What I'm more interested in is the artistic journey. When I talk to young directors I say, "Look, we always want to be somewhere we're not. There's always someone that's somewhere we would rather be and we can't work out how to get there." The only thing you can be is yourself and the most important thing is to find out why you want to be in this business. What are you trying to say? What is your voice? And how do you find a way to express it? And that will take time to find. When I started, I didn't know what my voice was or what I was consciously really into, but you fall into it by trial and error. I think following a career path means that you're trying to please someone else or you're trying to guess what's going to be a success and what people want to see and, you know, that's just always going to be miserable and unfulfilling. One lesson I have learned is that everything is uncertain and nothing is clear, so what gives me confidence and traction is knowing what I believe in and knowing what I believe theater can and should be about. I think sometimes it's dangerous for theater makers to think in terms of career path. I think it's a more interesting question to ask "How do I get access to space and resources to make the work that I want to make," rather than "Where should I be in five years?"

Artistic Leadership

Sarah Benson

The role of the artistic director in the UK and the United States

Benson is from the UK, but came to New York on a Fulbright Scholarship to pursue her MFA in Directing at Brooklyn College and has been there ever since. Since 2007, she has been Artistic Director of Soho Rep.

A lot of the artistic directors of theaters in the United States were once directors, but the demands of the job knock them out of it. In this nonsubsidized system, artistic directors have to spend a huge amount of time fundraising and building the business side of theater. I think a lot of boards are looking for someone who can do those things rather than predominantly looking for an artist.

In the UK, I see many more artistic directors thriving as artists (though that might start changing now as subsidies are decreasing). I think it's partly because there are sort of informal time limits on artistic directors' terms in the UK. People tend to cycle through every four to eight years. Afterward, they get absorbed by academia or continue a freelance career because they have continued their artistic work during their time running a theater. In the United States, I think artistic directors kind of get stuck in those positions because they've stopped practicing as artists, so there's nowhere for them to go. Their experience has pushed more toward the corporate than the artistic, so academia isn't as interested in them, and it's hard to continue with a freelance career because they haven't been directing.

At Soho Rep, the artistic director is a peer artist with the other artists. Historically, it has been really important to our board that the artistic director always be a working artist. I direct and work with other artists and I can constantly be around others who work differently than me and be inspired by their work. That's what feeds me and makes the job so terrific.

Anne Kauffman

Pushing the envelope

I find the British system of artistic directorship so inspiring. It seems to be considered a civic duty rather than a position of power to hold onto for dear life. Artistic directors in the UK do their five years or so of service, then they leave. And they are excellent directors, excellent working artists. In the United States, the turnover is not nearly that high. An artistic directorship here may not open for twenty years. That's a real issue in leadership. There are so many fewer opportunities to cultivate new leaders. And the percentage of actual directors in those positions is rather low. And the percentage of directors who are really pushing the envelope is even lower.

Blanche McIntyre

The skills of an artistic director

I probably will be interested in running a building in a few years, but the skills involved are different than those needed in freelancing. You need to know your audience, to know the community you serve and what it needs, as well as what it will need in two years because you have to commission the work now. You need to know how to balance a program in dialogue with other theaters in other places in the UK, and how to make the money work, and how a building works, top to bottom. They're such varied and difficult skills, and if you get it wrong, it hits hundreds of people. As a freelance director, I go from play to play in my thinking. Artistic directors have to think five years ahead. So, I'd love to, but it's a very different thing.

Vicky Featherstone

Creating worlds for people to flourish in

Featherstone comments on why some people are drawn to artistic directorship while others are not.

I think it's just different personalities. Some people like to create worlds for people to flourish in. And that can appear to be a more generous act than freelancing, but it's not. It's equally as egotistical as seeking one extraordinary production to direct after the next. It's just a different sensibility—with men as well. You know, some people really love that and some people don't.

Diane Rodriguez

The track to becoming an artistic director

In her capacities as Associate Artistic Director of CTG, Chair of the board of directors for Theatre Communications Group, and member of the National Council on the Arts, Rodriguez has witnessed the career trajectories of many artistic directors, past and present.

I think if your goal is to be an artistic director, there is a track to be on. Even when you're just starting out and you're directing in a very, very small theater, if you develop a relationship with the artistic director and the staff and they ask you back and you get to know the inner workings of the organization, all that helps. Then try to develop that same relationship with one or two more theaters in your city. But also, theaters want artistic directors who are connected nationally, so you cannot just stay in your town. Direct as much as you can in as many places as you can. And if you can't travel, go to conferences, take workshops, know the trends in the field by reading *American Theatre* and other sources. Online media and social media make it possible to be aware and connected without that much travel.

Lucy Kerbel

Fitting into the industry

Kerbel established Tonic Theatre and became its founding Artistic Director in 2011.

I knew I wanted to set up and lead a theater company that did something about gender, but didn't know what specifically I wanted to do. I was very lucky to be accepted in a year-long professional development scheme called Step Change that helps artists take a step in a new direction. I used it to make the transition from being a director to running a company. I was paid and spent a year setting up Tonic, getting mentoring, and shadowing people at the National Theatre and Royal Opera House to see how those organizations are run.

Spending time shadowing artistic directors, I realized that a lot of them would love to see more gender equality, but they're all so busy that they don't have time to really get at the root of the problem. Gender equality is on everyone's to-do list, but it's never urgent because no one's going to get hurt or fired if it isn't achieved. The roof of your theater isn't going to fall down, that funding application isn't going to fall through; therefore it never gets to the top of the agenda. So I decided to shape Tonic into an organization that helps the industry forward the gender agenda by doing that work with theaters.

I think if I hadn't had Step Change as an intervention, I wouldn't have had as confident an approach with Tonic. It was really audacious to sit down with the RSC and say, "You could be doing better. Work with us and we'll tell you how." Before Step Change, I would have thought it was just a bonkers idea that I could ever do something like that. But that program made me really question myself and reflect on what I was capable of and where I saw myself fitting into the industry.

Indhu Rubasingham

Giving back to the industry

I never wanted to be an artistic director, so it's hilarious that I am now. I'd been asked for quite a while to apply for certain jobs and I'd always say no (not that I was offered the jobs—I was just asked to apply). And I always thought it was something I didn't want to do. I had worked at the Tricycle a lot as a freelance director and I had this long association here. Then some personal changes in my life made me question things and this job as artistic director came up. Many people said, "You have to go for this job." At first, I could not find clarity on whether this was the right job, whether this was the right thing to do. And people were giving me different advice. My friend Lynn Nottage sort of told me off and told me that it was time to be an artistic director and give back to the industry, that being an artistic director is about fueling the industry whereas being a freelancer is about your own personal career. So I decided to apply.

Rubasingham discovered that applying for this position had an unexpected side benefit for her as an artist.

The application process was really interesting because it was quite an intensive personal reflective process. I didn't want to try and guess what the Board would want, but instead I wanted to be able to say, "This is what I believe in, this is what I would do, this is what I want theatre to be." That was quite a useful exercise that you don't normally do as a jobbing director, so I've since advised other mid-career directors to write or really clarify what they believe in and what they want to do. By accident, that application process really made me formulate my ideas and, even to this day, has formed the basis of the Kiln/Tricycle's mission and vision.

Roxana Silbert

Become the person who makes decisions

Silbert describes two reasons for women to step into artistic leader-ship positions—one that furthers higher goals and one that's simply pragmatic.

Initially, I didn't really want to run anything. I love directing. But as I became older, I knew that middle-aged women are the least employ-able people on the planet. There's a lot of focus here on young people and unemployment because of the current economic situation, but actually middle-aged women are the least employable because you're not attractive anymore. So I thought, "Well, if I can't be employed, I will have to become an employer." You have to become the person who makes decisions because you can't rely on the current people who make decisions to employ you. Also, if you want to change the world for the better, you have to be a decision maker. I have found the things I love most about running Birmingham Rep are (1) properly investigating the role of a theater like ours in its community and (2) having the ability to support other artists.

Community and Support

Kimberly Senior

I'm my own traveling institution

As directors often observe, they don't have any peers in the production process. Senior addressed this lack of peer input by pulling together a group of Chicago directors for regular meetings.

I realized quite quickly that actors always have peers because they're in rehearsal rooms together and they're on stage together. Designers have peers because they're part of a team. The director is like the cheese that stands alone. I started seeking other directors. We are in competition for the same jobs, but my version of *Hedda Gabler* is going to be different than yours just in the same way as actors. Why can't we get in rooms and talk to each other? Why can't we exchange resources? Whether it's actors or books or sources of inspiration. Can we come and see each other's work and talk about it? I don't think it's so novel or revolutionary what I've done, but now, in Chicago, this community of directors has emerged. We meet every six months at someone's house and we talk about different theaters, and we talk about our work, and we solve problems. There are people who I can call and say, "This scene doesn't work, help me." When I directed *Inana* by Michele Lowe, there was something I knew I was missing and I didn't know what it was. I brought in my directors and I talked through the problem.

Senior acknowledges that it can be hard to feel part of a community of artists as a freelancer and describes her approach to building community.

I want to stay a freelance director. I believe in that. I want that to be a viable career in this country. I'm going to stick it out even though it might be nice to get a steady pay check. And also to have that meaningful sustained relationship with artists, audiences, and staff that you can have when you work in one place. My version of that is I'm my own traveling institution. I have the desire to work with the same actors over and over and over again. You develop this language with each other and it lets you start out ahead on the project from the first day.

Anne Kauffman

A director's residency retreat

In order to make a living, a director has to direct a bunch of shows in a year. I was finding that my ambitions became smaller because I had no preproduction time—I was choosing shows small enough to manage in a schedule where I'm doing four or five shows a season. I felt exhausted and depleted and wanted time to dream big again. So, along with Sundance, I started a director's residency. I had won the TCG Alan Schneider Award in 2010. They give you a cash prize and one of the questions that they ask when they interview is, "What do you want to do with this money?" I said I want to start a residency for mid-career, freelance directors to give them time to think and plan. Other artists have residency opportunities, so why not directors? So I talked to various residency programs for playwrights to understand infrastructure and then did a survey through the Stage Directors and Choreographers Society, asking directors what their needs and wants were. Armed with this information, I met with Philip Himberg, who's the head of Sundance Theatre Institute, and it turns out he had been interested in developing a similar program. So we joined forces and I was fortunate enough to tap into a preexisting infrastructure in an organization with funding and name recognition. For several years now, we've invited six directors on a residency where they have freedom to work on any project they desire in an environment free of obligations and in the company of other directors. This is vital, this coming together of directors, since it almost never happens. This exchange of philosophies, experiences, practices, and histories has had great impact on the participating directors, and creates much needed community among us, while providing nourishment and revitalization.

The interesting and dispiriting thing is that, when other people in our industry catch wind of a directors' residency, they can't imagine what that might consist of. They ask, "What are you going to do? What work could a bunch of directors do without writers or actors?" It's dispiriting because it means that most people in this industry, in this country, have no idea what it is a director does. And this lack of understanding is at the core of why directors are often not thought of as independent artists. And this is a problem.

Maria Aberg

Peers

Some directors have stronger identification with a peer group than others. Aberg describes why she considers a certain group of directors her peers.

I definitely feel like I have directing peers. On the whole, they are people who are roughly the same age and roughly at the same stage of their careers. We more or less did the same jobs at the same time, so we started off assisting at the same time, did the National Theatre Studio course in the same three or four years, that sort of thing. I think it's also partly something to do with who you have the conversation with—the general conversation about work and life and art and how to do this thing that we do. And those conversations about work and how you make work aren't colored in any way by wanting to impress or trying to get one up on them. There's a generosity of sharing experience, artistically and personally. There is a slightly separate category of people in my generation who do the driven career path thing—mostly men actually—but I don't see my peers as doing that.

Nadia Fall

My partners in crime

I love working with designers. They're always my pals because being a director can be very lonely actually. Often you don't have anybody to look from a distance with you and go, "Is this okay? Am I making a right mess of this?" You need somebody to be your sounding board and really think through some of the decisions with you, so I find designers are my best allies, my partners in crime.

I do what I do ultimately because I adore actors. It's weird to give them the homogeneous title "actors" because they're all unique people; but there is a quality to performers that you don't find in other people, a childlike quality, craziness, and danger. I hang out a lot with actors outside of rehearsals, where some other directors don't (a successful older director told me that I'll probably do that less as I age). The theater is a small community, and you do end up working with the people you know and love as much as possible because you know they will deliver. I think even without having a building or a company, we end up creating an unofficial company of actors and creatives we like to team up with.

6
NAVIGATING GENDER, RACE, AND ETHNICITY

Wouldn't it be nice if this chapter wasn't here? If women and people of color no longer had to navigate through obstacles placed in their paths because of their gender, race, or ethnicity? If they no longer had to dedicate their energy to fighting for equality? As one of the directors said when asked a question about the benefits of diversity, "It's ridiculous that we still have to talk about this." Alas, they still do regularly have to deal with and talk about these issues. In this chapter, they share a woeful number of stories about bias and unequal opportunity. Hearteningly, they also share stories about successfully overcoming such obstacles. They describe strategies for gaining personal confidence and authority, as well as collective, coordinated strategies for fostering more equity in the theater industry. They go on to discuss the benefits that come from more equitable distribution of work, specifically the enhanced creative potential of diversified production teams and institutional staff. Finally, they share their thoughts on what unique qualities women directors may offer.

Obstacles

Leigh Silverman

It's not an equal playing field

There is just an accepted obviousness about hiring a guy to direct a show, whereas a woman has to prove herself in a different way. It's not an equal playing field, it's just not. Certainly Off-Broadway has changed a huge amount, but the closer you get to the money the fewer the women. Big, big shows are still directed by men. It's the Sheryl Sandberg thing, which is that men are hired for their potential and women are hired for their experience, their proven track record. Producers and artistic directors will look at a 22-year-old guy and say, "That kid's a genius, I bet he could do this huge show really, really well," but they won't say the same about a woman. There are some producers and artistic directors who will take risks on people; I just think there are more risks taken on men.

When I get together with my friends and female colleagues, it seems that all of us are trying desperately to hold on to our own sense of ambition and talent, but it's hard not to feel like you're just banging your head against the wall. Sometimes it's actually comforting when you see it happening again and again in other industries and realize we're actually part of a bigger society in which this happens in every corner, not just ours.

One effective strategy for reducing gender inequality has been for women to help create opportunities for other women.

I have spent a lot of energy and effort advocating for women to be hired on my shows and I have fought to have diversity behind the scenes and on the stage. It is just better for our theatrical ecosystem when we work toward gender parity and strive for diversity at every level.

Sarah Benson

Gender divide between commercial and nonprofit theaters

There are still not very many women directing in the commercial arena. I think those that are have often come in through new work or experimental work, whereas more of their male colleagues have said, "This is what I want to do," and just entered that arena. Commercial theater is part of the world of money and investment and that world is still male dominated, so most of the commercial producers are still male. It's changing, but I think there's still a male bias in that world. For instance, commercial producers often refer to a female director as a "woman director," as in, "I'd love to work with women directors." What does that mean? You enjoy working with good directors? In Downtown New York theater, there are so many incredible women working in every field (although admittedly there are still not very many women running the big nonprofits in New York).

Benson emphasizes the need to discover and challenge our own biases.

I think it's all of our jobs (especially in such a historically privileged form) to challenge our own assumptions around race, ethnicity, class, physical disability, and gender. What are our own built in biases? How can we surround ourselves with people who will disrupt our taste, our prejudices, the stories, and forms we are drawn to? How can we find more people who will disagree with us? We can only create a vibrant relevant theater if we are surrounded by work that is divergent and diverse in every way possible.

Lucy Kerbel

Men leapfrogging ahead

Kerbel describes some of the gender disparities she has observed as a director. These disparities prompted her to establish Tonic Theatre, whose mission is to advance gender equity in the theatre industry.

I would look around the rehearsal room and I'd realize that more often than not I was one of the very few women in the room. There'd be me, there'd probably be a female stage manager, I'd usually have a female assistant. Probably lighting and sound would be male, designer probably male, cast predominantly male because that was particularly directing Shakespeare. Even the new plays I was doing, the ratio was the same. Instead of having ten men and two women, as I would for Shakespeare, I had maybe four men and one woman. Unlike the rehearsal room, if I went to the admin offices I'd see loads of women and not many men. It wasn't that women weren't working in theater at all; there are loads of women, but not in senior creative and administrative roles. I thought that was odd, because when I thought back to when I'd studied drama, it was always disproportionately female. I thought of the youth theater groups I'd worked in, disproportionately female. Audiences seemed to be quite female. But when it actually came to who was getting the gigs, the directing and writing, the designing, the acting gigs, in the bigger, better-resourced theaters that I was working in, I realized it was mainly men. And, while some of the women directors my age were doing fantastically well, others were not progressing and it felt like more men were progressing than women. The men, unlike the women, were beginning to leapfrog ahead.

In Tonic's research, we've interviewed so many women who have said, "Do I feel like I've been massively disadvantaged because I'm a woman? Yes. Can I prove it? No," because no one ever says to you, "Well, we didn't give you that job because you're a woman and we don't think you're ballsy enough or intelligent enough or strong enough" or whatever. No one will ever say that to you, but you don't get asked to do stuff. That's part of the condition of being a freelancer, that you don't know why. For instance, with Shakespeare I'm offered comedies and *Romeo and Juliet*, but I've never been offered one of the history plays or any of the other tragedies. Is that because I'm female? I don't know. If it is, I can't prove it. Plus I look younger than I am and I'm petite. Does that come into play? Who knows.

In techs, the power is weirdly redistributed. When you go into a theater's building and the tech team is in-house, it's their space. You're beholden to them to open your show for you—they are the only people who can rig those lights, program the desk, and so on. Senior management for the theater isn't usually around during tech, so the production manager is the chief and it's almost like their own little principality. Unfortunately, this allows some people to behave very poorly toward female members of creative teams. I once had a board op sit there telling racist, misogynist jokes; but the show opened the next night and the team had made us feel very unwelcome, so I thought if I stopped to make a complaint I would be punished by the team and the show would not be ready to open. I once had a production manager scream at the female lighting designer and female playwright. I went to the executive director and he tried to do a bit, but the tech continued over the weekend when he was not around, so it didn't help.

Vicky Featherstone

Different paths

Since Featherstone was named Artistic Director of the Royal Court in 2012 and assumed the role in 2013, many media profiles and news stories have highlighted her gender.

The London-based media are preoccupied with female artistic directors. In nine years of running the National Theatre of Scotland, nobody talked to me about being a woman. Every so often, in more personal, in-depth interviews, people would ask about the challenges of having small kids and being a woman and running the organization. But that was only in an hour-and-a-half interview for a personal piece, you know? It was only when I got the job at Royal Court that reporters started asking me about being a woman all the time. I've been an artistic director since I was twenty-seven. I've never had a male boss; yet the London-based media perpetuate this sense that it's remarkable if women get these jobs.

Featherstone, who began her career after completing her under-graduate degree in the early 1990s, observes how the paths open to male directors of her generation differed from those open to female directors.

In my generation of directors, a certain kind of people went to Oxford and Cambridge and a certain kind of people didn't. Some aspiring directors started wanting a certain kind of success and could see a pathway to that kind of success through Cambridge especially. So they took that path and became really successful. And now, in the next generation, there is a whole group of young men who followed in their footsteps. They went to Cambridge in order to become directors, came out, wrote to the right kind of people who had also been to Cambridge, became their assistant directors, and are now directing incredibly successfully. There is a new old boys' club out there and it really is the boys. It's extraordinary.

As for the women in my generation, more of us have become artistic directors than ever before, but there are fewer female freelance directors than male. I would never have wanted to be a freelance theater director. From very early on, I wanted to run an organization and be an artistic director. But before I knew that artistic directorships were a possibility, it felt like the men were hitting it straight off and that was very far off for me, so a similar thing to what the younger women are describing now.

Roxana Silbert

Demographics of young directors

Silbert describes differences between the career paths of today's young male and female directors.

I think it is still true that if you're a young male director and you do quite a good show on the fringe, you get catapulted forward in your career, while female directors have to work harder and do it for longer. Men tend to get promoted on promise, women on results. But I don't think that's entirely a bad thing, because you do the groundwork. I've seen a lot of people rush to the top and fall off because when they get there, they don't really know what they're doing. They're not ready.

Despite these disparate trajectories, women directors are making inroads.

If you look the statistics of the number of female directors at the Royal Shakespeare Company (RSC) and the National until about seven or eight years ago, it would be almost naught. And now that's not true. I mean, it's just not true. I was a trustee on the JMK Young Director Award for eleven years, starting about fifteen years ago. Fifteen years ago, we found it really hard to shortlist any women because they didn't apply to the trust. Then there was a real definite shift and suddenly the applications were fifty-fifty. And sometimes the short lists were nine women and one man. So, somewhere in the last fifteen years, there's been a real cultural shift. A lot of female directors are getting jobs, they're on the main stages, they're running buildings. Now what we don't get are any applications from black and Asian directors. That shift has not happened.

She also observes a troubling trend in the class and racial demographics of young directors.

The young directors I see coming through now are not from the sort of class backgrounds that they have been over the past couple decades. Before my generation, it was all white, middle-class Oxbridge men; but then there was this window of opportunity. State schooling was good for my generation and I went to university on a full grant. When I came out of university, I could receive housing benefit when I wasn't working. These were things that made it possible for me to struggle through the first few years when I was on very small wages and not getting a lot of work. And those support systems aren't there anymore. And my fear is we'll go backward rather than move forward.

Leah Gardiner
You were born on the wrong side of the tracks

Gardiner, a woman of color, describes a rude awakening in her career.

Early in my career, I was doing a commercial show and a producer was trying to get me fired. I said to him, "I don't know what I've done to you," and he said, "Well, let's just say you were born on the wrong side of the tracks." I asked what he meant: "I went to the University of Pennsylvania. I graduated from Yale Drama School. How can I be 'born on the wrong side of the tracks?'" He asked, "You don't know?" and I said, "I have to very honest with you. I don't." It took me ten years to figure out that it was racism. It finally dawned on me that racism was the thing getting in my way. I should have known because my mentor was George Wolfe, who is a black man, but he was running The Public, one of the largest theaters in the country, so it didn't make sense to me that it would get in my way. Now that I've been in it for so long, I understand how racism and sexism work in the American theater. If you're of color and you're a woman, your experience is very different and it's just the way it is.

Paulette Randall

As a black woman, I'm always perceived as a risk

Randall explains why she does not fear taking artistic risks.

As a black woman, I'm always perceived as a risk anyway, so risk doesn't matter much to me. I go into a theater and they say, "Well, we don't know how to market this," or, "Oh it's a play about black people and we don't have that audience." That happens a lot, so I don't ever feel separated from the idea of my projects being a risk. Ever.

I knew really early on that I didn't have the connections of most white, middle-class, male directors—I don't have a member's pass into that club. So, you have to fight your battles in a very different way than others. And that's part of the fun of it, in a way. It's a challenge. You have to be cognizant enough and I guess maybe emotionally strong enough to say, "This is the way it is and I've made the choice and I know I'm going to have to make my own path." And it might feel a bit lonely to begin with, but you find kindred spirits along the way.

Unfortunately, experience does not inoculate directors from bias.

A few months ago, I told my agent, "I would love to work at this particular place." So he made a phone call and their response was, "Yeah, the only problem is we need to see her work." So I'm apparently Britain's leading black female director, I had a show in the West End last year,[1] but because they hadn't bothered to see anything I'd done, they weren't interested. So, if I'm struggling with this after doing this job for thirty-odd years, then what's it like for those who are just beginning and have no track record at all? Dear God. There are more actors of color, so that's changed. But nothing much else has. You can still go into a theater and if I'm the director, I'm probably the only black on the

---

[1] *Fences*, Duchess Theatre, 2013.

creative team. I've worked with three or four black male music directors, but never a black designer. So not much has changed in three decades.

Young Jean Lee

My ethnicity and gender gave me a boost

Luckily, as this example from Lee shows, sometimes being female and non-white can be a career asset. Lee was born in South Korea and grew up in Washington State. She has built her playwriting/directing career in the experimental Downtown New York theatre scene.

When I came onto the experimental theater scene in 2002, I felt like there was just such a hunger for somebody like me who was an Asian female. At that time, the experimental theaters were very white and, less so, very male. They were concerned about diversity and really wanted to have a woman of color in their season. My whole career was given such a boost by my ethnicity and my gender just because I found the right people and places who really were open to having a woman of color in their season at that time. It hasn't been difficult for me to find a place in this world. I think it has been actually a bit easier for me because of my ethnicity and gender. I think if I were to take a step out and try to do a commercial run or try to work in more mainstream theater or work in Hollywood or wherever, I would have a very rude awakening.

Diane Rodriguez

Connections and perceptions

Leadership in American theater is becoming more diverse, but the change feels glacially slow. It takes work. I heard an analogy at a Theatre Communications Group conference: searching for someone of color to lead your company or to be on your staff is like looking for your keys. When you lose your keys, you know they're somewhere, so you search your whole house. You look under the bed, under the tables, whatever, because you know they're there somewhere, you just have to find them. Same thing with diversity: you have to believe that people are out there, and you have to search everywhere to find them.

There's just so much education that has to be done, primarily at the board level. Most theaters depend on patronage—people giving us money. When a board searches for an artistic director, they want someone who will be able to socialize with those who have money because they need that patronage to survive. So they ask, "Does this person have the connections to bring in money?" White men may have had more opportunity to hobnob with wealthy patrons, which means that people of color and women need more of those opportunities. Or the board may just *perceive* that white male candidates have more connections and would be better at hobnobbing than women and people of color when, in fact, some people who have been successful leading, say, a nonprofit company of color might be very prepared to make that leap.

KJ Sanchez

Bias among gatekeepers

Increasingly, arts organizations rely upon a handful of placement companies to conduct national searches for their leadership positions. The employees of these companies are the gatekeepers who decide which names get passed onto a board for consideration. Before accepting an academic position as the Head of Directing at University of Texas at Austin, Sanchez was exploring artistic director positions. She relays a series of experiences she had with a representative of one prominent placement company.

His intentions are always great and he's made some really excellent placements recently, but his bias was so clear in our meetings. I met with him three times about three different positions. The meeting for the first position didn't go very well. When we emailed to set up the meeting for the second position some time later, he said something like, "Will we remember what each other looks like?" I said, "Oh, I look very much the same, except I have a few more grey hairs." I go to meet him, shake his hand, and the first thing he says is, "Like I said in my email, I wasn't sure I would remember what you looked like, but then I saw that pretty smile, and there was the KJ that I remember." That was problematic.

So then we go through my resume—for the last seven years I've been contracting with the Department of Defense with *Reentry*, I've written plays and done solo performances, I've directed this style and that style, and so on. I was pitching myself as this Renaissance artist, and this theater needed an artistic director with that breadth of scope. At the end of my pitch, he says, "Can I offer you some advice?" Unsolicited advice is fine, because part of their job is to help cultivate the pool of talent that they present to boards. But he says, "You need to rethink how you present yourself, because you've done so much that one might question if you have an inability to focus." And I couldn't help but think that, if I was a man, he might have said, "It's amazing how much this guy has done in a few years!" So that was pretty shocking.

Later I was shortlisted for a different organization and we met so he could prep me for my interview with the search committee. He was giving me some background information on each of the people who were going to be in the room and said some word that has two pronunciations (I don't even remember what the word was). He pronounced it one way, paused, and asked, "Is that how you pronounce that?" I told him how I thought it was pronounced. Then he laughed and said, "Imagine me taking English lessons from you." I was so taken aback. I said, "I'm sorry. I have to stop. Can we go back to what you just said? Why are you surprised you're taking English lessons from me?" He said, "I'm sorry, but I thought with your last name being Sanchez you identified as a person of color." I took a deep breath and said, "Okay, one thing you should know about so many Hispanics and Latinos in the United States is for many of us, Spanish wasn't our first language. For many of us, we've been here for generations and generations. My family has lived in the same town in New Mexico for 300 years. It was founded in 1680 by my ancestors. We never crossed a border. The border crossed us. I was not raised speaking Spanish. Also, assuming that people of color don't speak English is problematic."

To his credit, he was appalled. He thanked me for calling him out and said it was a major learning moment for him. He was very gracious about it. But the thing is, if we're worried about gender parity and diversity and inclusion in arts leadership, we need to look at who is holding the keys to the gate. If there are only a handful of people holding those keys and they all come from the same socioeconomic, ethnic, cultural background, that's a big problem. I hope that's changing now. I just noticed one of those search firms has some female leadership, so that's a step forward.

Strategies for Increasing Equality

Nadia Fall

Nothing is going to change without direct action

We need more parts for women, full stop. Not just playing the love interests and clichés that we are used to, but real and rounded people. I want to see new stories with female protagonists, written from a woman's point of view. It's so important that theater holds the mirror up to society and leads the way when it comes to reflecting our world. We need writers to come forward and write these roles and ultimately we need theaters to commission them in the first place.

We also need greater diversity in all senses of the word, including for disabled actors, who are so bitterly ignored from the equation. There's such injustice in it. Such injustice. I've been attending events held by a new charity called Act for Change (which now has an office at the National Theatre), and when I hear the stories of colleagues—especially actors—from disabled backgrounds not being given opportunities or being heard, my heart is broken. We're so programmed to think of what is "normal" that we're not even provoked to think out of the box. We're the poorer for it. We had a brilliant campaign in the UK by Channel 4 during the 2012 Paralympics where they tagged the paralympians as "Superhumans." It was so powerful that my son was like, "I want a special leg like that!" That led to a few more television shows hosted by disabled entertainers, and you just think, "We wouldn't have even known about these brilliant people if somebody hadn't given them a platform."

However, beyond equal representation on stage, I think we sorely need to focus on diversity behind the scenes: stage management, producing, designing, directing and many other departments are far from diverse. Nothing is going to change without some direct action: getting in to the education system to engage with a cross section of young people and let them know that these career opportunities exist in the first place, creating training opportunities and mentorships are all part of a solution.

Maria Aberg

It's not just going to go away

Aberg has cross-gender cast many roles in her productions at the RSC and other theatres.

Rehearsal rooms full of men are just part of the routine; it's basically accepted as the status quo. And in casting conversations where I try and push, even in tiny ways, to address the lack of roles for women, sometimes it feels like starting that conversation makes me a bit of a troublemaker in other people's eyes. You're perceived as the angry, yappy little dog in the corner and it would be easier for everyone if you'd just be quiet. When I have managed to push through with gender-blind casting, for example, in *King John*[2] at the RSC or in *Much Ado about Nothing*[3] at the Royal Exchange, it is often perceived as very controversial.

It's not just Shakespeare where there's gender imbalance. New plays are full of men too, because contemporary theater is based on the template we have. By and large, the plays that we write are based on the plays that we see, and since the classical, male-dominated canon continues to outnumber new work on our stages, that is still the template we base our plays on. If you go to the theater and see a world on the stage that's populated 80 percent by men, then that is going to define what you think good theater is. You subconsciously adopt an idea of what drama means, who drives story, what a protagonist is, and who affects change on stage.

I think the biggest obstacle to changing this gender inequality is the reluctance to realize that it's not just going to go away of its own accord. People need to acknowledge this is actually a problem that

---

[2]Royal Shakespeare Company, 2012.
[3]Royal Exchange Theatre, 2014.

needs immediate and direct addressing rather than just saying, "Well, you know, let's just of hope for the best. It'll be fine if we just plow on and let it straighten itself out." That's just rubbish. Lucy Kerbel of Tonic Theatre is a complete hero, and I absolutely believe that the work she is doing with the Advance project will change the makeup of British theater in the next ten years. I think what she is doing and advocating doing is absolutely brilliant because it's about shaping policy and actually making gender equity part of how a theater building is run. Lucy spent some time in Sweden researching their law mandating gender balance in professional theaters. The union stipulated what the gender balance had to be in every department of every theater across the country by a certain year. They simply went ahead and said, "Right, this is it and we're going to make it happen now whether you want it to or not." And of course it worked, of course it's brilliant. I really believe that's the way forward. People have such a terrible opinion of quotas and I think they are the best things that have ever happened. And I think people's arguments against quotas are driven by fear and laziness.

Lucy Kerbel

Tonic Theatre

I knew I wanted to make change in gender equality in the industry and was trying to work out what to do. I thought, "Well if it's just me on my own putting on plays about women, it's not going to change. The Young Vic won't even notice that's happening; but if I can use that same amount of energy to try and get the Young Vic to think about how they make plays, the effect is much, much greater." At that time, nothing was being done about it in this country. You would have small women's theater companies at the periphery making work about women, or you would have individual female voices talking about it, but nothing that went, "Let's get these big theaters together who have the majority of the money and the majority of the influence. Let's get them to do it. If we get the gatekeepers moving on this, everything will move with them." So I founded Tonic Theatre to help theaters make change.

One of Tonic Theatre's most impactful and well-known initiatives to date was the Advance project, in which Tonic helped eleven theaters research the underlying causes of gender disparities in their organizations and make concrete, realistic plans for correcting them.

The idea behind the Advance project[4] was bringing together a group of theaters who wanted to create change and who were excited about possibilities. It was not a slap on the wrist or a remedial class for cracked theaters. All the theaters I approached at first were ones I'd already been having conversations with. Then some who had come on board suggested others. Once we had a group, I said, "Okay, you guys have identified that this is a really exciting possibility, let's now make it happen together."

Paulette Randall

It goes back to whoever is batting it my way

Although Randall has been repeatedly hailed as the most prominent black woman director in Britain, she still finds that people regularly question her suitability for projects based upon her race, class background, and gender.

There's nothing worse than when you find yourself in a situation where you go, "It's because I'm a woman, why they're behaving like this," or, "It's because I'm black." It's not about me at all, it's about other people's reactions to me. It's not my issue. I don't have a problem with being female. I don't have a problem with being black. So, I have to find a way to make sure that that goes back to whoever is batting it my way. And that's tedious because it takes your eye off the focus of what you're trying to do. And it happens more often than people think.

I was doing *Twelfth Night*[5] at Nottingham and they have a thing where members of the theater can come and see a little bit of the rehearsal and meet the actors. This woman asks me, "Why don't you do one of your own plays?" And I said, "What do you mean, one of my

---

[4]*Advance.* Tonic Theatre. http://www.tonictheatre-advance.co.uk/ (accessed February 8, 2017).
[5]Nottingham Playhouse, 2010.

own plays?" "You know, one of your own." "No, I don't know what you mean," I said—because I wasn't going to let her get away with that. Then she said, "Well, why do you want to do Shakespeare? Because you've set it in Brazil." I said, "Shakespeare's been set on the moon. It doesn't make any difference." She replied, "Well, I'll be the judge of that." So, suddenly it wasn't just about putting a play on and seeing whether or not it'd be good, it was about putting a play on and seeing whether it would change the work of the Bard to a point that she would find acceptable. She was assuming Shakespeare belongs to white British people, not to me. Plus I'm working class and that's a factor as well. It's never been said to my face, but I've heard via other people that I've not gotten jobs because people have said, "Well, she wouldn't understand this play because it's very middle class." Yet there's the assumption that middle-aged white men can do anything, regardless of their class or race or gender. So it's not just theater we're talking about, is it? We're talking about the world, and theater is just a microcosm.

May Adrales

Diverse casting

I challenged myself to never have a cast that is just middle-class, white actors unless the play really requires it. I feel a responsibility as a director to put on stage the world that I think is true. I have a background you don't expect—Filipino from a very rural town. And there are lots of other people like me dotted around. There's a different kind of normal now in the United States and the theater should reflect that.

I've had pushback from writers who say, "This isn't a play about race," and I point out that just because a character is black doesn't mean it's about race. And I've seen casting directors omit people of color from their list, so I've had to bring them in to audition. But I used to get way more pushback than I do now. In recent years, the Asian American community has been much more vocal and organized about voicing their protestations.

I did a new musical called *In this House* and Chuck Cooper was available to play the main role.[6] That role was not written for an African

---

[6]Two River Theater Company, 2012.

American man, but Chuck Cooper had the voice and acting chops and charisma and was the best actor for the role. The audiences never questioned whether or not they thought that person should be black or white—they only talked about the story. I think that's the biggest testament to nontraditional casting. As long as it's true to the story that you want to tell, it doesn't become this political flag that you're waving; it just becomes normal within the story. I don't feel it can go wrong and it can open so many doors.

Kimberly Senior

Speaking in their own voices

I was directing Michele Lowe's *Inana* for TimeLine Theatre Company, which takes place in a London hotel room and the characters are Iraqi.[7] They were speaking with an Iraqi dialect and, before one of the previews, I thought to myself, "They're speaking to each other in their native tongue, why are they using a dialect? When I do Chekhov I don't have them speak with a Russian dialect but just plain old American accents." It was like half an hour before curtain and I go to the green room and say, "Guys, tonight no accents, no dialect." I felt like the thing that was missing was this kind of fire and human connection between them that, no matter how I kept at it, I hadn't been able to get to, so I thought maybe it was because there is this layer of distance when you're not speaking in your native tongue. We did it and there were so many great moments that happened on stage, but the music of the play was lost because it's actually written to be spoken with a dialect. Afterward, one of the actors (who is of Indian descent) said to me, "I'm sure we're going back to doing it with the dialect but I have to thank you because the moment before I went on I realized I could not remember the last time I spoke in my own voice on stage." He's an actor in his forties. I started to cry and I said, "Am I a part of the problem making this play?" Then another actor joked, "Yes, but we get to wear shoes. Usually I play characters with no shoes." I thought, let this be a promise to make plays where the actors are speaking in their own voices.

---

[7] TimeLine Theatre, 2015.

Leah Gardiner
Do bits at a time

Gardiner, a woman of color, earned her MFA in Directing at Yale School of Drama. Liz Diamond was among her professors at Yale.

When I was in grad school, I remember Liz Diamond sat me down and said to me, "If you ever do run a theater, I imagine that the audience will really be very diverse and that you will work extremely hard to make sure that that happens because you're diverse." That was something that really stuck with me. I'm interested in being an artistic director someday because I think that to have someone who looks like me and thinks like me, running a theater would be kind of cool. Whether I do it in New York or somewhere else in another part of the world, I don't know, but I think it's important.

Even as a freelancer, I've worked, on a very quiet, subtle level, to help transform the way we think about theater in this country. If I can just, between now and the time I die, do bits at a time, I think that for folks after me who look like me, there will be more opportunity. I'm looking forward to someone asking me to direct *The Sound of Music* at some point, you know? It's a musical that I absolutely love. Now, will I be the first person that they run to direct that show? Probably not, but I'm hopeful that if I'm ever asked by an artistic director what I'd really like to do and I say *The Sound of Music*, that they would embrace it. I'd like to help create a world where it won't seem like an anomaly to call someone like me to direct *The Sound of Music*.

When I directed *generations* by debbie tucker green, Ntomb'khona Dlamini was in the cast.[8] One day I told her and the cast that I had seen her play Serafina when I was a child. I sat in the front row and thought, "Oh my God, this is what I want to do. I want to make these kind of stage pictures and music. I want to make this kind of art." And I said to Khona, "It's because of you that I'm here. It's because of you that I am in my own little way helping to transform the American theater, to convince them that someone who looks like me can direct classics, can direct musicals, can direct straight plays, can direct world premieres and US

---

[8]Soho Rep, 2017.

premieres. I can do this because you inspired me." We in the American theater need to make certain that we are educating people like me, showing theater to people like me, so that all things are possible.

Young Jean Lee
The limits of the subscription model

Most mainstream American theaters generate a large portion of their revenue through subscriptions—a system in which patrons buy tickets for a theater's entire season year after year. This approach fosters patron loyalty and long-term support; it also pressures artistic directors to base their programming choices on patron preferences.

There are a lot of artistic directors in mainstream theater who would like to have a more diverse season, but they're subscriber-based. Their whole existence depends on their subscriber base of elderly, wealthy, straight, white people who are willing to pay astronomical ticket prices to see themselves represented on stage. In a decade or two, all those people are going to be gone and the audience demographic will be different, so theater will have to shift. In the short term, I don't think it is shifting very quickly, but the pressure is intensifying. This is a critical time when more and more pressure needs to be exerted on theaters to have a more diverse season, to hire more women, to hire more minorities, and so on. There are so many organizations that are really pushing for more diversity in film and theater: the Lilly Awards, the Kilroys, a lot of feminist playwriting groups. That's an important part of the process of change and I think these are signs that things will change in the future.

Diane Rodriguez
The Latinx Commons and open platform leadership

The Latinx Theatre Commons was founded in 2012 by a group of Latinx theatre artists. Their goal is to increase the visibility of Latino/a/x theatre and advocate for a greater representation of Latinx theatre artists in

American professional theatre. They sponsor an annual festival where Latinx artists share their work with one another and with producers from across the Americas.[9]

The Latinx Commons model has a lot of potential. I had a play featured in the first festival. It allowed me to launch my work to the wider field in a new way. Instead of holding our hands out and asking theaters to help us develop work, we are developing it on our own and inviting theaters to come in and find work to present. We're essentially curating these works as a service to theaters and artists.

The other fascinating thing about Latinx Commons is that there is no leader. There is a steering committee (which I've been on for three years). The festivals are organized by a group of people who each contribute in their own ways and it's all facilitated through open platform social media. I don't know where it will go, but many, many people are interested in this sort of open platform leadership model.

Liesl Tommy

Relentless pressure

Tommy sits on the selection board for the Susan Smith Blackburn Prize, where she reads many plays by female playwrights each year.

It's amazing to see the variety of writing by women. It's a very rich time right now, with writers who are pushing forms and challenging perceptions of diversity and masculinity and femininity and gender roles and so on. And the American theater is moving toward greater parity of male and female playwrights. But let me be clear: it's because of a relentless group of women who just won't ever stop saying, "Look at your season. Look at your season. Look at your season." We can't delude ourselves into thinking that parity comes because people want to do the right thing. Parity comes because of relentless pressure.

---

[9]"Latinx Theatre Commons." *HowlRound.* http://howlround.com/latinx-theatre-commons (accessed May 15, 2017).

Roxana Silbert

The artistic directors are genuinely concerned

The artistic directors of Silbert's generation have repeatedly expressed the need to create more equity in theatres. Silbert confirms that they are putting their words into action.

I think it's hugely different now. I met with Rufus Norris, the artistic director of the National Theatre, who is not quite a peer of mine, but not far off. He said that at his programming meetings, he wants to ask, "Is there a way of making this more diverse? Can we engage with a regional theatre on this?" And at the RSC we had an absolute commitment to diverse casting. There was never a season in which the intention wasn't to make as diverse as possible. So, I think there is a huge shift in terms of it being absolutely central to these policies. When we artistic directors look at a season, we will ask, "Is there enough for the Asian audience here? Is there enough for minority audiences here? Are there plays here that have women at the center of them?" For example, James Brining from West Yorkshire Playhouse rang up and said, "We really need something that's got women at the center of it because last season it was almost all plays about men, by men, directed by men." So the artistic directors are genuinely concerned.

Lyndsey Turner

Each generation's role

Turner began her professional career in the 2000s. She reflects on the obstacles faced by women directors in the past and present and speculates about how to clear obstacles for the future.

I feel a profound connection with my own generation of female theater makers, but also with those who came before. What I'm trying to work out is what my responsibility is to those who will come after me. How can they be supported but also challenged to take the conversation further?

The generations of female theater directors who preceded mine fought hard to get their foot in the door, and some of them got pretty bruised along the way. I cannot imagine what it must have been like for Buzz Goodbody or Annie Castledine when they were first starting out. I sometimes wonder how they were spoken to in production meetings, how their work was reported in the press, whether they had to infiltrate or resist the status quo in order to make the work they wanted to make. The fact that I find my gender fairly unproblematic in terms of my own work is, in large part, because these women went into battle on our behalf. I feel a responsibility to them to make the best work I can, and to champion and challenge the next generation of female theater practitioners.

Every six months or so, one of the "quality" newspapers will run an article on female directors. The subtext of these articles is one of surprise or curiosity about how a woman is able to run a rehearsal room—and that just points to a fundamental misunderstanding of what directing is. If you believe that directing is simply a matter of bossing people about, it follows that your interview will focus on the way in which a woman is able to find a space within that room to wield power. A friend of mine was interviewed for one of these articles, but when she read it in print, she found herself pretty upset by the idiocy of its premise. She said, "This story should be over by now." I started to wonder whether we're rather missing the point. Perhaps our generation's role in the great relay race of feminism is to endure the writing and rewriting of that "Female directors: Whatever next?" article in the hope that it's read by a teenage girl at a bus stop who, in that moment, thinks, "I could do that." Perhaps we just need to suck this one up so a future cohort can be inspired by those articles and move toward a day when the fact that a director is female will no longer count as remarkable or newsworthy.

Erica Whyman

We need to not give up

The women of my generation need to not give up. And I don't mean that flippantly. The women of my age—I was born in 1969—thought other women before us had changed the landscape and achieved much greater equality and that our job was to inherit the success of the revolution and live it. But we have struggled and fought to cling on to visibility and influence sometimes by our fingernails, and we are not living in an equal world, and we do not have a theater which fully represents our society. And it's tempting at a certain point say, "Okay, it's for the next generation to do," and perhaps to focus on more personal goals. But we need to not give up publicly fighting for equality. I think we've got a very exciting role to play with younger women artists who, I hope, are going to be bolder and braver.

I think we are entering a really lively moment in the discussion of feminism and equality more broadly. I sense, and hope, that many of us are ready to really own our feminism and act on it. I think younger men as well as women are open to tackling serious and complex ideas on stage, so whatever their behind-the-scenes confidence, an appetite to speak out seems stronger than for a generation. And I think we are living through very challenging times, politically, internationally, and that we will all need to be brave if we are to say what we really think or feel about the world.

Confidence and Authority

Anne Kauffman

Your personhood is the grease

When I started out, I was so afraid I wouldn't be taken seriously as a woman director, I actually attempted to de-sex myself. The superficial action was to dress like a man, to keep any evidence that I was a sexual being out of the room, to make sure my exterior hinted at nothing other than the seriousness of the task at hand. The more insidious and therefore more damaging action was to appear the authority in the room in a way that left my personality, my life experiences, and my point of view out of the room. In order to be an authority figure, I thought, it had to be only about the work and the "right way to do it," and not at all about my perspective on the work. Which sounds insane now . . . and was insane. By attempting to keep my gender out of the room, I essentially eliminated what made me, well, me. That all changed, gosh, when did it change? Probably in graduate school when I was part of a community of directors focused on teasing out our voices. It's really so astonishing to me now, that I engaged in such asphyxiating tendencies. When I allowed my sense of humor and my authorship back in the room while working on a distillation of the original *Spring Awakening*, I found that my relationship with the actors, their interest in the project, their work in rehearsal all became easier. More organic. Your personhood is the grease that enables the truly original creative process to happen.

Kimberly Senior

Being a female director is my superhero cape

I spent a very long portion of my career wearing my hair in a ponytail and wearing Converse and trying to not be attractive because I didn't want to distract anybody. Now I've realized if you're distracted by my breasts, that's actually your problem and not mine. I can still do my job in peace. You need to learn to figure that out.

I spent the first twenty years of my career rejecting the moniker of female director. You wouldn't call a male director a male director. The only time we put male in front of something is stripper and nurse and occasionally teacher. So why do I have to be female director? Can't I just be a director? I felt really adamant about that. Then, in 2015, I spoke at this annual event at the Goodman Theatre called Women on Fire. They bring together over two hundred women who eat together, listen to speakers, see a play, and talk about it afterward. I was meeting CEOs, doctors, working mothers, single mothers, and people who chose not to have children. I found myself feeling so moved by their accomplishments and their ease and their grace and how different each of them were. It wasn't like a room full of super-ballsy women in pantsuits. There were all different kinds of women with different stories. I'd never been in a room of two hundred women, and it was a huge turning point for me. I realized that being a female director, that's my superhero cape. I'm so proud for accomplishing what I have accomplished. Why turn my back on that? So now I wear that cape with pride. I haven't really faced enormous struggles. In fact, most of the struggles that I faced have been self-inflicted in many ways—my own esteem or confidence issues surrounding being a woman. My job next is to inspire younger women artists—whether in the classroom or the rehearsal room—to get there sooner. Get there. Don't waste your time.

Leah Gardiner

It's like being directed by my mom

How many times I've heard, "I've never been directed by a woman before. This is so cool. It's like being directed by my mom." Really? Or, I hear, "We were really interested in hiring you because you know, we wanted something different." Really?

KJ Sanchez

Dominance and gratitude

Earlier in my career, many years ago, I directed at two regional theaters within six months of each other. At both, the technical directors had the same approach to me, which was essentially, "Little lady, let me explain how building sets works." There was a real bias against me as a young, woman director. I hate to say this, but my strategy for both of them was just finding the right moment to cut them down. I had to stay internally on tilt—do you know that expression? It comes from training in the Marine Corps. Basically, it means that even though you are calm on the outside, internally you are tilting forward—as one does when you need to move quickly. So anyway, I was on tilt, waiting for an opportunity to change the dynamic between me and these guys. On one of those productions, it came when the technical director walked into the third production meeting and tried to make a cute joke by saying, "Okay KJ, what are we changing today?" suggesting I was always changing my mind. I said, "What we're changing is the use of the word 'changing.' We're going to say instead 'fixing,' because you didn't do it the way it should have been done. Now we're fixing X, Y, and Z." He went, "Oh. Okay." Then from there it was fine. I just had to find that moment in a meeting where I could clearly state my dominance to shift the culture of that whole room.

Thankfully, I don't have to do that anymore. I find that production managers and technical directors are so much more interpersonally

sophisticated than they were fifteen or twenty years ago. Gross gener-
alization, I know, but I think it's true. And I've changed too. I understand
who I am as an artist, I listen to myself, and I take pride in the fact that
I reserve the right to change my mind at any time—that's what makes
me a good director. So my first meetings with those folks are on much
more solid ground now. Part of the problem was a culture that had a
bias against girls, but part of it was also that I wasn't walking into the
room owning my leadership.

Sanchez shares another leadership mistake early career directors make.

The more often you thank everybody in the first few production meetings,
the more suspicious they're going to be of your leadership. You need
to walk into the room knowing you have every right to be there. I used
to think that an impassioned, teary-eyed thank you at 11:45 p.m. after
a long day of tech would win people. Instead, it's like, "You're keeping
us an extra fifteen minutes so you can tell us how grateful you are to
us for doing our jobs." Now I know that if I really want to thank people,
I shouldn't waste their time.

Liesl Tommy
I come from a very direct community

*Tommy, who grew up in South Africa but now works mostly in the
United States, demonstrates that expressions of authority are deeply
grounded in cultural norms.*

I'm not an early career director anymore, and now that I'm a little more
established, I don't fight quite the same battles I had to early on; but
I do still have to fight little battles. For example, I was in a meeting
recently and had come in kind of in a rush from a previous meeting.
I gave the artistic director a quick update on something and just said,
"Yeah, so I just decided that we have to do *x*." And he looked at me and
said, "*You* decided." I looked back at him like, "What the fuck?" Then he
kind of shook it off and carried on like that moment hadn't happened.
I wasn't raised in America. I come from a very direct community. That

American woman thing of asking for permission when I'm making a statement never ceases to amaze me. That's just not my thing.

Maria Aberg
The performance of confidence

Directors feel pressure to project confidence when they meet with artistic directors and other potential employers. This can pose a challenge for women because, in this historically male-dominated field, men have established the cues employers look for when assessing confidence.

There are times where I have felt that it would have been very helpful if I were able to switch on that confident young man thing that confident young men do. I think that a lot of the time that particular variety of male confidence is a performance of confidence rather than the real thing, but because that performance is often expected you can feel lacking if you don't have the ability to collude in that idea of what confidence looks and sounds like. I've certainly felt that sometimes, but I don't know if I'm reluctant to join in the performance because I'm a woman or just because of who I am as a person. Of course, it would be wonderful to go into a meeting with an artistic director and have an actual two-way conversation about ideas, but most of the time that's not how it pans out. I don't really know why. Maybe it's because, as an artistic director, you don't often have the energy or time or head space to engage in that kind of conversation with everyone who comes through the door, so it's quite helpful to just sit back and say, "Tell me what you want to do, give me your vision, give me the show of who you are." Or maybe it's because many artistic directors are men and that's how they're used to evaluating ideas and people. Although a lot of the time that's also how it is with female artistic directors. And I again don't know if that's because that's what the job actually requires or if it's because they're emulating a model of being an artistic director that they have seen men exhibit on their way up to that position.

I have noticed recently—and perhaps it has something to do with the increased number of female artistic directors—that the hard edge of trying to press your way forward in your career seems to be softening. I certainly don't feel it as much with a female artistic director as I do with a male equivalent. I hope that's what's happening. Less trying to show off to artistic directors and critics and generally "play it like a man."

Aberg describes what "playing it like a man" looks like to her.

It's the act of ego, which carries with it resonances of wanting to slightly intimidate or challenge or turn things into a bit of a battle. I suppose "playing it like a man" also, to a certain extent, means ignoring the fact that you're a woman. I don't know exactly what that means, but there's something about being slightly more ruthless or not allowing yourself to be quite as open or not as much of an individual – a little bit more cold and professional.

Lucy Kerbel

The circumstances we've built

As part of Tonic Theatre's research into gender inequities in the British theater industry, Kerbel and her colleagues conducted focus groups and interviews with various theatre professionals.

At one point, I did a focus group of young women sound and lighting designers. I was talking to them with my research hat on, but just for a moment I pulled out and looked at them with my director hat on. They were really sweet, but timid. For a moment as a director I thought, "I don't know if I would trust one of you in a tech. Because if the shit hits the fan, I don't know, maybe you would just break down and cry. You seem so fragile." I found that a really troubling thought because they might be brilliant designers, and what a shame that I might ignore one of them and pick someone else who is aggressive but might not be anywhere near as good because of the circumstances that we've built around techs. Plus, I'm judging that when the shit hits the fan, they'll break down and cry, but I don't know—they might be absolutely fine.

I could hire another designer who's filled with bravado who, when push comes to shove, could just completely melt.

An established lighting designer musing about young designers told me, "I meet too many young women who think they're not good enough and too many young men who are incapable of self-questioning." That sense kept coming out in our research—men not self-doubting or self-questioning enough, but the women self-questioning too much.

Another researcher I worked with had lots of conversations with playwrights and literary managers about pitching conversations. What she found is that, generally, male playwrights talking to literary managers and artistic directors make their ideas sound artistically exciting but low-risk, whereas the women playwrights will make their ideas sound artistically exciting but high-risk. Now, if you're an artistic director choosing someone for a £60,000 show and you have one low-risk candidate and one high-risk, you're probably going to go for the low-risk one. I think we're confusing emerging artists, because director training programs are about exploring and playing and taking artistic risk, but often when they go to pitch to a theater, exploring and risk is not what the theater is looking for. A lot of directors say they never know what those meetings are for. Are they being asked to pitch an exciting idea? Or explain why they would be a safe bet for that £60,000? Or just to have a nice chat?

In her interviews, Kerbel asked women directors if they thought their male peers' "performance of confidence" (to use Maria Aberg's phrase) put women at a disadvantage when vying for jobs.

I spoke to some of the RSC assistant directors about this issue of confidence in the pitching meeting. One young woman said, "You know, I don't think that we should encourage women to change so they become more like men. I think confidence comes in many different forms. For me, having a collaborative conversation is my way of sharing I am confident. If I go into pitch meeting with an artistic director and I say, 'I'm thinking of doing this, but what do you think?' that's not me doubting myself. It's me having the confidence to say to that person, 'Challenge my ideas,' rather than saying, 'This is what I'm going to do.' "

Erica Whyman

State clearly that you could and would deliver

As Deputy Artistic Director of the RSC, Whyman regularly hears pitches from young directors.

In the women fifteen to twenty years younger than me (in their late twenties/early thirties now) there has been a notable falling off in confidence. Vicky Featherstone [Artistic Director of Royal Court] has said she thinks it's because we all became obsessed with ourselves and it became all about the individual and, that women, broadly speaking, performed less well in those circumstances. It became all about whether you're the winner, whether you're the best, and more women than men said, "Oh, I don't want to be in that race because I'm sure I'm not the best."

The irony, the terrible irony, is that the person who is the best does not win the gig—the person who's perfectly comfortable saying that he's the best wins the gig. The person who's relaxed about that as an idea. And he's usually a man. When I meet with assistant directors at the RSC, the young men will come straight in with a pitch for the Swan (the smaller of our two main stage theaters). They know that probably I'm not going to offer them a show in the Swan, but the trick is to come in and say, "I'm who you want directing on one of our main stages." And the women will come in and say, "Well, I've got this little thing that might work in the studio space and I've got this thing which I appreciate somebody else is probably directing and . . ." A woman is much less likely to come in and go, "I'm the person you want." So, you're already navigating a relationship with someone who's not sure they can do it. Now sometimes you can take someone from there all the way to really doing it, but that takes more effort and energy. Those of us programming theaters don't and can't always put that effort and energy in. Often what we're looking for is the guarantee that this person can stick with it whatever the risk.

Whyman describes how her perception of "performing confidence" has changed in her years as an artistic and deputy artistic director.

When I was younger and working freelance, I was furious at my perception that I was being judged wholly on how I performed in a pitch—usually a pitch where I was being asked to perform to somebody else's criteria. I was at the National Theatre Studio in 1997–1998 on a bursary, and part of that bursary was to make a piece of work that would be shown as a work in progress in the studio. So the Director of the Studio (who was a woman, as it happens) told me, "You come to me when you've got a good idea." And so I did a lot of thinking about it, which was not what I was meant to do because I'd already betrayed that I didn't immediately have six ideas (a version of the performance of confidence, I think). I then went in with my idea, laid it out very carefully, and she said what I now know she always said: "Here's why that's no good. Go away and think of another idea." And I did that a couple of times and then thought, "Oh, this is never going to work, because these are the ideas I want to make." And I became absolutely livid with the profession and decided, "If I don't run a theatre, I don't want to do this," because I didn't want to be in this false dynamic of consistently having to say, "I'm like him," or, "I'm a star," instead of, "I've got an interesting idea that I want to develop and talk about properly." So, I have nothing but sympathy for the women who are reporting frustration with having to perform confidence in that way.

But something has shifted for me. Now I realize that you can choose when to use the performance of confidence and using it sometimes in the right places gets you the opportunity to have those conversations. I've seen too many women come into pitch sessions and fail to mention that they are absolutely sure they can do it. And the people they are pitching to—people who have been trusted with resources that they have to decide how to spend—do at least need to hear that those resources are going into safe hands. So, on the one hand, I think the theater is unnecessarily obsessed with the performance of confidence. The industry is really blinkered about who is actually any good. It's only interested in who's "hot," who has had great reviews, who has just done something that somebody you know went to see and thought was terrific. We spend no time at all tracing what was the actual experience of the actors or the audience in these productions. But, on the other hand, I do think that some women do miss the moment to state clearly that they could and would deliver.

Roxana Silbert

Generational differences in confidence

Early in my career, when I was in my thirties, I was desperately under-confident. No, actually, not under-confident—I thought I could do it if I was given an opportunity, but I didn't know how to speak the language of the British establishment upper middle class, so I did appallingly at interviews. That's why I decided to take a different route into the industry through new plays. But now, when I meet women directors in their thirties, I think they're ridiculously articulate and confident. There was one incident at RSC when I was in rehearsal at the same time as another female director (who is in her thirties). The producer wrote the two of us an email asking if we would move out of our rehearsal rooms into some really inadequate rooms. I replied by writing the most impassioned five-page email as to why this had broken my heart. My colleague wrote, "I'm afraid this will not be possible. Love, X." And I thought, "That is the difference!" I still find it so hurtful, while she is just so confident. Also, I feel that these younger female directors are much bolder in their artistic vision. I see a very different kind of theater coming out, which I actually really love.

But with young women now in their twenties, I find that their relationship to their confidence is tricky. Sometimes they undersell themselves. There's one girl who's been an assistant of mine, and often people would ring me up for a reference and say, "We really, really liked her but she came over as really under-confident. Will she be able to cope with blah, blah, blah?" She is a velvet glove with a hand of steel—she's really confident and capable, but just doesn't feel the need to project that. Then there are other young women who come in and are so aware that they need to pitch that they're rather aggressive and a bit frightening. And I have to say, "If I'm going to work with you I need to know who you are and you're just showing me that you're tough, tough, tough." Which of course, isn't real confidence either.

Silbert gives an example of how a young female director's positive attributes—in this case competence and reliability—can actually undermine her chance of advancement.

In one of my organizations, we had two assistants at the same time, a girl and a guy. The girl was incredibly capable. You could give her anything to do and she would sort it out, so she was given more and more administrative and managerial tasks. The boy was a bit hopeless and insecure. He couldn't really be trusted with anything that required any responsibility, so the jobs he was given were to direct, because he was a sensitive soul who was all about art and acting. I remember noticing that and thinking, "We have to stop that." Because her generosity was being punished and his flakiness was being rewarded.

Vicky Featherstone
We can never stop talking about feminism

I was in Scotland for nine years then came back to London. Since coming back, I've noticed a massive shift here that is very different from what's happening in Scotland at the moment. There's a confidence crisis among the generation of women below mine—those in their mid-twenties to mid-thirties. Since coming to Royal Court, I've been meeting everybody I've missed out on over the last ten years. The men of that younger generation come in here and talk really confidently, ask me really hard questions, really challenge me. And the women come and are much less certain. They're quite unforgiving of themselves. And they all ask me how to be successful and have kids. They can't imagine how they can do that. Something is making them think you can't have all that. And if I'm more easily convinced by the men in these conversations and have to seek to find my trust of the women, then that's really fucked.

It was very different with the women in my generation. Starting out, I was an assistant director to Jude Kelly at the West Yorkshire Playhouse. She was in her second year as an artistic director and was trying to run this massive organization with two small kids—a five-year-old and a three-year-old. It was really, really hard for her and she'd had no role models; but she was an amazing role model for me and taught me how to be and how not to be. I saw her struggle to balance work and family, but I never asked her how she did it. I just assumed I would figure it out. Her generation did the hard job and enabled my generation to be really confident. Jude definitely carried a chip on her shoulder at that time about having to man up. I couldn't understand why. I thought, "You don't have to be like that. You don't have to be either aggressive or downtrodden; there's a middle ground." And now Jude totally exists in that middle ground. But back then, there I was at age twenty-three watching her and thinking, "I don't get that at all." I'd just been to university on a really feminist course with brilliant women tutors, studying women playwrights, and doing sessions with women directors. I never questioned my right to be doing what I was doing. And that has changed.

I think it has changed because we stopped talking about feminism. I think a lot of men in my generation would say they felt emasculated by feminism. That it was hard for them to be instinctively who they were around the power of that feminism. And so when that feminism went a bit quieter I think there was a backlash against it from the next generation of men. That sort of thrusting—and I don't mean that literally—male confidence came back. Maybe it's because they didn't see us fight enough? I directed Abi Morgan's play *The Mistress Contract* here at Royal Court.[10] Her last idea in the play is that, because of nature, we can never stop talking about feminism. We never definitively reach equality due to the physical power that men fundamentally have over women; therefore, in every generation, it needs to be rediscussed and recalibrated. I'd never, ever thought that. It's an extraordinary idea—that we never reach equality and we have to be continuously discussing it and trying to get to it. There's never a tipping point. It gets there and we all go, "Ah, fine," but then with the next generation we need to get there again. I didn't use the word "feminism" for years, but I feel really strongly about using it all the time now.

Nadia Fall

Hold your nerve

Nobody knows the piece of work you're making more than you. Different people will always have different tastes and opinions about any work. You have to choose the people you listen to and take notes from very carefully, it should only be a very small number or you'll be running around like a headless chicken in rehearsals or previews. That's why it's great to work with a good artistic director whose vision and taste you can really trust, so that when they tell you to cut half an hour in previews (like Nick Hytner did when I directed *Dara*), you can trust they're right.[11] Not to say it's easy to hear! At the same time, there are some things that you absolutely know in your "waters" are important to hold on to, so do hold your nerve on those gut decisions.

Hold your nerve with your career as well. If this is what you need to do because you don't know another way to live then you've got to do it no matter what people tell you. Keep going. Keep finding ways to make work. Young directors may not have a lot of money at their disposal, but they're lighter on their feet. At the beginning, you can beg, borrow, and steal to put something on. It gets harder to ask favors the second or third time around!

Benefits of Diversity

Diane Rodriguez

Solidarity and understanding make us good leaders

Why do we continue to have to prove that diversity is valuable? It's tiresome. I see it at the National Endowment for the Arts level where the agency constantly has to prove that art is valuable with surveys, and data and charts.

If theaters don't understand that we don't live in a homogenized society, then we have to focus on theaters where more opportunity lies. We've had fifty years of a social movement and the theater in the United States is still controlled by a nondiverse group of men and a few women.

The point is not to hire women of color for only works specific to their community. A good director is a good director. Work of color is not the only thing we can direct. I'm directing a reading at the Pasadena Playhouse of Tennessee Williams's *Eccentricities of a Nightingale*, and

---

[11]National Theatre, 2015.

I so understand Alma.[12] She's not a woman of color but a woman who has so much female angst that we all relate to her.

We female directors of color, like most directors, can direct a range of stories that have universal themes; but often we don't even have the opportunity to direct on the regional theater level, let alone direct works of color.

It has gotten better, for sure. Look at the wonderful May Adrales who has had such success with *Vietgone*.[13] She's Filipino American, directing a story about Vietnamese. Or there is Liesl Tommy who directed *Party People* by Universes.[14] She's South African and the Universes ensemble is African American and Latino; so, she's not directing work from her specific ethnic community. We understand and relate to each other's stories because they are often stories of struggle in a dominant society that looks at us as the other. And that solidarity and understanding make us good leaders in a rehearsal room as excavators of stories about struggle, prejudice, sometimes done with humor, sometimes with tragedy.

Roxana Silbert

Diversity opens up more diversity

Elizabeth Freestone did research that was published in the *Guardian* and I came out as having directed more plays by women than anyone else in the country.[15] That's not strategy. That's because I'm attached to those stories because I connect with them. The former artistic director at the National Theatre said, "Women don't write plays that have a strong enough narrative motive to carry the Olivier stage." I think that's to do with what he thinks a story is. Women's voices were outside his experience of the world and how he sees it. That's why it is absolutely necessary to have diversity in leadership. And it's not just about

[12]Pasadena Playhouse, 2017.
[13]South Coast Repertory, 2015.
[14]Oregon Shakespeare Festival, 2012.
[15]"Women in Theatre: How the '2:1 Problem' Breaks Down." *Guardian*, December 10, 2012. https://www.theguardian.com/news/datablog/2012/dec/10/women-in-theatre-research-full-results#data (accessed December 10, 2012).

playwrights. As a result of there being more women artistic directors, there are more women designers, lighting designers, sound designers, and so on because women gravitate toward other women. Diversity opens up more diversity.

Nadia Fall

We need that alternative gaze

Our modern age is global in every possible way: our politics, our economics, the internet, the media, what we buy—"diversity" is in our lives and part of all our histories whether we like it or not. It just makes no sense not to have that reality reflected in our theater. And aside from an argument about accuracy—which is that we should paint the stage as multifaceted as we find our world—we need diverse stories to understand each other and to remember that we have more in common than we have dividing us.

As audience members, most of us have witnessed a classic play reinvigorated by diverse casting and/or diverse creatives; why is that when the words are the same? I think it's because the conduits have different perspectives, something unique and necessary to offer and we need that alternative gaze. Not just because it is politically correct to redresses an historical imbalance but because quite frankly our art is richer and better for it. Theater culture is slowly changing, as theaters attempt to actively make their buildings more diverse and inclusive. However I think there are elements, some theater commentators and critics, for example, who are extremely territorial. They don't mind diversity in certain theaters and spaces, but if you try and inject change into the traditional larger spaces, they scream blue murder. Also, they want diversity packaged at a safe distance; a play set in a colonial past or a diversely cast Shakespeare is acceptable, but attempt to put forth a contemporary piece, set in our city, looking at issues of race, for instance, and they're not comfortable. I think theater audiences, however, are keener than ever to embrace diversity, and through such programming we are drawing in new audiences: often younger and more diverse themselves. We need this if we are going to see theater flourish for the next generation.

Tina Satter

Realizing what you take for granted

Satter talks about the influence that trans actors in her company, Half Straddle, have had on her work.

My entire artistic output and then, consequently, personal and political life has been utterly informed by working with and becoming close with the trans actors Jess Barbagallo and Becca Blackwell (and others, but those two in particular). It has made me consider how for granted I've taken my entire life the ability to be seen by the world exactly how I wanted to be seen in my personal identity—and what it means for queer and/or trans bodies to not ever have that feeling and the intrinsic safety that comes with it. I never make work from the top down around that idea, but it comes from the inside of every piece organically because those people are in the work, and their bodies are in the work. And, even if they aren't, I can't stop making work that never ever shows a heteronormative dynamic. Because, in the vein of carving out spaces, we must constantly carve out and put forth playful, serious, complicated, failed, and successful spaces of feminist and queer identities.

And it bears out. Every single time we do a show, we hear especially from young audiences and young artists who see the work, that they very rarely see these kind of spaces so fully made—that it's not preach-y work, but totally takes for granted and moves around these wholly female and/or queer worlds and just shows people of so many ranges and types falling in love, fucking up, finding transcendence, and always trying to be themselves.

Indhu Rubasingham

Attracting a different community of collaborators

Rubasingham is a British native of Sri Lankan descent who has focused her career on directing plays by international writers from diverse British backgrounds, a focus she carried into her role as Artistic Director of Tricycle Theatre (later changed to Kiln Theatre).

I think because of the way I am or the person I am, I attract a different community of collaborators and artists than if I was a white, male, middle-class artistic director. The sympathies and empathies and allegiances and tastes are going to vary, which again is the biggest argument for having a diversity of leaders in our theaters. That's why I'm really committed to our creative learning program. How do we remove obstacles that allow people from those diverse backgrounds to enter the industry? I'm not interested in token gestures. How do we recognize talent and give them the best opportunities to grow and develop? How do we recognize and therefore remove the obstacles that prevent this talent from emerging and therefore flourishing? How do we ensure a diverse pool of excellent and talented artists that will feed our industry and enrich it?

Lucy Kerbel

There can be different types of good

All of us see predominantly white, male, able-bodied, middle-class work. Naturally, we tend to make work in the same way because that's what we've learned is good. Writing the book *100 Great Plays for Women*, I learnt that I needed to broaden my own conception of what could make a good play. When I started, if I'm honest, there were probably plays that I read earlier on in my research that aren't in the book because they didn't emulate or reflect what I had been taught to think was a good play, so I discounted them straight away. There are a lot of plays we consider great now that, when they first came out, a lot of people went "What is this?!"

I once had a friend working as a tour guide at a big stately home in the north of England. He was giving me a tour and there was lots of art on the walls. We turned one corner and there was this startling picture that was like a mixture of a progressive rock album cover and flower fairies. It was Georgiana, Duchess of Devonshire, flying through the clouds with her dress billowing behind her and was painted in the eighteenth century or something. I didn't know if I liked it, but it was different than every other painting. My friend said it was the only painting by a woman in the collection. Just then, a guy came past, looked at it, and went, "God, I don't know what that is," and moved on. Doesn't that encapsulate it? We take a quick look and go, "Don't know what that is, that's no good," and we move on to the next thing that we recognize and go, "Now that's good." Was that painting by that woman better than the others? Was it worse? No, it was just different. Was it different because she's a woman? Who knows, but probably she had a different way of seeing the world. Possibly that's why it was different. I think we're very quick, unfortunately, to attribute levels of success rather than just accepting that there can be different types of good.

When you have theaters that are run almost exclusively by one type of person, they are far more likely to hire people like them. If it's all white guys from Oxbridge, a white guy from Oxbridge walks in to a pitching meeting and they go, "Yeah, we get this guy." Maybe a white girl from Oxbridge walks in and they go, "Oh we should have a woman on this season, and she seems great." Then she gets in. But that black guy who might have grown up next door to the theater, but doesn't have that same way of presenting himself or that same educational background, might miss that chance. I would advocate for greater diversity in creative decision-making in theaters. Even if you have one artistic director, they can be surrounded by a team of people who are familiar with and will champion work of all different types and artists of all different types.

Gendered Aesthetics

Kimberly Senior

What is essentially feminine about me

In an interview with The Interval, *Senior talked about embracing her feminine side.*

For many years, I tried to hide things that were called essentially feminine or female about myself. Like, I'm really proud of the fact that I can drink most men I know under the table, since that felt like a skill that was important to acquire to be heard. And I was like, "I'm not going to live my life according to my feelings, because those are female, and no one will listen to me if I feel things deeply." And then I was like, "Wait a minute, you can't be an artist if you don't fucking feel things deeply." Men [in the arts] have been trying for centuries to feel the way women feel, so that they can access what we're doing. I made this shift to being like, what would it be like to walk through life feeling vulnerable and emotional and sensitive all day long? And, suddenly, that's when I noticed the leaf on the ground and I want to hug a stranger. Maybe there's a tremendous bravery in vulnerability. And maybe there's a tremendous bravery and risk in loving another person. There's no strength without fragility. Once I opened my heart up to using what is essentially feminine about myself in my work, there was suddenly a rich, vast treasure chest that I had never used before, and it's been kind of amazing.[16]

Senior gives a few examples of how increased vulnerability and comfort expressing emotion has enhanced her work.

When directing *Disgraced*, I was very technical about it at first, knowing it wasn't my story.[17] Over the years, I learned I needed to locate my own rage, my own identity struggle to help the story be told through the actors. It wasn't until I reckoned with my own emotions, and left my "textbook" behind, that I felt I was really able to unlock the play.

When I was directing *Rapture Blister Burn* by Gina Gionfriddo at the Goodman Theatre, there was one scene that just moved me to tears every time, but I felt like I couldn't let the actors see me cry, so I would kind of avoid the scene.[18] Eventually we *had* to work on it! When they saw how moved I was, we were able to really decipher what moved me (as an audience member really), and once we discussed that, I was able to actually begin to work on the scene in a deeper, more meaningful way.

Mostly it's about how I talk about my work. I'm not afraid when pitching now to say things like "this play really moves me. I'm a mother and it deals with that subject in a beautiful way." It's about learning that being vulnerable is an asset and opens the room for others to be the same way. And vulnerability isn't just about feelings; it's also about admitting you're wrong, asking questions, taking risks.

---

[16]Victoria Myers, "An Interview with Kimberly Senior." *The Interval*, September 3, 2014. http://theintervalny.com/interviews/2014/09/an-interview-with-kimberly-senior/ (accessed September 3, 2014).
[17]American Theater Company, 2012.
[18]Goodman Theatre, 2015.

Maria Aberg
Exploring an area of vulnerability

Aberg is known for her bold, high-concept interpretations of classic works.

When I hear people say things like "women focus on the emotional core of a piece and men focus more on bold choices," I instinctively I want to dismiss them, but maybe there is something in there. I guess, by and large, I would say women are more likely to be vulnerable or want to explore an area that exposes some vulnerability in themselves or in the piece that they're doing. But I don't think that if you focus on emotion you can't do big, bold gestures as well or the other way around. They're perfectly compatible. And I think both men and women are capable of making very hollow, high-concept work with big, empty gestures.

Erica Whyman
An urgency to be in the room together

Whyman describes pressures and double standards faced by women directors.

Women directors are required to behave differently than their male counterparts. The best formulation of this I've heard was from Polly Findlay in one of the debates during our 2014 Roaring Girls Season at RSC. She said, "If I was a female dentist, I don't think I would be required to talk about the fact that I was a woman almost every week." It becomes a feature of who you are. I have talked more about my gender with journalists than I have about my work. And yes, it's important and it's interesting, but it's hard to fight for airtime to actually talk about the work you make. Also, the media and, to a degree, our male peers expect us to take a special interest in work by women or about women; but then a number of them mock us or undermine us for doing so. So, you can find yourself in an absolute catch-22. I've had letters saying, "I can't believe you've put on another play that's just mainly got white men in it." And I wonder how often male directors are challenged in that way. So there's a sense of responsibility to women and to diversity as a whole. I also think that critics (often male) are less ready to accept bold approaches to a play or production from women and expect us to "behave" better in relation to a play's history, while our male counterparts are positively encouraged to confound those expectations.

There's also an expectation—which most of us live up to—that women directors will be more collaborative in the rehearsal room. And I don't regret that, but that expectation, I think, is slightly greater for women than it is for men. Also, in the journey to becoming a successful freelance director, there's this whole tricky area of being an assistant director. A woman is expected to be a very, very good assistant director for as long as possible and then to miraculously make a sudden shift to being a brilliant, wholly authoritative director in her own right. In contrast, men are broadly expected to not assist for terribly long because the sooner they get on with saying who they are as a director, the better. So we create quite a lot of good female assistant or associate directors who continue in that role for a long time since they get paid to do it and they're in a rehearsal room and it's better than doing nothing, but often at the expense of finding their own voice or status as a director.

Whyman identifies a recent shift in British theater toward more feminist plays.

In the last five years, there's been a lot of very good writing by women; but only in the last twelve to twenty-four months has there been much feminist work. Starting around the time of the economic crash, the Royal Court found a generation of new young women's voices. Strong voices, smart voices, writing about a whole range of things—but not really writing about feminism. And, if you'd asked me five years ago, I'd have gone, "Well, thank god they're not," in the sense that a truly changed world would not need the women to take a special interest in women's rights or in equality. Genuine equality would mean the women would never be relegated to a corner of the world marked "women" or "feminism." But something else is happening now. We might credit Phyllida Lloyd for starting it with her all-female production of *Julius Caesar* in

2012.[19] But I think she was picking up on something happening in the world, actually—younger women feeling ready to say, "This is rubbish, isn't it? We haven't got it right."

Vicky Featherstone hosted a preshow discussion at Royal Court in March 2014 called "Why Write a Feminist Play?" with playwrights Abi Morgan (*The Mistress Contract*) and Nick Payne (*Blurred Lines*). Several of us from RSC went because we'd just commissioned the writers for *Midsummer Mischief* and we'd been doing lots of thinking about gender. I assumed there would be fifty or sixty of us in the audience for this discussion, but the Royal Court's large Downstairs theater was full. To the rafters. With people not able to get in. And it was full of all generations of women. And I could see that Abi and Vicky and Nick were not quite expecting the level of heat in the room. They started by having a very gentle, civilized conversation about whether the two writers thought their plays were feminist and it was interesting. But the question and answer session came alive with people saying, "Thank God you're doing this," and, "At last I can say how much we need this work and how angry I feel about the state of the world." It was fascinating and it gave us real hope. Then, when we produced the *Midsummer Mischief* plays here, that was what happened again.[20] There was a kind of urgency to be in the room together and talk about the issue, which is something theater can sometimes provide.

Blanche McIntyre

My antennae are not great

When asked if she perceives a difference between the aesthetics of male and female directors, McIntyre states the following:

I wouldn't like to draw a straight line between the female and male approaches. There are male directors like Peter Gill and Paul Miller who are incredibly detailed and interested in human behavior, and Rob Hastie, who does incredibly finely observed, very humane work. Then there are female directors like Maria Aberg, who I rate very highly, who do strongly conceptual work. And Katie Mitchell is the queen of deconstructed film and Foley work in theater. So I think it's more zigzag than one expects. I can say that I find high-concept, high-technology work pretty dull; but I don't know if that's because I'm a woman.

Admittedly though, my antennae for this kind of thing are not great. I was one of four sisters, and my mother, as well as being a fantastic mother, has been incredibly successful in her career. Then, from the ages of five to nineteen, I went to an all girls' school where the ethos was "achieve as highly as you can, ambition is great." When that's your home environment and your school environment, you don't gender behavior in the same way. When everybody is a woman, you don't say, "That's masculine behavior," because it can't be—it's being expressed by a woman. So I was about nineteen or twenty before I started thinking about sets of behavior as particularly female or particularly male. And, in fact, my radar is still well off.

Caroline Steinbeis

Putting a gender label on things would be missing the point

Steinbeis questions whether aesthetics can be categorized along gender lines with any reliability.

I find the male/female debate a little reductive. The art we make is determined not only by our gender but also by a far more wide-reaching and complex web of socioeconomic factors. It is to my taste to create work that is both emotionally complex and bold in choices. And I find a great deal of the work created by my peers—many of whom also happen to be female—hugely exciting on these terms. It's inquisitive and playful, and it has a great deal of muscle and ambition behind it. It communicates that there is a huge amount of satisfaction gained from the work we make, that we love what we do; this is something we all share. But how we go about making our work is so subjective that putting a gender label on things would be missing the point.

KJ Sanchez

It's fine for a man to be obtuse

It's totally fine for a man to be obtuse. Robert Woodruff is an incredible director who was one of my first mentors. I was in a production of *Orestes* that he was directing.[21] In a note session, he said to us, "All right. There's the thing, and then there's the deal. You've got to figure out when is the thing the thing, and when is the thing the deal." Everyone in the room went, "Ohhhh," then had to define it for him or herself. Nobody asked him, "What are you talking about?" We all somehow knew it was brilliant and right, but we had to fill in the blanks to get there. We had to meet him halfway on that particular note.

Women are not given the benefit of the doubt in that way. A man can say something so sweeping, so metaphoric, so veiled, and no one will say, "Wait, what do you mean?" Yet sometimes I say something that's not that obtuse and the actor will repeat it to make sure he or she really understands what I'm saying. If you want to look at it in a generous way, you can think of it in terms of Marshall McLuhan's hot medium verses cool medium. A note like, "When is the thing the thing, and when is the thing the deal," is a very cool medium—you've got to project your own meaning. I think women are required to live in a hotter medium. We have to be crystal clear.

Tina Satter

Trying to break down the paradigm

Satter is known for using a variety of experimental forms to explore gender identity in the plays she writes and directs for her company, Half Straddle.

I am constantly exploring feminine identity in my work because it feels important to me to keep shoving that up in the cracks of media, culture, and art. To keep saying, "Now you're going to see a bunch of

---

[21]La Jolla Playhouse, 1992.

women, you're going to see these queer people, you're going to see a pink world that also talks about this." But I also keep making work in that playground of space because I'm artistically, emotionally, and personally fond of it. My choice to pursue those themes never comes from "How can I keep doing that?" but instead from "I have this idea . . ."

My work is not interesting because it's six women and two trans people on stage. It's interesting because it's eight people on stage making something you've never quite seen before in the space of theater. That something is often related to gender identity, but it's more than that. For example, in *House of Dance*, Jim Fletcher played a teacher in a dance studio who teaches a tap class to a fifteen-year-old trans kid.[22] There's also a piano player, who was male and clearly had some kind of crush on the teacher. The strange male tap teacher—everyone knows who that is as a type. But Jim didn't fit that type. He's this big guy, much bigger than Jess Barbagallo who played the kid. And I anchored him in a slightly stylized way so he became more someone intriguing thing to look at, less a man being a tap teacher. I wasn't trying to fight against what I thought male-ness was about, because that isn't interesting to me. I wanted to display this broken person of whatever gender trying to get through teaching his tap class. But because of prescribed social and gender roles, the audience came in expecting the characters to unfold a certain way and they didn't, which left the audience either to feel disrupted and frustrated, or to feel, "Cool. Pressure off. Let's see where this goes." And that's an exciting space to be in when you see art I think.

---

[22]Half Straddle, 2013.

7
THEATER TODAY

As working professionals, these directors have many insights to share on the current state of the theater industry. This is a dynamic moment in theater history. Recent and pending shifts in economics, public policy, and entertainment consumption patterns are profoundly affecting the aesthetics of theater and the demographics of audiences: inflation increases production costs; austerity policies decrease subsidies; core older audiences age and contract; younger audiences immersed in high-stimulus media crave new dramatic forms; theater literacy decreases as education policies de-emphasize the arts; increasingly diverse British and American populations seek diverse voices and new stories. It is a time of many challenges, but in a creative industry, challenges and limitations can foster brilliant innovation. So even as they face many obstacles, these directors see exciting opportunities on the horizon. In this chapter, the directors share their observations on how the industry stands and their opinions on how it should move forward.

Changing Aesthetics

Roxana Silbert

European influence in the UK

Silbert describes how British theater has changed since she started her career in the 1990s.

You see a lot more influence from European work now. Thirty-odd years ago, two young women called Lucy Neal and Rose Fenton decided they wanted to bring international work to London. They set up the London International Festival of Theatre (LIFT) that still runs every two years. And as a result of that, directors started to see a lot more international work. Then the Iron Curtain came down and lots of things happened politically that meant it became easier for British directors and writers to go to Eastern Europe and see work in that tradition. So, physical, devised work used to be the visual form and new writing used to be very text-based, but eventually exposure to the European tradition allowed people to explode the text and make it theatrical and visual. As a result, the lines between devised, physical work and new writing have broken down.

Caroline Steinbeis

A marriage between Brecht and Stanislavski

Steinbeis was born in Germany and grew up there and in the UK. As an adult, she has lived, trained, and worked predominantly in the UK, but has also directed in Germany, Austria, and other countries.

I feel a strong affinity to German theater. Over recent years, I have started looking for the melting points on which a marriage between Brecht and Stanislavski is possible. This comes out of my desire to challenge the discursive and narrative led theater we have in the UK and reach a wider audience with productions that are not based entirely on naturalism and founded on psychological motivation. Of course, there is a well-established and ongoing movement away from naturalism in the UK but our mainstream theater still revolves around this artifice, which feels stifling to me. When German theater is at its best, an alienation effect is unlocked that combines the spoken word with a startling image and this bares an emotional truth and meaning that far transcend what naturalism can achieve.

There seems to be such a lot of space for cross-pollination between these two approaches; but it may mean a certain level of interference with your source material, which is still very unusual here in the UK. The fact that a director has this prerogative is a not a given here, so you have to create the conditions where you can do this kind of work. Ultimately we set our own boundaries, and if the conditions for your working process aren't what you need them to be, it's up to you to change them. We work in such an open and unpredictable art form, with millions of variables, so the only thing we can take responsibility for is surrounding ourselves with people who are interested in pushing for the same answers.

Maria Aberg
Questioning the superiority of language

Born and raised in Sweden, Aberg moved to the UK to study directing and has based there since, but works in several European countries, including Germany.

I lived in Germany for a bit and met the German director Andreas Kriegenburg who said that because of the history of Germany in the twentieth century, they lost faith in language as a means of communicating any kind of definitive truth or value. It was so corrupted by its use as a political tool and in other ways that theater was forced to develop a sort of counter tool for communication, which I really love as an idea. And I think it's brilliant that we in the UK are starting to question the superiority of language as the most powerful and most precise way to communicate. That's a difficult transition in the UK though, because English is not just a language that is particular to Great Britain or America or where ever. It's a world language and I don't think we're going to arrive at a point where our reliance on the English language lessens in the same way the German language did in Germany, unless something radical happens.

Blanche McIntyre
I grew up with words as my comfort zone

McIntyre describes how she sees the difference between the "British model" and "European model" of directing.

Like many British directors, I'm quite text-based. In Britain, the director tends to follow what the writer wants or is assumed to have wanted, and most productions start with a text. I don't think anything draws me to a text-based model specifically—I'm the child of publishers so I grew up with words as my comfort zone. But I don't think one model of work is better than another. At the end of the day you're aiming for a communication between the audience and actors, and there are lots of ways of getting there. I talked yesterday to a young director who had worked in Romania and he was describing the Romanian approach to directing as plotting the emotions, as you would on a musical score, and stretching the text to cover them. But he contrasted that with the Hungarian approach, which apparently is more text-faithful. Of course, all European theater isn't the same. But "the European model" is a handy shorthand for British theater makers to describe a way of working that embraces the presented aspect of theater and is interested in pushing the possibilities of form as much as exploring behavior. I saw a production of *Lady with a Lap-Dog*, an adaptation of a Chekhov short story, in Russia a few years ago, which used two clowns. I heard of a *Seagull* done in Avignon at the same time as mine where everyone wore seagull masks. It's about taking away the assumption that what is being presented on stage is naturalistic in order to look more closely at what is actually happening, which often sets the director's vision above the writer's.

Lyndsey Turner

New approaches to Shakespeare

Turner directed one of the most high profile Shakespeare productions in recent years—the Barbican's 2015 Hamlet *starring Benedict Cumberbatch.[1] She observes how today's female directors are changing the aesthetics of British Shakespearean production.*

Arguably, British theater has traditionally been dominated by independently educated, male Cambridge graduates. And one of the cornerstones of the work produced by some of the nation's most influential theaters in the 1970s and 1980s and early 1990s was the recontextualization

---

[1]Barbican, 2015.

of the Shakespearean canon. So, for instance, "we're going to do *Measure for Measure* in Freud's Vienna" or "we're going to do *Winter's Tale* in Fellini's Italy." It's a noble tradition, and in the great productions, something is uncovered about that play or that period of history which truly rewards the endeavor; but when the work isn't good, it feels like you're watching something thuddingly literal: an attempt to bend a work of the imagination into a well-behaved historical cliché.

What I find sublime in the work of someone like Maria Aberg is that she understands that Shakespeare's Vienna isn't really Vienna. Shakespeare's Denmark isn't Denmark. Shakespeare's England isn't even England. They are fictive spaces. They're imaginary worlds. Those forests don't really exist. They're projections of something else. So being a Swede and an iconoclast and a profoundly metaphorical thinker, she's able to set *King John* in King John-world.[2] I feel like some of the strongest Shakespearean work I'm seeing comes from women who don't feel as if they are bound either by the text or by historical verisimilitude.

Vicky Featherstone

Theater must not be boring

I think that theater has turned a corner in an important way over the last ten years or so. More and more it's following the rule that "theatre must not be boring." That's something my peer group has always wanted and, now that we've got more senior positions, it's happening. People weren't really allowed to discuss this before, so theater remained something that had to be good for you and had to be worthy of respect from a certain group. The exciting thing about theater now is that it feels like it is allowed to use more populist forms but still be intellectual. You can break down those barriers now, so it feels like—when it's at its best— today's theater is a more holistic product of the world we actually live in.

For example, *Black Watch*, which I helped develop when I was at the National Theatre of Scotland, has a hugely populist form.[3] It's got direct address. It has singing in it—some songs the audience won't recognize, some they will. It has an accessibility in its form that isn't about

---

[2]Royal Shakespeare Company, 2012.
[3]National Theatre of Scotland, 2008.

a secret someone has studied and then put on stage. It's saying that we range widely in our experiences and if you can create a cohesive dramaturgy around that then it's justified to put those different shapes on stage together. It's about using what you have to communicate; about using different mediums to express different points of view. And I think that's been a big breakthrough, because before this kind of theater was seen as a populist form and therefore not worthwhile in many areas, but I think it has become polished and elevated.

Sarah Benson

Going beyond naturalism

Naturalism has become so embedded in people's assumptions about what they're going to see when they go to the theater that it's hard to see it's just another convention, like melodrama was a convention. People like Shaw used the naturalistic form brilliantly, but then it became entrenched and conventionalized and stopped meaning anything theatrically. Now it's become this dead delivery system for content—content I can learn about in a newspaper or novel or by watching YouTube. I have no reason to show up with my body to see it. When people look back at theater history five hundred years from now, they'll study what is happening right now as this crazy thing where you have actors in a laminated reality pretending the audience isn't there, acting in a style perceived as being "reality" when it's actually far from how people really behave and talk. I would love to stop seeing so much work that just takes naturalism as a given. It's that lack of interrogation I find tired. I'm most excited about work that is honest and transparent about the fact that it's performance. I think a lot of young theater makers are in the same boat.

It is changing and I hope that in ten years we've shifted toward really embracing what can be incredible in the theater, which is the potential for changing how people feel. We need to use the form to do that, rather than just the using the form as a way of serving up content. I hope we can really start to merge form and content and embed the transformation that we want to feel in audiences in the form itself. I'm really excited by artists such as Aleshea Harris, Jackie Sibblies Drury, Clare Barron, Isabelle Lumpkin, Becca Blackwell, and Christina Masciotti who all feel like their practice is about colliding form and content in a spectacular way.

Tina Satter

Grants can shape theater too much

Grants can shape theater too much. For a while, every grant application wanted to know, "How does this work fit into the community? What is it doing for the community directly, actionably? Are there community members in it?" Everything was so social-action-oriented. Of course, that's really important and there should be theater with that as a mission. But when everyone has to take that angle to get funding? That feels like the wrong way to do both theater and social action. It all becomes about marketing and creating work that fits grant questions instead of doing what you want to do. Let the art come from the inside out. Let artists tell you what they want to do and why it's important.

Kimberly Senior

We don't have to reinvent the wheel

Senior points out that dramatic form doesn't have to break molds to be exciting.

How do you write a contemporary play? When Ayad wrote *Disgraced*, he set out to write an Aristotelian tragedy. Anytime that someone would suggest something else he would be like, "That doesn't fit into the model. I'm writing the model." We don't have to reinvent the wheel. We're on that journey, so why not pay respect to that journey? Why not say, "I'm completely inspired by the idea of a rousing titan fear?" What do pity and fear mean and how does that translate to the twenty-first century?

Diane Rodriguez

New leadership in American theater

There are future leaders waiting in the wings who could really change things. They have come up through very different terrain than their predecessors and explored a lot of new aesthetics. We're still very much into plays now, but we know there are other possibilities in theatrical work and in the process we use to create new work. Joe Haj exemplifies this potential. He's done incredible ensemble-driven work and now is running the Guthrie, this very large and influential theater. He'll not only be able to bring in a new aesthetic, but will be able to help his regional theater audience contextualize it. That could be part of a huge, exciting shift in how we do theater in this country.

Changing Audiences

Erica Whyman

New obstacles, new appetites

In the sixteen or seventeen years since I've been a director, I think there has been a change in the way theater sits in people's cultural education in the UK. When I grew up, theater was aspirational. If you took your children to the theater, you knew you were doing something good for them. I don't think that's true for as many parents now. Many see taking their children to the theater as an expensive, intellectual, luxury thing to do, for which they think they need a certain kind of confidence or knowledge; therefore, we tend to lose the middle of our audience. You end up with an audience that is under twenty-five or over forty-five.

Also, people have got far more choice of things they might do in an evening now. And people are bombarded with the kind of marketing spin devoted to the big commercial shows and to cinema, which has lowered the visibility of noncommercial theater. If you talk to people about theater and they haven't been, their instinct is to think of the big commercial show because that's what they see in their world, whether they've actually been or not. That's changed, I think. So that's the negative story—we're fighting for airtime in a much more complicated universe. There are greater barriers to encouraging those people to think of the theater as something that they might enjoy.

The positive story is that I think there is a greater appetite for ideas onstage than there was ten or twelve years ago. At that time, I was very frustrated with British theater. I was running The Gate in Notting Hill and trying to interest people in international theater. It was after Mark Ravenhill's *Shopping and Fucking* and Sarah Kane's best work—that moment when in-your-face British theater had been really celebrated right across Europe. But in the tailwind of that moment, theater had become quite narrow in its focus. We were looking at issues in very naturalistic ways and I found it rather depressing. Everyone was trying to avoid messages, and it was a somewhat celebrity-driven culture, and so it was harder to engage people with complex ideas or get them to think of theater as a place for ideas. (Of course, you did see some great triumphs like Kneehigh and Shunt who, in a way, rejected ideas and were saying it's about story and entertainment and engagement with audiences, and that served audiences very well.) Since the economic crash in 2008, I think something has happened. I discern a positive change, which is that there is an appetite to be in the theater and absorb difficult and complex subject matter and talk about it afterward. And I'd go as far as to say I think it's because the world is really confusing. For instance, there has been a rise of feminist thinking that was deeply unfashionable even five years ago.

Caroline Steinbeis

Hungry for new experiences

It seems to me that British theater makers are becoming very progressive in reinventing the type of dialogue they want to have with their audiences. Programming houses are responding to audiences who are hungry for new experiences. This is reflected in the type of artists who are being invited to make work across the country at the moment. It is energizing and heartening to feel so much confidence and trust; it's infectious. We have learned to achieve big things with very little money in this country, so despite the increasing financial pressures on the industry, the output continues to be risk-taking and surprising. And this is exactly as it should be. Theater must feel energized if it wants to reach wide audiences.

Tina Satter

Speaking to younger audiences

Satter and her company, Half Straddle, explore gender and queer identity in all of their plays.

Young art-maker people really click into our work. That feels exciting. It's amazing to make something that makes young, queer people think, "That really confusing, androgynous actor just made me (a) feel like I wanted to make out with them and (b) feel like I wanted to stand up for them." When an audience member sees a show that makes them think something is possible in that core, essential way, that is real. That is so meaningful to us as a company.

Karin Coonrod

Giving the audience a whole lot in a short time

Audiences are more interested in shorter pieces now. I've done quite a lot of really long plays in the past, some even with two intermissions— *Bernarda Alba*[4] and *Victor or Children Take Over*.[5] But now I'm more interested in really just packing it in, you know? Giving an audience a whole lot in a short amount of time. I've done *Phoenician Women*,[6] *The Tempest*,[7] and *Love's Labour's Lost*[8] all without an intermission in around two hours, as well as adaptations of literature, like *The World Is Round Is Round Is Round*,[9] in even less time than that. It's like a machine that starts and then finishes.

Leah Gardiner

Hope for diversity

Gardiner praises the efforts of various theater organizations and individuals—including audience diversification expert Donna Walker-Kuhne—who are developing more inclusive, diverse audiences across the US.

---

[4]Columbia University, 2005.
[5]Arden Party, 1996.
[6]Columbia University, 2009.
[7]La Mama, 2014.
[8]Public Theater, 2011.
[9]Compagnia de' Colombari, 2013.

Whenever I'm asked to do a show, the first thing that I ask the artistic director is, "What are your audiences like?" Because they are vastly different from one city to another. And they're changing. We're still looking at a very homogeneous, middle-class audience base, but in the big cities, you're seeing a lot more people of color in the audiences now. I would say even ten years ago there was a lot of blue-haired ladies, whereas now I think Theatre Communications Group and Donna Walker-Kuhne have worked extremely hard across the nation to really create a much more inclusive audience. And some theaters are really working hard on audience development and trying to educate America through the art form of theater; not so much by busing in busloads of underprivileged children to see a Wednesday matinee, but more about building diverse audiences from the ground up.

Kimberly Senior

We need to really know our audiences

I think for us to advance our work, we have to engage our audiences in a really authentic way. That doesn't just mean providing programming for them and giving them a really cool panel discussion or an amazing piece of literature—not to denigrate those things because they're also fantastic, but they're supplemental and secondary. I think we need more primary access to and relationship with our audience so that we can know them, not so that they can know us. I don't always know the audience because I'm freelance and not institutional, so recently I have made such an effort to get to know them. I make myself available for talkbacks and conversations and going over to a board member's house for dinner. Audiences are different at LCT3 in New York than they are at La Jolla Playhouse in California than they are at TimeLine Theatre in Chicago, but we tend to be wrong about who they are unless we take the opportunity to really know them. And we have the opportunity because we're living in a culture and at a time where everyone thinks their opinion matters. People are used to asserting their voice so we need to capitalize on that; actually, harness it in a way that it's talking back to the art and changes what we do.

Vicky Featherstone

There's no such thing as an audience

Featherstone has programmed theater for a wide variety of audiences in her role as artistic director for three different companies: Paines Plough, National Theatre of Scotland, and Royal Court.

There is no such thing as "an audience." You have to be very sophisticated in conversations about audiences and I think often we can get quite blanket about it. The experience and desires of the audiences in Scotland are very different to those here in London, so it's quite important to break them down into different groups.

Blanche McIntyre

Theater has become fractured

I think we're living in an age where theater has become fractured. There are companies that make political theater, and often tour it to nontraditional places; Out of Joint has just been taking a wonderful verbatim play around the country, called *Crouch, Touch, Pause, Engage*,[10] about rugby, coming out, economic decline, and town spirit in Wales, and it speaks beautifully to British regional audiences about the specifics of Bridgend and Gareth Thomas and about wider issues too. Then there are regional theaters that serve their communities brilliantly and make work specifically for them. But in the commercial sector, because the money involved is vast, the plays usually have to entertain first and that makes it hard to be controversial. Plus, when you've got a theater whose pull is international, your collective is bigger and less unified so it's harder to speak directly. So all these theaters are speaking to such different audiences in such different ways.

---

[10]Out of Joint, 2015.

Roxana Silbert

Growing gap between London and the regions

I perceive what's programmed in London and what's programmed outside of London to be very, very different. London has a much more experimental strand of work. The work that the Royal Court does in the main house would not sell in Birmingham. You know, we've taken Beckett. It's Beckett. But even that is a hard sell for us. The work that Rupert Goold's doing at the Almeida, which is phenomenal and can transfer into the West End in London, wouldn't sell in Birmingham. I doubt it would sell in Liverpool or Plymouth, either, without a very, very famous person in it. There is a growing gap between how progressive London can be and what you can do regionally. On any scale.

London is very big and there's a lot of wealth there. So, there are people that go to the theater three times a week, five times a week. That is their hobby and they love it. Birmingham is not a rich city; it's a working-class city. People don't have a lot of money and they're not going to take risks in the same way. Plus, it's very difficult to get in and out of town, so late nights are quite tricky for people. In our 140-seat theater, The Door, we can almost put on anything we like and it'll do okay for a few nights. But our main stage has to make money in order that I can put on more experimental, forward-thinking shows that don't make money at The Door. So we have very different contexts in which we're programming and making work. And how I would program at the Royal Shakespeare Company and at Birmingham are also completely different because you're in completely different social contexts. The economic downturn has had more impact in the regions because we do not have the same capacity as London to raise money from philanthropy. Eighty percent of philanthropic giving in the UK goes to London. So while five years ago Birmingham Rep could subsidize its work, now we have to make money from the program. That means I can't take risks. I have to program work that I will believe will break even or make money.

Coproducing is one strategy regional theaters have adopted to cope with decreased funds.

Birmingham Rep was closed for four years before I came, and before my predecessor left about six years ago, she would have been able to say, "This is the spring season and these are the plays I'm doing on the main stage and this is who I want to direct them," and then it would be all produced in house. Now I probably couldn't produce a single play on my own. I have to find a partner for everything I do. And I have to have at least one or two commercial shows in each season that will move into the West End and make us money. So I am on the phone to other theaters all the time.

Silbert also notes another growing gap between London and the regions—availability of actors.

The tradition used to be that actors would start in the regions and then come into London and then go into telly and cinema. That would be quite a normal route. Now most actors live in London and really don't like leaving. There are little nucleuses in Manchester and Newcastle, but a lot of actors are in London and they just don't want to leave home, especially if they have a family. So, getting actors of profile and some-times just getting really good actors is hard unless there's a transfer to a London venue at the end of it.

The Director's Shifting Role

Polly Findlay

Director as organizer

Findlay is British and based in the UK, but has also directed in mainland Europe.

In the UK, there's a line of thought that says that directing is about organizing. Your job is to get into a room and organize something to make it clear and comprehensible. I don't mean everyone operates that way, but there's a tradition of it here. The limitation to this approach is that when your instinct is to organize, it's hard to create an environment where actors can come up with something individual and brilliant. Generally speaking, the mainland European directing tradition feels more political—you're using the play to express something that you think to be true about the world. There is a thrilling cross-fertilization beginning to take place between these British and mainland European traditions, with more and more directors beginning to work in a way which exploits the creative tensions between different theater cultures.

Nadia Fall

Being utterly present in the rehearsal room

In Britain, the director is part producer, so you have to look at everything. You'll have a meeting about marketing and the image in the morning. Someone will talk to you about the program in the afternoon. You'll have a discussion about costumes in a tea break and after work you might have a conversation about the rights to a song you want to use. And now with iPhones, everyone expects a response to everything right away, at all times of day. You have to juggle all that, but not when you're in the rehearsal room. You have to protect the sanctity of that room. Although you can't solve the bird's eye problem of the whole play while you're sitting in that room, you can solve that little scene you're working on. And if that's really good then maybe tomorrow you'll make another really good bit and then the next day you'll tie them up together and then you'll have something. That's the most important work of the director. You can only do that work if you're utterly present in the rehearsal room and keep "producer you" at bay as much as possible.

KJ Sanchez

We're writers now more than ever

We as directors write the visual, three-dimensional narrative for the play. What a great responsibility that is and what a great opportunity it is, especially now that playwrights are writing such episodic work. Now when you work on a new play, it often has twenty-three different locations. Our job is to weave the fabric that holds all of those scenes together. I think we're writers now more than ever.

Priorities for Producers

Lear deBessonet

Exquisite and rigorous and populist

There's more awareness that it is depressing to make shows with only white people in them. I'm really happy that that seems to be changing. It's a trend that I hope goes a lot further. I recently heard [playwright and actor] Lisa Kron say, "We need people from lots of different demographics and different experiences to tell the story of the world."

DeBessonet has been on the staff of the Public Theater since 2013.

I think the Public Theater is one place where there is a really compelling and diverse idea of what theater can be. It's a place where Shakespeare in the Park can coexist with Under the Radar and experimental stuff and plays by writers like Suzan-Lori Parks and Richard Nelson and Tony Kushner that the Public has had long relationships with. There's a current moving under all of those that's saying, first of all, that they can all live in one house. It's not a coincidence that *Fun Home* and *Hamilton* both came out of the Public. That's a tribute to [Artistic Director] Oskar Eustis and his belief that populism isn't a bad thing. That making a piece that is exquisite and rigorous doesn't mean that that piece won't find a large audience. It should find as big an audience as it can and engage as many people as possible with those ideas.

May Adrales

A platform for important conversations

I directed a reading of *A Power Play; or, What's-Its-Name* by A. Rey Pamatmat at the Eugene O'Neill Center, which is about the political world behind gun control.[11] I really want to get it produced, but most of the theaters I've sent it to thus far have said it's too much for their audience to deal with something so radical. But this is a discussion

---

[11]O'Neill Playwrights Conference, 2017.

that's going in our world right now and it's directly affecting our communities, so we should be doing this play. That won't happen until companies decide to use their theaters as a platform for that kind of conversation.

For example, The Foundry Theater does an effective job of bringing people together from different backgrounds to talk about plays. They have an ambassador program in which they invite various sectors of the community, such as activist, religious, and political groups, to come together and witness a play and talk about it with theater artists. The experience enriches everyone's understanding of the play.

My production of *Vietgone*,[12] which ran at South Coast Rep, Manhattan Theater Club, Oregon Shakespeare Festival, and Seattle Rep and is set in a Vietnamese Refugee Camp in Arkansas, was not billed a political production, though it was deeply political. It challenged the Western historical understanding of the Vietnam War. It upended stereotypes of Asian Americans and humanized refugees in America in this critical present time. I believe no one left without questioning their own assumptions. These theaters supported fully the production, which was singular and unlike their usual programming. They gave us a platform for change by taking a chance on the work.

Paulette Randall

Programming for black audiences

Randall argues that to build an audience of a particular demographic, theaters need to regularly produce plays about that demographic.

It's really funny, whenever you talk to programmers about producing more plays about black people, they say, "But, you know, we don't get many black people into the theater so we don't program many plays for them." Well, if you don't put on many shows for black people, they're not going to regularly come. If you keep offering something regularly, then people will start going, "Oh, alright then, thank you very much." When we did *Fences*[13] in the West End in 2013, there were two other

---

[12]South Coast Repertory, 2015.
[13]Duchess Theatre, 2013.

black productions on in London at the same time—*The Color Purple*[14] and *The Amen Corner*.[15] So, suddenly it was news because it's unusual to have three on at the same time. It shouldn't be news. It should just be a regular thing that happens at the theater. So when it's that rare, you can't expect a whole lot of black people you've never seen before to suddenly decide, "Yes! We're going to go and do that thing!" when it's not become part of their norm.

Indhu Rubasingham
Prioritizing diverse programming

When Rubasingham took over the position of Artistic Director of the Tricycle Theatre (later changed to Kiln Theatre), she a made a commitment to helping the unheard voice become part of the mainstream and refocused the theater's mission and programming away from the overtly political toward plays that offer different lenses on the world.

In my first season, all four plays were directed by women, all of the leads were nonwhite parts, two of the plays were world premieres, and two of them were by women. Statistically that's unheard of in London. But it wasn't like I consciously went, "I want all of the plays to be directed by women." I did consciously want different lenses to the world and the unheard voice being part of the mainstream because those things are part of my mission statement. That's why it's important to have diversity of voices among cultural leaders, because then you get a diversity of programming choices and ways of making work. I opened my first season with *Red Velvet*, which I'd been working on for a long time as a freelance director but we couldn't get it produced.[16] Theaters were interested but they wouldn't commit to it. It took me becoming an artistic director to program it and finally get a production of it. In order to change the cultural landscape, you've got to show that these plays are of high artistic quality and are commercially viable and that audiences are hungry for these different stories. When you show that,

---

[14]Menier Chocolate Factory, 2013.
[15]National Theatre, 2013.
[16]Kiln Theatre (then Tricycle Theatre), 2012.

it suddenly becomes a model that other theaters or other places might be interested in. Diversity is often used in sense of it's a good thing to do and "it's politically correct." This doesn't interest me, as diversity is imperative for the future of the arts. We need a diversity of stories and perspectives and therefore artists. This will make the arts relevant, vital for all kinds of audience and therefore be intrinsic to the commercial and artistic success and viability of cultural organizations.

Sarah Benson

Keeping the staff really close to the work

Benson is Artistic Director of Soho Rep, which has a small core staff.

I'd like to see more sustainable, art-driven theaters in New York City and around the country that are not bloated with infrastructure and can thrive without huge scale. At Soho Rep, we've only got seventy-three seats. That affords me a lot more artistic freedom than many of my colleagues running larger theaters with many more seats to fill and subscriptions to sell. We also have a tiny staff. There are five of us full time and so everyone's very close to everything. Obviously there are challenges with that in terms of sustainability, but people aren't silo-ed into departments and it really feels like we're all making stuff together. The challenge always is figuring out how to grow while still having everyone stay really close to the work. That has to be our measure of success.

Nadia Fall

We need to make some plays quickly and give others more time

Sometimes we make plays very quickly that respond to what's going on politically and help us digest this ever-more complex world we're having to cope with—like some verbatim-style plays. Other new plays take longer; their beauty is in their nuanced language or storytelling. I want to see things that have taken years to come to market alongside quick, documentary responses to the world that I live in today. I think we need both of those types of new work in our theaters.

One of the most valuable things producers can give directors is time. If somebody said, "Okay, Nadia, in this rehearsal process what is the one thing that you want more of?" I would always say time. It's so precious. I know we can be indulgent and we always think, "If I had a little bit more time I'd make it better. I would do this, I would do that . . ." But with subsidies going down and money getting tighter, theaters are asking us to make the work in shorter and shorter periods. Now, in commercial theater it can be just two weeks. That's a really big problem. When you put such a constraint on making something, the work suffers. You cannot achieve depth without time to work.

Theater's Contribution to Society

Diane Rodriguez

Theater is a communal ritual

Everyone says this, it's nothing new, but theater is a communal ritual. We don't have many of those anymore, so I do think people come to the theater for that experience. Whether it's an urgent story or something gorgeous to look at, people crave it. If you invest in new work, work that's relevant to people, they want to know "what's going on over there at the theater?"

Blanche McIntyre

There's something democratic about it

The thing that makes theater different from film or television is that the audience helps create it. A quiet audience makes for a very different kind of performance. The show changes shape. With a noisy audience, you have a completely different show, sometimes you have a different play, although the words are the same. The audience brings half the experience. I've just done *Comedy of Errors* at Shakespeare's Globe.[17] Of course, comedy is a particular kind of beast that requires more energy from an audience, but the mood at the Globe, when it's

---

[17]Shakespeare's Globe, 2014.

full—and it's regularly full—is like a rock concert. The actors say it's terrifying. You go out there, shaking, you're surrounded by one-and-a-half thousand people, you can see all their faces, talk directly to them, they laugh or they don't, they heckle or they don't, and you come back off again feeling like a god and you want to go straight out and do it again because you feed off their energy. I think that is seductive. There is something about the audience as a powerful creature that I find exciting. Film doesn't care if anyone's watching, but a piece of theater can see the response it's creating. There's also something democratic about it. When you're watching a film, you look where the director wants you to, whether it's close up or wide shot; in live theater, you can get bored and look at the lighting or set. Or you follow that person's story or this other person's story—your choice of what to watch is your own and so you have more control over your experience.

Kimberly Senior

We are not advancing the culture

For a long time, I think theater was a vehicle for social change. Our theater was able to be a step ahead of our culture in terms of what we were discussing. Now I'm nervous that we're in a moment where our culture is actually ahead of our theater. The conversation that's happening surrounding gun violence? Our plays are not ahead of that yet. The conversation on gender identity? Where are the plays? Why aren't our theater artists putting out the new ideas? I think it's about fear and economics. I think we're terrified of asserting something that means we're going to lose our funding. Or lose our audience. We're in a fractured, fractured time right now, and instead of diving into the fracture, instead of seeing the fissure and expanding it in a plate tectonics way, we're trying to pull things together, to heal. To be like, "See? We're all the same." But we are not advancing the culture.

Erica Whyman

A space where ambivalence can be explored

I think the theater remains a space where ambivalence can be explored, because you can air many different viewpoints in the same moment—conflicting but equally intriguing eyes through which to see. Shakespeare, of course, is the expert—we find both Othello and Iago compelling for different reasons—one may be more the villain, but Shakespeare insists that both men are equally flawed, ambitious, skilled, and equally fascinating. Similarly, Claudius endeavoring but failing to pray is a remarkable moment of humanity, truth, a lonely man alone with what he has done—and yet, we the audience are, in almost the same breath, willing Hamlet to kill him. And of course, it is in the very essence of the theater that no one audience member is the same but we sit next to one another, witnessing the same events through different eyes and ears. Edward Albee, Harold Pinter, and contemporary writers like Mark Ravenhill or Alice Birch are intent on confounding our prejudices— leaving us arguing about who is to be liked/trusted/respected in their plays or in our world.

Tina Satter

It makes a whole new space right there

We have finite air, but theater goes into the air and can make a whole new space right there. It's infused with everything we already know, but it's a new space. Right in that moment, in the room. I mostly feel this feeling seeing certain kinds of visual art—where the pressure is less pointed (than it is on theater) to know exactly *where* you are, *what* you are seeing every second—it's like these forms and feelings from this painting or installation of course are in relation to or from or working against what we know, but paired here and done in this way, we have this new space and energy and interaction. I'm thinking of Rothko and Ryan Trecartin and Karen Kilimnik and so many more—and I want the theater I see and make to also do that. It's also like an excellent short story, where you feel that charged inner excitement as your reading of "oh, I know this feeling a bit, I get this," so it's very satisfying and then it totally expands or juxtaposes itself in a wholly unexpected way, and then because of that piece of art or story, you now know this new thing, this new space, this new feeling! If live performance and theater can't attempt to do that, then where? Live humans doing stuff is made for that transaction.

Lear deBessonet

Justice and hard won joy

From devised work to large-cast, community-based productions to Off-Broadway productions of Brecht, deBessonet has an enduring focus on theatre that promotes social justice.

I think often there's a thought that if you have any concerns about social justice, the nature of how you'll engage that in your work is to make very dark pieces that feature the atrocities and the tremendous abuses of power that plague humanity. And obviously I believe that work does need to be done and it is important, but I don't think it is the only way to make work that is meaningfully engaging questions of justice. Composer Todd Almond and I, very early on in talking about doing *The Odyssey*[18] in San Diego, talked about how we felt like, because of the divided nature of American society and the sort of caste system that we live within, that actually just to have people of really different life experiences in a room together, by choice, having a good time, that that alone was a political act. There really aren't very many spaces that exist in our society where something like that can happen, so that has fueled the way we have thought about our pieces.

For me, joy is not disconnected from the difficulties of life. It's not disconnected from sorrow. In the case of the Public Works projects and some of my other community-based projects, so many of the individuals that are part of them have encountered extraordinary obstacles in their lives. So the joyfulness in those plays is a hard-won joy. To me there's something that's different between joy and giddiness or silliness. Joy just cuts a lot deeper because it's knowing the sorrow and the injustice of the world and, in spite of that, grabbing onto a deeper will to live and deeper life force. And harnessing that life force together with other people. I think that's what people are responding to in those shows.

---

[18]Old Globe, 2011.

Vicky Featherstone

One of the most consistent art forms

I am fascinated with the fact that, with every new turn in technology, people start to question whether theater is under threat. This has been happening forever. Actually, what we do fundamentally is no different than what we did two thousand years ago. Theater is one of the most consistent art forms—it's an individual standing up in front of a congregation of other individuals and communicating directly with them by telling a story in some way. However fancy the video or technology, that hasn't changed. I think the form is incredibly robust and therefore unbelievably fundamental to us, because otherwise it would have changed. People may want to see film or television or other entertainment on demand, but with theater *the experience* is what we really, really crave. The current human need for affirmation of a live experience is really enormous. So theater is at its best for a large group of people, when it feels like an event; thus, it's very important to me for it to feel like an event every single time. It's the experience of witnessing, of sharing an experience together in a room.

Metaphors for the Role of Directors Today

Diane Rodriguez

Directing is like painting

Directing is like painting for me. It's composition and seeing color and moving people. A play is like a painting that moves. So you come prepared with all your little tools to rehearsal, but you don't really think about them. You create a piece in the moment with what the actors bring to you. Out of all that I do—directing, writing, and acting—directing is the most fun because it's about working with actors to shape the whole picture.

Leigh Silverman

Director as conduit

Silverman describes the director as a "conduit" for the creative choices of all her collaborators.

They have to enter and then exit through the body of the director. Any impulse that someone has I'm either going to like it or not like it. If I don't like it, I'll offer suggestions. If I do like it, I'll then try and figure out how that is going to match up with the next impulse and the next impulse. Whether it's a design choice, a writing choice, a production choice, or an acting choice. I think that's why directors are both everywhere and nowhere in every production.

You have to stay completely in control and yet be utterly flexible. There's a nimbleness that's required and yet you have to take people with you. You can't leave people behind. I think that's hard because you're all the time managing personalities, managing other people's anxieties, managing your own anxiety, managing expectations, managing the noise of the world. You're just trying to make a thing that everyone is on board with. And even when people aren't on board, you're still trying to make it. Everything passes through the director so that you can get everybody in the same car, going to the same destination.

Patricia McGregor

The tuning fork

How do I know if something "works"? For me, it's a personal litmus test. I have to sit in a seat and feel like somebody hits a tuning fork on the stage and it resonates with me. As the director, I'm the first audience member. I'm always thinking about the young people and the old people, the black people and the white people, all those who will be in the audience; but at the end of the day, I can only feel what resonates with me. We have to do everything we can to hit the strongest note so it will resonate to the core of the audience member, so I organize every-thing to hit in me in the most meaningful way and then hopefully it will mean something to other people too.

Sarah Benson

Directing is a giant improv

Benson explains how preparatory research and analysis inform the rehearsal process.

Directing a play is sort of like this giant improv. You prepare, you get yourself in the right frame of mind, and then you start and have to roll with it. That preparation and frame of mind affect how you cast, how you create a rehearsal room, how you make all the choices you make.

CONCLUSION

What I Did Not Find

Traits of a female director. When I embarked upon my initial set of interviews, I intended to speak with ten to twelve directors and write an article that addressed the research question "How does gender influence the work of women directors?" I quickly discovered that I was not going to find a clear answer to my question because it rested upon a couple of naïve assumptions: (1) the productions of women directors will have something in common simply because they are women and (2) the influence of gender will be easy to discern. Both assumptions were wrong. After researching and interviewing over two dozen female directors and reading about dozens more, I cannot confidently name one dominant characteristic specific to women in this field. Women directors vary in their process and aesthetics as much as their male counterparts. Additionally, most of the directors I asked struggled to trace clear lines of influence from their gender to their work. In retrospect, I should not have found this surprising. Because directing is an inherently integrative field where its practitioners apply a vast array of skills and knowledge to make nuanced, complex, aesthetic judgments, it is difficult to parse out how the myriad factors considered by the collaborative team ultimately influence the process and production, particularly with factors as deep-rooted and habitual as gender roles and gender expression.

Sexual harassment. In these interviews, which I conducted between June 2014 and June 2017, some of the women describe dealing with sexist behaviors, but none describe behaviors that would commonly be considered harassment. Perhaps that would have changed had I continued doing interviews into the fall of 2017 when the #MeToo and #TimesUp movements opened the floodgates and such stories began pouring out of people across the theater industry. No doubt, many female directors, including perhaps some of these interviewees, have faced sexual harassment or assault. The proliferation of these movements via social media brought this dialogue into public discourse on an unprecedented scale, hopefully marking a lasting shift from a culture of shame amid victims to a culture of shame among perpetrators. Vicky Featherstone stepped forward during this troubling moment to help lead a conversation about how to address abuse and protect people in the industry; I feel certain that many of the other women represented in this book will also do their part to lead us to a safer, more respectful future.

Fear of artistic failure. Not one director expresses anxiety about the prospect of artistic failure. On the contrary, Rubasingham expresses admiration for directors' work that has "an honesty and a vulnerability, and an exposure to risk, which means they may fail,"[1] and explains that when she has "played safe" at the Kiln/Tricycle, the box office receipts have lagged.[2] Featherstone echoes her sentiment, saying she only feels comfortable when her team is "taking a journey toward the unknown or into a risk" and saying, "Oh my God, what are we doing?"[3] This desire to push the boundaries of the familiar, to—in the words of Anne Kauffman—"enter the room a little unknowing" in order to be "lithe in experimentation," clearly outweighs fear of artistic failure for most of these artists.[4]

What I Found in Several Cases

Enthusiasm for shifting audience appetites. Several directors expressed enthusiasm over signs that the dominance of the naturalistic mode is waning and new forms are emerging. Benson sees naturalism as a style that has outlived its vitality: "People like Shaw used the naturalistic form brilliantly, but then it became entrenched and conventionalized and stopped meaning anything theatrically. Now it's become this dead delivery system for content—content I can learn about in a newspaper

---

[1]Rubasingham, Chapter 5, Success.
[2]Rubasingham, Chapter 1, Season Planning.
[3]Featherstone, Chapter 1, Season Planning.
[4]Kauffman, Chapter 2, Preparing for Rehearsal.

or novel or by watching YouTube. I have no reason to show up with my body to see it." She believes that younger generations agree: "I'm most excited about work that is honest and transparent about the fact that it's performance. I think a lot of young theater makers are in the same boat."[5]

This enthusiasm for nonnaturalistic work is evidenced by the recent success of productions with new, more populist, forms, such as *Hamilton* and the National Theatre of Scotland's *Black Watch*. Featherstone describes this emerging populist theater: "It has an accessibility in its form that isn't about a secret someone has studied and then put on stage. It's saying that we range widely in our experiences and if you can create a cohesive dramaturgy around that then it's justified to put those different shapes on stage together. It's about using what you have to communicate; about using different mediums to express different points of view. And I think that's been a big breakthrough, because before this kind of theater was seen as a populist form and therefore not worthwhile in many areas, but I think it has become polished and elevated."[6] This "polished and elevated" populist theater may be contributing to a shift in audiences that Whyman has observed in the UK over the past decade: "I discern a positive change, which is that there is an appetite to be in the theater and absorb difficult and complex subject matter and talk about it afterward."[7]

Influence of international traditions. One development that several directors say has contributed to recent shifts in British dramatic form is the increasing influence of European work. McIntyre observes that, while there is great variety of form in European theater, the phrase "the European model" has become "a handy shorthand for British theater makers to describe a way of working that embraces the presented aspect of theater and is interested in pushing the possibilities of form as much as exploring behavior."[8] Several British directors are excited by the greater malleability of text enjoyed by European (particularly German) directors, which allows them the option to privilege the visual and auditory aspects of the play over the narrative—or, as Silbert puts

---

[5]Benson, Chapter 7, Changing Aesthetics.
[6]Featherstone, Chapter 7, Changing Aesthetics.
[7]Whyman, Chapter 7, Changing Audiences.
[8]McIntyre, Chapter 7, Changing Aesthetics.

it, to "explode the text and make it theatrical and visual."[9] Directors who have worked in both Central Europe and the UK, such as Aberg and Steinbeis, seem particularly keen to broker what Steinbeis calls "a marriage between Brecht and Stanislavski."[10]

Central and Eastern European staging traditions have not influenced theater in the United States as directly as in the UK, but American theater practitioners certainly have incorporated processes and forms from non-American and nonmainstream performance into their work. Rodriguez is optimistic that emerging leaders informed by diverse influences will spearhead further innovation not only in form, but also process: "There are future leaders waiting in the wings who could really change things. They have come up through very different terrain than their predecessors and explored a lot of new aesthetics. We're still very much into plays now, but we know there are other possibilities in theatrical work and in the process we use to create new work." She holds up Joe Haj—a Palestinian American who has done workshops in Gaza as well as ensemble and devised work—as an example of this new type of leader. "He's done incredible ensemble-driven work and now is running the Guthrie, this very large and influential theater. He'll not only be able to bring in a new aesthetic, but will be able to help his regional theater audience contextualize it. That could be part of a huge, exciting shift in how we do theater in this country."[11]

Anxiety about misrepresentation. The current cultural and political climate in the United States and the UK has fostered an acute awareness of how groups of people are represented in performance, while social media has created a platform for people to question and challenge publically any representations or cultural appropriations they judge problematic. This context can make directors anxious about the prospect of misrepresenting groups or individual figures. For example, Lee describes her anxiety about representing African Americans in the first production of her play *The Shipment*, in which the first half is structured like a nineteenth-century minstrel show: "Finding the right tone [was] the challenge of the entire rehearsal process. For the play to work, the tone [had] to be *that* tone. If the stereotype section of *The*

---

[9]Silbert, Chapter 7, Changing Aesthetics.
[10]Steinbeis, Chapter 7, Changing Aesthetics.
[11]Rodriguez, Chapter 7, Changing Aesthetics.

Shipment were done with a high comedy tone, it would be horrific."[12] Aberg describes similar anxiety about her production of John Webster's *The White Devil*, in which she staged one scene in a bondage club in order to highlight the misogyny inherent in the play's world: "In week two, I sat everyone down and said, 'Right, we need to have a conversation about how we do this because I don't want to get it wrong.' I wanted to make sure we didn't tell a story that we didn't want to tell, but I also wanted to make sure that I didn't make any of the women or men feel uncomfortable portraying any of the things that we were about to portray. I just wanted to make sure that everyone could really stand for what we were going to do."[13]

Lack of a clear career path. Several interviewees express concern that women and people of color do not have access to the clear, established career path open to some men. Randall explains, "I knew really early on that I didn't have the connections of most white, middle-class, male directors—I don't have a member's pass into that club. So, you have to fight your battles in a very different way than others."[14] In Britain, many white, male, middle-class directors make the connections they need to enter this "club" by training at Oxford or Cambridge and then being hired to assist by older, male Oxford and Cambridge graduates.[15] Of course, many young female directors also assistant direct, but, as Whyman explains, this does not tend to lead them down a path into the director's seat as quickly as their male peers: "A woman is expected to be a very, very good assistant director for as long as possible and then to miraculously make a sudden shift to being a brilliant, wholly authoritative director in her own right. In contrast, men are broadly expected to not assist for terribly long because the sooner they get on with saying who they are as a director, the better. So we create quite a lot of good female assistant or associate directors who continue in that role for a long time since they get paid to do it and they're in a rehearsal room and it's better than doing nothing, but often at the expense of finding their own voice or status as a director."[16]

---

[12]Lee, Chapter 2, Analyzing the Play.
[13]Aberg, Chapter 4, Empowering Actors.
[14]Randall, Chapter 6, Obstacles.
[15]Featherstone, Chapter 6, Obstacles.
[16]Whyman, Chapter 6, Gendered Aesthetics.

In the United States, female directors have to take a particularly circuitous route to success in the commercial theater sector. Benson observes,
"There are still not very many women directing in the commercial arena.
I think those that are have often come in through new work or experimental work, whereas more of their male colleagues have said, 'This is
what I want to do,' and just entered that arena."[17] Silverman, who has
directed on Broadway several times, confirms this inequity: "There is just
an accepted obviousness about hiring a guy to direct a show, whereas
a woman has to prove herself in a different way. It's not an equal playing
field, it's just not. Certainly Off-Broadway has changed a huge amount, but
the closer you get to the money the fewer the women. Big, big shows are
still directed by men."[18] Women of color are even less likely to be hired to
direct commercial productions; Gardiner states it bluntly: "If you're of color
and you're a woman, your experience is very different and it's just the way
it is."[19] However, women of color are making some inroads, such as Liesl
Tommy's 2016 Broadway debut with Danai Gurira's *Eclipsed*.

One route of entry that does seem to be more open to women is
through the fringe. Many mid-career directors, particularly in the UK, first
made a name by directing fringe shows and subsequently worked their
way up to more and more prominent theater venues.[20] Unfortunately,
as McIntyre observes, the price of mounting a show at a fringe festival
has skyrocketed over the past decade, so increasingly directors from
working class backgrounds are being shut out of this option.[21]

Many aspiring directors in both countries now attempt to enter the
field through postgraduate study. MFA programs in the United States
and MA courses in the UK offer young artists intensive training and
hands-on experience. McGregor points out that this kind of course is
an excellent way to gain a great deal of experience in a compressed
time.[22] The main drawback of these programs is their cost. As the
price tag for higher education climbs, students must take on increasing
debt to complete a postgraduate course. Kerbel fears this will further

---

[17]Benson, Chapter 6, Obstacles.
[18]Silverman, Chapter 6, Obstacles.
[19]Gardiner, Chapter 6, Obstacles.
[20]Silbert, Chapter 5, Getting Established.
[21]McIntyre, Chapter 5, Getting Established.
[22]McGregor, Chapter 5, Getting Established.

discourage working class people—female and male—from entering the field.[23]

Increasing opportunities for women directors. Male directors still clearly have more opportunities on both sides of the Atlantic. Both Leigh Silverman in New York and Roxana Silbert in Birmingham observe that, like in other industries, employers tend to offer opportunities to men based on potential and to women based upon proven performance, which means that young male directors tend to leapfrog forward faster than their female counterparts. The good news is that there has been some positive shifts toward greater gender equality among professional directors. As Silbert observes, in the UK "in the last fifteen years, there's been a real cultural shift," evidenced by the fact that the JMK Young Director Award's shortlist is now regularly balanced between female and male directors— although between 2008 and 2017, men still won the prize in seven out of ten years.[24] Women artistic directors lead more major British theaters now than ever and Royal Shakespeare Company's 2018 Stratford summer season was directed entirely by women. There are some heartening trends in the United States as well. For example, six women won Tony Awards for direction between 2008 and 2017, verses three in the previous decade and none in the first five decades of the award.[25] So there is a shift toward more gender diversity in the United States, but, as Rodriguez says, "the change feels glacially slow."[26]

Another hopeful sign is the increasing prominence of organizations dedicated to fostering greater gender equality in the industry. Tonic Theatre is leading the charge for change in the UK and Lee sees an optimistic trend in the number of US organizations dedicated to this issue: "There are so many organizations that are really pushing for more diversity in film and theater: the Lilly Awards, the Kilroys, a lot of feminist playwriting groups. That's an important part of the process of change and I think these are signs that things will change in the future."[27] Tommy underscores the need for the sort of initiatives these groups

---

[23]Kerbel, Chapter 5, Getting Established.
[24]Silverman and Silbert, Chapter 6, Obstacles.
[25]*Tony Awards.* https://www.tonyawards.com/en_US/history/pastwinners/index.html (accessed November 14, 2017).
[26]Rodriguez, Chapter 6, Obstacles.
[27]Lee, Chapter 6, Strategies for Increasing Equality.

undertake: "We can't delude ourselves into thinking that parity comes because people want to do the right thing. Parity comes because of relentless pressure."[28]

What I Found Throughout

Director as relationship builder. The interviewees use a variety of language and metaphors to describe the role of the director, but underlying all of them is a fundamental commonality: the director's role is to build and facilitate relationships, specifically (1) between a play and an audience and (2) among members of the collaborative team.

One of the director's core tasks is to build a relationship between the play and the audience. In deBessonet's words, the director's job is "to reveal a piece" to the audience, "to let the piece be itself and be seen."[29] Steinbeis says "the job is to create a dialogue between the play and the people coming to see it."[30] Findlay sees her role in productions of classic texts is "translating" them in such a way that they can be "decoded by a contemporary audience."[31] Featherstone describes her task as bridging the "gap between the performance and the audience," and argues that "brilliant theater is where that gap is active, not inert. It's where you can feel the intangible dialogue going backwards and forwards in that space."[32]

Some directors build the relationship between the play and the audience by developing a specific interpretation of the text then striving to clearly communicate that interpretation to the spectators. As Turner describes, there's a strong tradition of this approach in the UK, particularly evident in Shakespearean productions of the late twentieth century, where it was common to set a piece in an anachronistic period and interpret it through a specific political lens. Turner and several of the other directors indicate discomfort with this model. As she observes, "It's a noble tradition . . . but when the work isn't good, it feels like

---

[28]Tommy, Chapter 6, Strategies for Increasing Equality.
[29]deBessonet, Chapter 2, Analyzing the Play.
[30]Steinbeis, Chapter 2, Communicating with the Audience.
[31]Findlay, Chapter 2, Analyzing the Play.
[32]Featherstone, Chapter 2, Communicating with the Audience.

you're watching something thuddingly literal: an attempt to bend a work of the imagination into a well-behaved historical cliché."[33] Aberg rejects this kind of thesis-driven theater: "I think presenting something where the ideas are solid, sealed, and compacted and the statement, mission, and opinions are fully defined is absolutely pointless. I just see no reason to put that in front of a live audience."[34]

The directors I spoke with are less interested in conveying their interpretation of a play to the audience than in giving the audience access to the play's world and ideas so that individual audience members can grapple with them on their own terms; in other words, they are more interested in building a relationship between the play and audience than in showing the audience what *they* think the play means. Even the two most arguably auteur-ish of the directors I interviewed—Lee and Aberg—prioritize giving the audience access over communicating their own interpretations. Lee both writes and directs and describes herself as "a person who requires a high level of control,"[35] yet she does not seek to use that control to convey one message: "I try to provoke a multiplicity of responses by force. To ensure that you're unable to leave with a single interpretation. A bunch of questions get raised, and then there's no satisfying resolve."[36] Aberg is known for high-concept work and admits that when directing a classic play, she "can be quite selfish about which ideas [she would] like to communicate to the audience through the prism of the text,"[37] yet she sees a theater production as fundamentally "a conversation between actors and audience" in which the ideas of the play should be made "porous enough for the emotional and intellectual contribution of the audience to penetrate."[38]

The process of building and facilitating a relationship between a play and an audience is a collaborative one, and the director's other fundamental role is to build and facilitate relationships among the collaborative team. As Gardiner says, leading such a team is about "making certain that everyone feels that (1) they are being heard, (2) they are being seen, and (3) their participation matters."[39]

---

[33]Turner, Chapter 7, Changing Aesthetics.
[34]Aberg, Chapter 2, Communicating with the Audience.
[35]Lee, Chapter 2, Playing Multiple Roles.
[36]Lee, Chapter 2, Communicating with the Audience.
[37]Aberg, Chapter 2, Working with Playwrights.
[38]Aberg, Chapter 2, Communicating with the Audience.
[39]Gardiner, Chapter 2, Working with Playwrights.

Benson argues that "there is more of a collaborative model evolving" between directors, playwrights, designers, and actors.[40] Her argument seems to bear out when you look at the way most of the interviewees in this book talk about collaboration. From Coonrod's observation that "there's a growing hunger among actors for making something together"[41] to Chavkin's practice of having writers at auditions to help identify "actors who get how the text wants to be spoken"[42] to Turner's success with bringing the designer into dialogue with the playwright well before the writing is finished,[43] these directors are embracing and facilitating rich dialogue between diverse members of their production teams.

As McIntyre quips, "Theater is made by a bunch of people for another bunch who are watching it in the same moment."[44] The director must help all those people build meaningful, stimulating relationships with each other and with the world of the play. While the directors represented in this book have a wide variety of approaches to this task, they are all masterful at building exciting, creativity-fueled relationships both behind the scenes and onstage.

Looking Forward

It has been a privilege to meet and learn from these extraordinary theater artists. Their wisdom about directing techniques, the collaborative process, and mentorship have enhanced my creative practice, and their insights about professional opportunities and challenges have significantly expanded my understanding of the theater industry. I hope you, the reader, have also learned something valuable and found inspiration from their words. I look forward to seeing how these women shape both onstage worlds and the theater profession in the decades to come.

---

[40]Benson, Chapter 2, Playing Multiple Roles.
[41]Coonrod, Chapter 4, Empowering Actors.
[42]Chavkin, Chapter 3, Acoustic Storytelling.
[43]Turner, Chapter 3, Discovery in the Design Process.
[44]McIntyre, Chapter 4, Empowering Actors.

INDEX OF DIRECTOR NAMES